The American Assembly, *Columbia University*

PRISONERS IN
AMERICA

Prentice-Hall, Inc., *Englewood Cliffs, N.J.*

Library of Congress Cataloging in Publication Data
Main entry under title.

Prisoners in America.

Background reading for the forty-second American
Assembly, held Dec., 1972, at Arden House, Harriman,
N. Y.
    Bibliography: p.
    1. Prisons—United States—Addresses, essays,
lectures.   2. Corrections—United States—Addresses,
essays, lectures.   3. Criminal justice, Administration
of—United States—Addresses, essays, lectures.
I. Ohlin, Lloyd E., ed.   II. American Assembly.
HV9471.P77   365′.973   73–1221
ISBN 0–13–710822–2
ISBN 0–13–710814–1 (pbk)

Printed in the United States of America.

10 9 8 7 6 5 4 3 2 1

PRENTICE-HALL INTERNATIONAL, INC. (*London*)
PRENTICE-HALL OF AUSTRALIA, PTY. LTD. (*Sydney*)
PRENTICE-HALL OF CANADA, LTD. (*Toronto*)
PRENTICE-HALL OF INDIA PRIVATE LIMITED (*New Delhi*)
PRENTICE-HALL OF JAPAN, INC. (*Tokyo*)

Table of Contents

iii

Preface

"We can no longer delay confronting the chaos of the American correctional system." This was the general agreement of seventy Americans who met at Arden House, Harriman, New York, December 1972, in the Forty-second American Assembly. Attempts to provide rehabilitation in American jails and prisons have failed, they asserted. Their report also said that "cynicism and public mistrust permeate the criminal justice system." (The report may be had in pamphlet form from The American Assembly.)

The Assembly participants further agreed that most American correctional institutions are and can be no more than "mere warehouses that degrade and brutalize their human baggage." The conditions of confinement coupled with unrealistic expectations of rehabilitation have contributed to the unrest and riots for which American jails and prisons have become infamous. "More effective ways must be found to do the job."

And that is what this book is about—finding ways to do the job. Edited by Lloyd Ohlin, professor of criminology at Harvard Law School, the volume was first used as background reading for the Arden House Assembly. But its analyses and recommendations are designed to make our correctional system more effective and therefore more rewarding for the public at large, which in the main has shown remarkably little interest in corrections. The book therefore is meant also for the general reader.

The American Assembly is a neutral forum and as such does not express official opinions. The ideas found in this volume belong to the authors on their own. And The Ford Foundation, which generously underwrote this Assembly program, is not to be thought of as sponsoring any of the views herein.

Clifford C. Nelson
President
The American Assembly

Lloyd E. Ohlin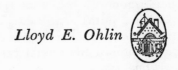

Introduction

An intense and critical reappraisal of the system of correctional services is now in full stride in the United States. Critics are raising fundamental questions about the role of corrections in the criminal justice process, the relative balance of punishment and treatment as correctional objectives, and the effectiveness and desirability of many current policies and practices. The basic goals and direction of the existing correctional system were charted over a hundred years ago in the Declaration of Principles of the National Prison Association in its first Congress in Cincinnati in 1870. Today there are increasing doubts whether this resolution of basic correctional issues appropriate to the nineteenth century is any longer capable of guiding the policies of an urban, postindustrialized society. Public concern about the capacity of the criminal justice system to control the crime problem is at a peak. There is now a new readiness to reexamine basic philosophical assumptions about the place of punishment and treatment in a system of crime control and to consider whether new directions and policies should govern the use and development of correctional resources in the future.

The amount of serious effort that has been devoted to restudying

LLOYD E. OHLIN *is professor of criminology at Harvard University Law School. Among other positions, he has been associate director of the President's Commission on Law Enforcement and the Administration of Justice, special assistant for juvenile delinquency to the Secretary of the U.S. Department of Health, Education and Welfare, and supervising research sociologist of the Illinois Parole Board. Dr. Ohlin is the author of several books, including* Sociology and the Field of Corrections.

1

correctional issues in recent years attests to the saliency of the problem as a central concern of domestic public policy. The recommendations of the President's Commission on Law Enforcement and the Administration of Justice in 1967 to increase the effectiveness of the criminal justice system assigned a key role to the reform of correctional practices. The National Commission on Violence in 1969 critically probed the special problems of treatment posed for the correctional system by offenders disposed to individual or collective acts of violence. The current National Commission on Correctional Goals and Standards is preparing more detailed blueprints for the future development of correctional programs and practices. In 1971, the American Friends Service Committee in a report entitled *Struggle for Justice* raised fundamental challenges to basic features of our existing correctional system such as the individualized treatment model, preventive detention, involuntary treatment, the indeterminant sentence structure, and the exercise of broad administrative discretion in the disposition of convicted offenders. The American Bar Association is sponsoring intensive studies by a Commission on Correctional Facilities and Services. A privately endowed Committee for the Study of Incarceration has been formed to study fundamental philosophical assumptions about corrections with a view to charting new objectives for the future. The Board of Trustees of the National Council of Crime and Delinquency has recently issued several controversial policy recommendations for the reform of the nation's correction system. The National Institute of Law Enforcement and Criminal Justice in the Law Enforcement Assistance Administration (LEAA) of the United States Department of Justice is funding national assessments of the system of correctional services for juvenile and adult offenders. The block grants by LEAA to state planning agencies in criminal justice are encouraging some review of state and local commitment of resources to correctional services. Furthermore, the foregoing projects represent only a part of the current ferment of studies, experiments, and reform now in progress in the correctional field.

Challenge to Corrections

The purpose of the Forty-second American Assembly program is to facilitate public discussion and resolution of key issues which the correctional system must answer to formulate new guidelines for its future development. The papers contained in this volume discuss a number of specific issues about the operation of our existing systems of correction. Threading through the problems and proposals for reform in these papers run a fundamental set of questions about the philosophy, goals, and policies of a correctional system in a free society which no single conference could hope to resolve. Answers to these questions will only gradually emerge from the total process of study, reappraisal, and experimental innovation now in progress. Consideration of more specific issues and proposals, however, should take place with an awareness of the nature of these basic challenges to the correctional task and the circumstances which have raised them to prominence at this point in our history.

QUESTIONING PREMISES

Current challenges to correctional practice reflect uneasiness that we are too readily disposed as a nation to resort to criminal sanctions as a measure of social control when other less drastic measures might prove more effective and less costly. This concern is expressed especially in the papers by LaMar Empey and Edith Flynn but becomes a central theme in the paper on diversion by Elizabeth and James Vorenberg. We appear less certain than we once were that it is desirable to use the criminal justice process and ultimately the correctional system to control drunks, vagrants, drug addicts, and truant or rebellious children. These cases impose an enormous drain on correctional resources yet ordinarily they present problems intractable to services the correction system is able to provide. In fact the problems are more often exacerbated rather than solved. As the authors of these papers suggest, development of more effective measures of social control outside the criminal justice system would undoubtedly prove more beneficial to society in the long run.

Perhaps a more fundamental issue for corrections is whether the responsibility of administering a system of punishment can ever be made compatible with a system of individual treatment and rehabilitation. Apparently an inevitable and essential feature of any system of criminal law and its administration is the use of punishment as a measure of social control. Considerations of elementary fairness, deterrence, and promotion of respect for law are held to rely on the just administration of punishment. If the correctional system cannot escape its obligation to administer the punitive sanctions decreed by the court, can it at the same time direct a program of treatment that provides successful rehabilitation opportunities for individual offenders? Many of the basic conflicts, failures, and dilemmas of the correctional system are traceable to the obligation to organize personnel, programs, and resources to punish and to treat simultaneously. The papers presented in this volume, in particular the discussion on adult prisons by Donald R. Cressey, offer numerous illustrations of the self-defeating costs that derive from an inability to balance successfully the achievement of these objectives. Sometimes the result leads to an ambivalent vacillation of decisions and resource commitments from one goal to the other. More often than not, because of the perception by correctional administrators that the public gives priority to the goal of punishment, a rhetorical and superficial overlay of allegiance to the rehabilitative ideal masks the basic organization of corrections around custodial and punishment objectives. The result is a system especially vulnerable to charges of hypocrisy in its attachment to treatment goals.

This obligation of corrections both to punish and treat leads to other self-defeating contradictions as well. The administration of punishment relies for its acceptance and effectiveness on the fairness with which it implements the principles of equal treatment and "just deserts." In contrast the achievement of treatment goals relies on a flexible adaptation of rehabilitation resources and opportunities to individual needs and problems. Thus in a system that tries to do both the individualization of access to treatment resources may be seen as evidence of favoritism and discrimination, a denial of equal treatment, while the administration of "just deserts" may be perceived as a repudiation of the motivation for treatment. This contradiction is so pervasive in corrections in the United States that some authorities now urge abandonment of the attempt to build a system embracing both goals at the same time. They advocate a return to a system where fixed penalties are administered to fit the crime rather than the criminal with only clearly defined exceptions being permissible. The administration of penalties would be undertaken in a fair and humane way. The system would have no formal obligation to treat or rehabiliate those committed to its care, though it might be permitted to provide treatment opportunities on a voluntary basis for those who desire to make use of them.

Systems of criminal justice in the United States have always reserved for their correctional administrators enormous discretion to individualize the application of punishment and treatment measures. For example, correctional administrators have had almost unlimited discretion in the classification and segregation of prison-

ers, assignment to work, educational and treatment programs, administration of disciplinary measures, selection for furloughs or
work release opportunities, release on parole, parole revocation, or
discharge from parole. The broad scope of this discretion has been
justified as an essential requirement for custodial security and the
administration of punishment and the individualization of treatment. It has been charged that the allocation of such broad administration discretion in a correctional system designed both to
punish and to treat offenders is inevitably discriminatory. It may
result in the imposition of long and punitive periods of confinement inconsistent with the seriousness of the offense for which the
prisoner was sentenced, or to favoritism in the distribution of rewards and treatment advantages. Illustrations can be found in the
papers by Empey, Cressey, and Daniel Glaser. In general the lack of
any adequate system of internal or external accountability for the
use of this discretion can, it is argued, open the door to arbitrary
and prejudicial actions which can only create for offenders exposed
to it dehumanizing and demoralizing conditions of uncertainty and
destructive insecurity.

This increased concern about the virtually unlimited power
which correctional administrators exercise over the destiny of offenders, especially within the context of a system of indeterminate
sentences and individualization of punishment and treatment measures, has raised a whole range of new questions about the constitutional rights of convicted prisoners. Until recently, the courts
have generally adopted a hands-off policy in matters pertaining to
the administration of the correctional system and its decisions in
handling prisoners. Increasingly questions are being raised as to
whether convicted prisoners should in fact lose most rights to which
they would otherwise be entitled. What rights should prisoners have
to the exercise of their religion, to communicate to the press, to
receive publications of their choice, or to have guarantees of due
process in classification and disciplinary decisions? Are they entitled
to counsel at parole selection or revocation hearings? To what kinds
of channels should they have access for the redress of grievances? As
Glaser notes in his paper, in the absence of more clearly defined
standards for the administration of discretion within the correctional system, there appears to be an increasing disposition to turn
to the courts to invoke constitutional limitations on the exercise
of this discretion.

The existing correctional system has developed over the past hundred years with relatively quiet acceptance of its basic philosophy, general policies, and use of resources. It remains to be asked why these kinds of challenges to corrections are being raised today.

The answer seems to lie in the convergence of a set of trends dramatically exposing the inadequacies of the existing correctional system to public attention more than any other time in the past century. Perhaps most important, an aggressive civil rights movement during the decade of the 1960s focused public attention on issues of equality, individual rights, and the functioning of basic social institutions as they related to poor and powerless minorities in American society. This period witnessed virulent attacks and challenges to the authority, legitimacy, and relevance of basic policies governing education, welfare, housing, employment, and administration of justice. Fundamental questions were raised concerning the distribution of power, resources, and access to opportunities and rewards, especially from the standpoint of the most disadvantaged groups. It seems inevitable that such challenges should expose the correctional system to special scrutiny as the final repository for the society's failures and violence-prone rebels.

A second major trend during the decade of the sixties was a rising tide of public insecurity and fear of crime in the streets as expressed by individual acts of robbery and assault and collective protests and riots. With each passing year, reported increases in the volume and rate of such street crimes gave a focus for more general concern about growing disrespect for law and established institutions. It led to increased public demand for more effective crime control and increased support for the entire system of criminal justice. Proponents of more punitive treatment of convicted offenders exploited these heightened fears about crime to attack the permissiveness and ineffectiveness of treatment programs which result in premature release of offenders and attenuation of the effects of punishment measures.

The combined effect of the rising rate of crime and increased support for law enforcement meant increasing numbers of offenders processed by the criminal justice system during the 1960s and a greater burden for the over-taxed correctional services available. Many years of neglect, low budgets, rising costs, untrained staff, and overcrowded ancient facilities unsuitable for treatment programs made it impossible to handle effectively the increased volume of offenders, and larger numbers were diverted to parole and probation supervision. The failure of the system was also made more evident by demands for change by articulate, militant minorities, politically conscious of the efficacy of collective protest and dramatic public exposure. The result was an increasing wave of major disturbances and riots in jails and maximum security prisons culminating in the tragic events of Attica in September 1971.

In addition the decade of the sixties witnessed an effective exposure of correctional problems by private foundation and government-funded research and evaluation programs designed to test the effectiveness of alternative types of correctional policy and practices. As the research evidence accumulated it became increasingly clear that very few of the correctional programs were having any appreciable impact upon rates of recidivism or on the ever increasing volume of crime. The evidence leading to this conclusion is found throughout the papers contained in this volume but is most fully described in the paper by David Ward on evaluation of correctional services. As he reports, the enlightened administrators of the California correctional system not only pioneered innovations in correctional services but subjected these new experiments to more systematic evaluation than they had ever received before. These studies provided factual grounds for questioning widely accepted doctrines about the effectiveness of both traditional and more progressive strategies of correctional treatment.

Finally it should be noted that the saliency of increasing public concern about crime as a political issue in national, state, and local elections since 1964 was responsible for a tremendous increase in the allocation of federal resources to crime control and prevention measures. The work of the National Crime Commission resulted in the passage of the Safe Streets Act in 1968 and the creation of the Law Enforcement Assistance Administration in the Department of Justice. The budget of this agency steadily increased, reaching a total of $750 million in fiscal year 1973. It was anticipated that this budget would exceed $1 billion in the next fiscal year. A program of block grants of money for criminal justice programs to the states begun in 1968 resulted in the creation of state planning agencies to allocate these funds to state and local criminal justice and crime prevention agencies. Corrections has received an increasing proportion of these expenditures, rising to 35 percent in fiscal year 1973. The availability of these large sums has raised new possibilities as

well as new questions about the most appropriate strategies and
policies for correctional agencies to pursue. Many old practices are
being questioned, and more frequently new evaluation requirements are being demanded as the price for funding new proposals.

Key Trends and Policy Issues

All of these trends have converged to focus critical attention on
correctional policies and practices. The types of issues being raised
today and the emerging trends and proposals are referred to
throughout the chapters that follow. It would not be possible to
summarize them all in this introductory statement. However there
are a few central trends in policy which repeatedly arise throughout
these chapters that deserve to be singled out for special attention.

DECRIMINALIZATION

One of the most conspicuous trends is the increasing pressure to
decriminalize certain forms of proscribed conduct in favor of other
measures of social control and other types of treatment services. The
arguments for pursuing such a course are given special treatment
in the papers by Edith Flynn on jails and Elizabeth and James
Vorenberg on diversion. As already noted, for example, the criminal justice system is confronted with a heavy and unmanageable
problem by the repeated arrest and confinement of alcoholics for
drunk and disorderly conduct. But similar issues are also raised by
repeated arrest of persons for vagrancy or of chronic drug abusers.
The issue of decriminalization also arises clearly in Empey's discussion of the juvenile justice system and the tendency to commit
youth to juvenile training schools for such child offenses as truancy
and runaway and stubborn or ungovernable behavior. Though
these juvenile proceedings are intended to be civil in nature, commitment to an institution on a delinquency petition continues to
carry much the same stigma as a criminal conviction. Diversion of
these cases to other types of child guidance services would not only
greatly relieve the pressure on existing youth correctional resources
but would correct a major source of serious injustice in the system
as it now operates.

It is becoming increasingly clear that the resort to criminal sanctions in these various types of problem cases generally does more
harm than good. Adequate treatment resources are not available
and the imposition of punitive sanctions and the stigma of criminal

process appear to have little or no deterrent effect. A major policy issue, however, is raised when the decriminalization of such offenses is achieved without adequate provision for alternative services to take care of these problems. As the Vorenbergs point out, a policy of decriminalizaiton must be coordinated with policies leading to the development of alternative services.

DIVERSION

The diversion of offenders from the criminal justice system to alternative treatment resources different from those traditionally provided for such offenders emerges as a constant preoccupation of the various systems discussed in the following chapters. It is such an important trend and raises such significant policy issues that it seemed desirable to devote an entire chapter to a consideration of current practices, possibilities, and the key issues. These are described in the chapter by Elizabeth and James Vorenberg.

DEINSTITUTIONALIZATION

The following chapters repeatedly refer to the growing evidence that prolonged periods of confinement of offenders in correctional institutions is a self-defeating policy. As Donald Cressey describes in considerable detail such confinement leads to increased criminalization of offenders and it also tends to degrade and dehumanize them. Though it incapacitates offenders by preventing them from committing crimes in the outside community while they are confined, on the average they are more likely to do so when they are released than if they had been exposed to a less corrupting form of punishment. It also now seems apparent that the costs of such prolonged confinement far exceed the preventive values achieved.

It is still evident, however, that some proportion of the convicted offender population will require prolonged confinement in maximum security institutions. How are such dangerous offenders to be identified? Is it desirable to subject such offenders to a prolonged period of preventive detention in anticipation of future acts of violent crime? How can the length of this confinement be determined and where should the responsibility lie for such decisions?

ENRICHMENT OF ALTERNATIVES

A growing trend in corrections today, as noted throughout the following chapters, lies in establishing a wide variety of community-based residential and nonresidential treatment facilities and opportunities. Though often resistance from neighborhood groups has been very strong, the argument is persuasive that the problems of developing a stake in a legitimate career must ultimately be solved in the communities where offenders will reside.

The chapters by Empey, Flynn, Glaser, and the Vorenbergs raise a number of difficult questions. How can the understandable concerns of neighborhood residents about the establishment of such facilities be met? How much use should be made of the services of volunteers and former offenders as compared to those of professional staff in the operation of such facilities and the provision of essential services? To what extent should public correctional agencies resort to the purchase of service arrangements with private organizations and agencies? Should public correctional agencies retreat from the provision of direct services in local communities except where security requirements and the potential involvement of the use of force is indicated? To what extent should compulsory forms of treatment for convicted offenders be supplanted by voluntary treatment centers and opportunities?

RIGHTS OF CONVICTED OFFENDERS

Throughout the following chapters there is increasing evidence of appeal to the courts for definition of the rights of prisoners and the limits of administrative discretion. This trend raises a number of policy issues many of which can be resolved by the establishment of appropriate correctional standards and guidelines. The disposition to establish such guidelines on the part of correctional administration would provide a desirable alternative to the increasing involvement of the court in the determination of correctional policy. However, whether this occurs or not, it is likely that there will be increasing pressure to curtail administrative discretion in the handling of prisoners.

The following chapters again raise relevant specific issues. What types of limitations should be placed on administrative discretion? What types of procedures should be developed to review the exercise of this discretion? What channels should be established for airing the grievances of prisoners in confinement or under supervision in the community? How much should prisoners or ex-offenders be involved in the governance of correctional institutions or treatment programs? Should the management and daily operation of correctional facilities and services be made more visible and accessible to public inspection? How can such public access and visibility be attained within the limits of acceptable security arrangements?

POLICY EVALUATION

The history of correctional practices shows numerous examples of the tendency to protect policies and practices from effective public exposure and evaluation. The isolation of penal institutions in rural areas and the low visibility of the daily operations of probation and parole agencies tend to insulate correctional services from public attention except when riots or other major disturbances occur or when a particularly atrocious crime by a released offender arouses public indignation. This situation is further aggravated by chronic neglect of these services by the public's desire to forget about the problems they deal with.

In the chapter on evaluation, David Ward asks what forms of policy review and evaluation of effectiveness can be instituted to maintain honesty and initiative for innovation. In addition one may question where the responsibility for such evaluation should be lodged and how supported. What types of evaluation responsibility should be built into the correctional system itself as a routine practice and what provisions should be made for a periodic review by external agencies, boards, or commissions?

Though no one conference can expect to resolve fully such a broad range of issues it can answer some of them. Furthermore, it can sort out basic problems and in the process identify those that require more extended public debate and empirical inquiry. It is our hope that this volume will contribute in a helpful way to the accomplishment of these ends.

LaMar T. Empey

1

Juvenile Justice Reform:
Diversion, Due Process, and Deinstitutionalization

Background

The current court-correctional system for juveniles in the United States grew out of a reform movement started in the nineteenth century. This movement led to the removal of dependent and neglected, as well as delinquent, children from the criminal law process and substituted a special system for them. While there is some disagreement over the roots of this movement, certain things about it are important to this discussion.

The first is the concept of *parens patriae* derived from the English Chancery court. Theoretically, the notion of *parens patriae* permits the state to intervene in the lives of all children, not just those who are strictly criminal in behavior.

Secondly, the development of the juvenile court seems to have been accelerated by the attempts of social reformers to counteract the effects of the industrial revolution, of rapid urbanization, and

LaMar T. Empey *is professor of sociology at the University of Southern California and associate director for research of its Gerontology Center. Previously chairman of the Department of Sociology and director of the Youth Studies Center at Southern California, Dr. Empey has written several books and numerous articles on the handling of juvenile offenders. His recent books include* The Provo Experiment: Evaluating Community Control of Delinquency *(with Maynard L. Erikson),* Explaining Delinquency: Construction, Test and Reformulation of a Sociological Theory *(with Steven G. Lubeck), and* The Silverlake Experiment: Testing Delinquency Theory and Community Intervention *(also with Mr. Lubeck).*

of the infusion of many new cultures and peoples into American life. Anthony Platt argues that the social reformers—the "child savers" as he and others have called them—were rural and paternalistically oriented prohibitionists who believed in the strict supervision of juveniles and the careful regulation of their leisure time and access to worldly pleasures. Efforts to humanize the lives of adolescents have been mixed with a sense of moral absolutism through which attempts are made to "save" youth from cigarettes, alcohol, pornography, and anything else that might rob them of their innocence.

Finally, the third set of forces that had a marked impact upon the development of the juvenile justice system stemmed from the historical treatment of offenders, adults as well as juveniles. With the growth of Freudian psychology and the social sciences in the late nineteenth and early twentieth centuries, the belief grew that law breaking, especially among children, was not always a deliberate or sinful defiance of social norms but might be an unconscious response to an underlying emotional conflict. The delinquent child may be sick rather than wicked, in need of treatment rather than punishment. Consequently, just as the doctor seeks to restore the physically sick child to physical health, so this reform ideology urged that provisions be made for restoring the delinquent child to emotional health.

The juvenile justice system today strongly reflects these historical trends. They have resulted in a series of practices that emphasize three things: (1) the right of the state to exercise wide jurisdiction over the lives of young people—the dependent, the neglected, and the "incorrigible"—as well as the law violator; (2) the use of the court to maintain the moral as well as the legal standards of the community; and (3) the implementation of treatment procedures designed to correct the emotional and social problems of children.

The first special court embodying these practices was established in Illinois in 1899. Within 25 years, similar courts were found in every state but two. Today they are found in every state and territory. Yet, because they combine elements from criminal, chancery, and administrative tribunals, they simply cannot be equated with any other court in this country. They are unique.

EMERGENT PHILOSOPHY AND PRACTICE

The sharp contrast of the juvenile court philosophy to that of the older criminal court is obvious. The judge is supposed to act as a wise parent rather than a stern arbiter of justice. Historically, he has been given broad powers by legislative bodies to depart from strict rules of legal procedure, and to utilize the kinds of evidence that are ordinarily excluded from criminal law proceedings. The adversary system, with its climate of confrontation, is replaced, at least hypothetically, by an aura of informality and understanding.

Ideally, professional specialists—social case workers, psychiatrists, and other clinicians—are supposed to be working partners in the process. On the basis of their recommendations, the court might resort to a wide range of correctional resources—probation for the child who can remain in his own home, foster placement for the child who must be removed from the control of a neglectful family, or placement in a minimum security facility, a forestry camp, or possibly in a secure institution. In short, the announced purposes of the court-correctional system are to understand the child, to diagnose and treat his difficulties, and to help him adhere to the moral as well as legal standard which the community wishes to preserve.

HIGH DELINQUENCY RATES

According to its critics, however, the juvenile justice system has not lived up to expectation. On the grossest of levels, there is perhaps no better body of evidence to which critics can turn than the persistently high delinquency rates among juveniles. During the decade of the 1960s, for example, crimes of violence per one hundred thousand population (murder, forceable rape, robbery, and aggravated assault) went up 104 percent, while crimes against property (burglary, larceny, and auto theft) went up 123 percent.

More burglaries, larcenies, and auto thefts are committed by young people, ages 15 to 17 years, than by any other group. Fifteen-year-olds are arrested most often with sixteen-year-olds a close second. For crimes of violence, those from 18 to 20 are the most responsible with the second largest group in the 21 to 24 age range.

Many juveniles are arrested, of course, for acts far less serious than those just mentioned. In 1966, it was estimated that between one and one-half million persons under 18 were arrested, with approximately half of them being referred to court for trial. Overall, the evidence indicates that delinquency is at a very low ebb before the onset of adolescence, rises sharply after its onset, hits its peak around 16 or 17, and then declines sharply. Obviously, traditional forms of crime are very much a youthful phenomenon.

Since delinquency rates are a function of the way a total society is organized, it would be blatantly unfair to place all blame on the juvenile justice system for youth crime. Yet, it must share some of the blame. Therefore, before making any suggestions for changes in court policy, it is necessary to sort out the kinds of problems the system might address and those which might be better left to others.

First, consider the "brave idea," as Edwin M. Lemert puts it, that the juvenile justice system can remedy or prevent all delinquency by itself. This idea is seriously deflated by a number of research studies of unreported or hidden delinquency which reveal that the amount of undetected delinquency—acts that remain a secret and untreated by officials—is high among all segments of the youth population, among middle and upper as well as lower class juveniles. Youth unknown to the police often commit as much delinquency as those who are known and punished. Moreover, the estimates are that from 90 to 95 percent of all these delinquent acts either go undiscovered or unacted upon by the authorities. Hence, as Murphy *et al.* suggested in 1946, "even moderate increase in the amount of attention paid to [them] by law enforcement authorities could create . . . a 'delinquency wave' without the slightest change in adolescent behavior." Clearly, the justice system has relatively small impact on youthful behavior.

Secondly, consider the fact that, despite these high rates of delinquency and a lack of intervention in most of them by the court, the preponderant majority of young people grow up to be law-abiding citizens. Forces are obviously at work, other than those of the juvenile justice system, to bring about conformity.

These findings are striking in light of the fact that the usual tendency is to focus upon means for changing the juvenile justice system alone, or for tinkering with the correctional segment of it, as a means of reducing juvenile misbehavior. Clearly, that perspective is a limited one. For that reason, this paper will adopt a broader perspective, one that attempts to do two things: (1) to analyze the problems that are thought to characterize, not only the internal workings of the juvenile justice system, but its relation to the broader society; and (2) to review some of the reforms suggested as a means of addressing these problems.

Basic Problems

JURISDICTIONAL NET

The first basic problem has to do with the ambiguity and all-encompassing character of the legal statutes that define delinquency.

It is ironic, but true, that children can be found guilty and sanctioned, often severely, for acts which, if committed by adults, might not even have resulted in arrest. The jurisdictional net of the juvenile court is so broad in most states that, given almost any set of compromising circumstances, a child can be defined as delinquent. Consider the comment of the President's Commission on Law Enforcement and Administration of Justice:

> The provisions on which intervention . . . is based are typically vague and all-encompassing: growing up in idleness and crime, engaging in immoral conduct, in danger of leading an immoral life. Especially when administered with the formality characteristic of the courts' procedures, they establish the judge as arbiter not only of the behavior but the morals of every child (and to a certain extent the parents of every child) appearing before him. The situation is ripe for over-reaching, for imposition of the judge's own code of youthful conduct . . . One need not expound on the traditional American virtues of individuality and free expression to point out the wrong-headedness of so using the juvenile court . . .

Overreach of law—Roscoe Pound expressed grave reservations over the extent to which the health, education, and morals of children have come under the jurisdiction of the juvenile court, to say nothing of attempts to use elaborate legal means to control truancy, curfew violation, running away, smoking, and drinking. "When these matters are committed to courts," says Edwin N. Lemert in *Instead of Court,* "they necessarily delegate the work of enforcement to administrative agents, such as probation officers, whose capacity to achieve these ends is questionable." How can a probation officer or a policeman insure proper morals for a child, or an adequate education?

There are some social science propositions, Lemert comments further in a Crime Commission task force report, that merit consideration in examining the capacity of the court to address extra legal problems:

> A salient one is that the family, even though attenuated or disturbed by conflict, morally questionable, or broken by divorce or death, continues to be the institution of choice for the socialization of children. Neither the Spartan gymnasium, nor the Russian creches, nor the Israeli Kibbutz nurseries, nor scientifically run homes have been found to successfully duplicate the socio-psychological mystique which nurtures children into stable adults. Explicit recognition of this might very well preface the juvenile court codes and statutes of the land . . .

Neither the modern state nor an harassed juvenile court judge is a father; a halfway house is not a home; a reformatory cell is not a teen-ager's bedroom; a juvenile hall counselor is not a dutch uncle; and a cottage matron is not a mother.

Yet, the facts are that, when familial, school, and other youthful problems are written into the statutes as grounds for court action, this encourages parents, neighbors, schools, and others to pass on their problems to the court rather than trying to solve these prob-lems themselves. The basic problem is that legal definition and practices tend to be arbitrary, artificial, and insensitive to many subtle and difficult issues. It is questionable whether they can even be expected to substitute for the forms of learning, socialization, and control exercised not only by the home, but by peers, school, and community. Worse still are some of the psychological and social effects of legal action on juveniles themselves. A growing chorus of writers have suggested that, rather than solving many problems, the policies and practices of the juvenile court have made them worse.

Labeling and Stigma—In 1938, Frank Tannenbaum argued in *Crime and Community* that the final step in the making of an adult criminal occurs when youth become enmeshed in society's legalized methods for dealing with them. To be sure, the most vul-nerable group are those who are truant from school or considered to be the troublemakers in the neighborhood. They cause difficulties in the classroom, defy their parents, and frighten the neighbors. Ironically, however, as the community imposes increasing legal sanctions upon them, they are not really integrated back into the institutionalized track that leads to successful adulthood as one might hope, but are separated ever further from it. Thus, a self-fulfilling prophecy is set up that tends to evoke and make worse the very behavior that was complained about in the first place. Evil is dramatized, not eliminated.

All of this suggests, of course, that society must be concerned, not merely with the deviant behavior of children, but with the way it responds to delinquency. If deviant behavior has high visi-bility, and if society reacts severely to it, then the long-run results for the child may be disastrous. Not only must he deal with the stigma associated with his delinquent status, but must respond to more subtle cues regarding what is expected of him. Paradoxically, responses from youthful associates, delinquent and nondelinquent, as well as from officials, may tend to affirm his delinquent status. Hence, to the extent that he is sensitive to the expectations and actions of others, his behavior may easily mirror, not his normal role, but a deviant one.

Lemert also suggests that once a person is labeled he is expected to adhere to an additional set of official rules that apply only to him. But rather than helping to reduce his problems, they may only increase them. When a delinquent is placed on parole, for example, after having been incarcerated, he is often forbidden to live with an "unfit" parent; to associate with his former girl or boy friends, or to evidence any failures at school. Any failure to adhere to these special rules will, in itself, constitute a new act of deviance. Hence, the justice-correction system, in attempting to "treat" the delinquent, can actually escalate the grounds whereby his future behavior may be termed delinquent.

This increase in rules, coupled with the tendency for the delinquent to begin behaving in accordance with the expectations of his deviant status, may result in what Lemert calls *secondary* deviance. This kind of deviance evolves out of the adaptations the labeled person makes to the problems created by official and conformist reactions to his primary deviance. The stigma of being defined as delinquent results in a record for the child, both formal and informal. It is translated into heightened surveillance by officials, rejection by conformist children and their parents, lowered receptivity by school officials, and, eventually, an encumbrance when employment is sought. When these effects are added to those of minority or lower class status, the chances are decreased that the child can ever make his way back on to the institutional track that makes for successful adulthood.

Implications—The implications of the idea that there is an overreach of juvenile court law are manifold. First, they suggest the need to scrutinize, and likely reduce, the grounds by which a child can be defined as delinquent. By no means is it being suggested that predatory crime should not be identified and sanctioned, but the present body of ill-defined rules by which children can now be labeled as delinquent—drinking, smoking, "in danger of becoming delinquent," "out of control," truant, etc.—is excessive. Far from being socially harmful, some acts may be defined as delinquent because, and only because, they are proscribed legally.

Secondly, because the effects of legal overreach often tend to be the opposite of those desired, it is important to recognize that conformist self-concepts are forged *outside*, not within, the strictures of the juvenile justice system. Healthy and nondeviant identities are not likely to be produced by legal processing. Since, in the last analysis it is these that are being sought, the juvenile court system cannot be expected to solve problems that might better be left to families, schools, welfare agencies, and other community groups. By concentrating more narrowly on criminal kinds of behavior it might be more effective.

Thirdly, the analysis has implied that the forces that result eventually in the making of a delinquent or adult criminal do not reside solely within the individual. Rather, society and the juvenile justice system itself can easily contribute to that end. The labeling and stigmatizing processes that they generate may, in some cases, escalate the likelihood of further delinquent acts. In seeking to understand and correct the juvenile, therefore, the court's role in the process must be carefully scrutinized.

LACK OF DUE PROCESS

Not only have juvenile court statutes been criticized for legal overkill, but the failure of the court itself to protect the constitutional rights of the child has also been criticized. The Supreme Court documented this problem in a comment from its landmark decision on the now famous 1966 Kent case:

> While there can be no doubt of the original laudable purpose of juvenile courts, studies and critiques in recent years raise serious questions as to whether actual performance measures well enough against theoretical purpose to make tolerable the immunity of the process from the constitutional guarantees applicable to adults . . . *There is evidence, in fact, that there may be grounds for concern that the child receives the worse of two possible worlds: that he gets neither the protections accorded to adults nor the solicitous care and regenerative treatment postulated for children.* (emphasis added)

In a second landmark case, the Gault case, the Supreme Court held in 1967 that the code and practices of the state of Arizona deprived children of procedural safeguards guaranteed by the Fourteenth Amendment. Gerald Gault was a 15-year-old boy charged with making an obscene phone call to a neighbor. As a result of the juvenile court process, Gerald was incarcerated in a state institution where, according to law, he could have been held until the age of 21. By contrast, the maximum punishment he could have received, had he been an 18-year-old adult, would have been a fine of from $5 to $50, or imprisonment in jail for not more than two months.

Although the severity of this penalty is questionable enough by itself, it was but one of a long list of dubious court practices which the Supreme Court noted in reversing the original decision: Gerald was arrested and held in detention without notification of his parents. A petition authorizing the charges was not served on the Gaults prior to trial; in fact, the petition that was used made no reference to any factual basis for taking court action. It recited only that "said minor is under the age of 18 years and in need of the protection of this Honorable Court [and that] said minor is a delinquent minor."

Although the police and court action that led to the incarceration of Gerald was based on a verbal complaint by one of his neighbors, that complainant never appeared in court to give sworn testimony. In fact, no one was sworn in at the hearing, nor was any transcript or recording kept, nor was Gerald represented by counsel. Gerald was alleged to have confessed to making the call, but his "admissions," in court or otherwise, were never reduced to writing. His first "confession" was obtained out of the presence of his parents, without counsel, and without any advice as to his right to remain silent. In short, due process, so carefully pursued in adult criminal proceedings, was totally disregarded.

While the Gault case is only one, and possibly an extreme case, the Supreme Court suggested that the failure to exercise adequate safeguards is a general one that characterizes many jurisdictions, not just this one. Rights are granted to adults that are withheld from the juvenile. "Juvenile court history," said the Supreme Court, "has again demonstrated that unbridled discretion, however benevolently motivated, is frequently a poor substitute for principle and procedure." Citing Roscoe Pound, who had written that "the powers of the Star Chamber were a trifle in comparison of those of our juvenile courts," most of the justices concluded that "due process of law is the primary and indispensable foundation of individual freedom."

The justices also suggested that the observance of due process need not compel the states to abandon any of the benefits of the juvenile court. But since they did not indicate how this could be done, some important questions remain unanswered: can the anonymity of the juvenile be protected under the procedures of due process? Can counsel for juveniles be used without resort to the older adversary system? Can the needs of juveniles be addressed if too much formalism is inserted into the process? Although such questions as these must be answered, there is a growing consensus that more must be done to insure the protections of due process. It is difficult to see how a sense of justice and responsibility can be engendered in the young so long as they experience an arbitrary use of legal power by seemingly all-powerful police, court, and correctional authorities.

INDIVIDUALIZED APPROACH TO CORRECTIONS

Sources of Offenders' Difficulties—The need for enhancing the credibility and effectiveness of the juvenile justice system extends to its correctional segment as well as to the courts and police. One of the most profound puzzles which court and correctional personnel face is that of identifying the roots of the delinquency problem they wish to correct. In the introduction to this chapter, it was noted that, in the historical approach to corrections, society has tended always to locate the sources of delinquency *within* the offender: he was sinful and evil; he was rationally pursuing his own selfish gratifications; or he was biologically deformed in some way. More recently, with the rise of the juvenile court movement, the youthful offender has been more likely to be seen as a psychologically disturbed individual in need of treatment. Yet, as in the past, the sources of difficulty are still individually centered.

This focus upon the individual is an important one because it implies that, if correctional programs can change the offender, the crime problem will be eliminated. In recent years, however, a growing number of scientists and professionals have questioned this long-held assumption. The delinquency problem, and the forms of intervention needed, are far more complex than that.

Most people would now agree, for example, that distinctive biological features do not characterize delinquents or criminals. In fact, as Jack P. Gibbs has suggested, the possibility that such characteristics exist, even for particular criminal types such as murderers or bigamists, not only lacks scientific verification, but defies logic. "Since legislators are not geneticists, it is difficult to see how they can pass laws in such a way as to create 'born' criminals." But the same kind of thinking has been applied to the search for unique psychological characteristics, attitudes, or values as well. That search has not been particularly successful either. As Starke R. Hathaway *et al.* put it in 1960, personality measures "are much less powerful and apply to fewer cases among total samples than would be expected if one read the literature on the subject." Summaries of other studies suggest (1) that known offenders are more like than different from the general population, and (2) that measures of personality which yield deviancy variations reliably still do not distinguish criminal behavior types. It appears that legislators are unable to identify psychological aberration by passing laws just as they cannot identify born criminals.

These kinds of negative findings, as a result, lend support to those who argue that the causes for crime cannot be found solely in the structural characteristics of the offender any more than solely in the structural characteristics of society. Rather, it is the processes of interaction between the two that are more likely to hold the secret.

This emerging assumption places more emphasis than in the past upon the compelling pressures exerted upon the offender by persons living in his community, by the social groups to which he belongs, by our overall culture, and within it, a host of dissonant subcultures. It is the cultural and subcultural matrix from which the offender comes that prescribes his goals and his standards of conduct. And it is this matrix which will heavily influence whether he will become a success or a failure, a criminal or a law-abiding citizen.

With regard to the delinquent behavior of working-class and ghetto youth, a large body of existing theory has emphasized these very points. Born into conditions of poverty and deprived of the kinds of intellectual and interpersonal experiences necessary for achievement in a success-oriented society, lower class children are handicapped, if not doomed to failure. The result is a growing sense of frustration that not only alienates some of them from conventional roles and expectations, but turns a significant number to membership in delinquent groups where the tendency is to repudiate conformist values. Adherence to delinquent norms, alternative sources of satisfaction, and illegal activities are the result. Delinquency has been spawned.

As indicated in our analysis of court statutes and practices, it was also made clear that delinquency and crime, and reactions to them, are social products and are socially defined. Society, not individuals, defines rules, labels those who break rules, and prescribes ways for reacting to the labeled person. Hence, there are times when the societal process of defining, labeling, and reacting is problematic, times when it is far more influential in determining who shall enter the correctional process and what the outcome will be than techniques designed solely to change offenders.

Isolation of Offenders—The court process is especially problematic when, without due process, it labels young people who have familial, educational, and self-destructive problems as "delinquents." When this is done, and "offenders" are placed in correctional programs for lawbreakers, the process not only tends to encourage the adoption of a negative self-image by those so treated, but is a means of isolating them from, rather than integrating them in, effective participation in such major societal institutes as schools, businesses, unions, churches, and political organizations. These institutions are the major access to a successful, nondelinquent career. Those who are in power in them are the gatekeepers of society and, if offenders and correctional programs are isolated from them, then the personal wishes and characteristics of offenders will have only marginal bearing on whether correctional programs succeed or fail.

Existing correctional problems, then, can be divided into two general types: the first, an ideological or philosophical one that has tended to locate all difficulties within the individual offender; and the second, an operational one that tends to isolate most correctional practices and organizations from the mainstream of American institutional life. The point is that correctional programs are not organized to bring about changes in the economic, educational, and social functioning of the community. Rather, they are seen as appendages to it where, if possible, the community seeks to dump the problems it cannot or will not handle itself. Hence, as Judge Ted Rubin put it in 1968:

> Cursory supervision on probation has been an inadequate device for competition with pathological families and pathological environments. Welfare agencies have tended to shy away from giving services to delinquents. To counter this reluctance, many courts have set up their own programs, which have often been underfunded, inadequately supervised, short-lived and consequently ineffective.

Whether this pattern will ever change is difficult to say. It is clear, however, that, given the questionable effectiveness of incarceration for any purpose but the protection of society from serious, predatory offenders, more will have to be done to make correctional programs an ongoing part of the fabric of community life. For many offenders, correctional programs lack credibility because they seem incapable of addressing the very problems that are of greatest concern to them

—their relationships to family or schools, their inability to resist the pressures of delinquent associates and to gain the acceptance of nondelinquent ones, or their lack of opportunity for a job. To seek changes in the offender, therefore, without concomitant changes in the community, is to address only one side of a two-sided problem.

In summary, our analysis of the problems of the juvenile justice system has implied the need to reduce the ways by which many juveniles are now inserted into the legal process, to insure that the protections of due process are provided for those who are, and to find ways for making the whole system of juvenile justice, especially the correctional segment, a more effective part of the entire community.

Suggested Reforms

The reforms for the juvenile justice system that have been suggested have one overriding theme; namely, the need to revise existing court and correctional practices in such a way that young people with problems can be integrated more effectively into, rather than separated from, the conformist and rewarding features of the community. This theme has not been articulated very well, but much more than in the past it emphasizes prevention rather than control, correction of the entire system as well as correction of the individual. Relying less upon legal machinery, attempts are being made to find ways to give young people a stake in conformity rather than merely reacting to deviant behavior once it appears. Many unanticipated problems are undoubtedly inherent in such an approach, but its emerging features are symbolized by three fundamental concepts: *diversion, due process,* and *deinstitutionalization.*

DIVERSION

Perhaps more than anything else, the criticisms of the juvenile justice system outlined above suggest that an impossible burden has been laid upon that system. Expectations that it can both prevent delinquency and simultaneously correct almost every conceivable youth problem are unrealistic. Therefore, steps should be taken to divert from the system many of the juveniles and the problems that heretofore it has been expected to correct. "If there is a defensible philosophy for the juvenile court," said Lemert in 1967 in a Crime Commission task force report, "it is one of *judicious nonintervention*" (emphasis added). The court "is properly an agency of last resort for children, holding to a doctrine analogous to that of appeals courts which require that all remedies be exhausted before a case will be considered." Since the powers of the juvenile court are extraordinary, it should deal only with extraordinary cases. Consonant with Lemert's idea, two major recommendations have been made by which they could be implemented.

Narrowing Juvenile Court Mandate—The first step would involve a narrowing of the juvenile court mandate by reducing the number of legal rules which define that mandate. Norval Morris and Gordon Hawkins in *The Honest Politician's Guide to Crime Control* have advanced a number of arguments in favor of such a reduction. Although they were speaking with reference to crime as well as delinquency, many of their points are applicable here.

> We must strip off the moralistic excrescences on our [juvenile] justice system so that it may concentrate on the essential. The prime function of the criminal law is to protect our persons and our property; these purposes are now engulfed in a mass of other distracting, inefficiently performed legislative duties. When the criminal law invades the spheres of private morality and social welfare, it exceeds its proper limits at the cost of neglecting its primary tasks. . . .

Thus, these authors would distinguish between those acts that are predatory, and those that are not, and alter the rules to eliminate many of the latter as crimes.

The same kinds of suggestions have been made with respect to legal rules that apply only to juveniles. A number of different people and organizations, including the President's Commission on Law Enforcement and Administration of Justice, have suggested that young people should not be prosecuted and receive penal sanctions for behavior which, if exhibited by adults, would not be prosecuted. Some also suggest that legal rules should not put police and judges in the position of having to decide what is moral or immoral conduct for young people. Such decisions are better left to other institutions and processes.

Efforts to revise legal statutes or reduce sanctions might also help to encourage respect for the law, and to reduce the hypocrisy in which legal authorities are often forced to engage. Consider a comment by the National Commission on the Causes and Prevention of Violence as it applied to the current widespread use of marijuana:

> Since many of our youths believe marijuana to be relatively harmless and, yet, are faced with legal sanctions, they are led into a practice

of law evasion which contributes to general disrespect for law. . . . The present harsh penalties for possession and use of marijuana are a classic example of what legal scholars call "over-criminalization"—treating as a serious crime private personal conduct that a substantial segment of the community does not regard as a major offense; prosecutors, judges and juries tend to moderate the severity of the statutory sanctions, and the resulting hypocrisy of all concerned diminishes respect for the law.

As a result of these considerations, some authorities have recommended that sanctions for the possession or personal use of marijuana, and some other drugs, be reduced or eliminated and concentration placed upon finding greater resources for reducing drug dependence, and for apprehending the suppliers of them.

Morris and Hawkins argue that if these kinds of changes were instituted, three major benefits would result. First, the numbers of people defined as delinquent or criminal would be reduced by as much as three million cases annually, a sizeable prevention effort indeed. In numerical terms, this kind of reduction might be far greater than that which could be achieved by more traditional and limited kinds of correctional programs. Moreover, the pressures on police, courts and corrections would be greatly reduced, leaving society's agents of control with much greater means for combatting serious forms of crime—violence, burglary, robbery, and other predatory acts of this kind.

Secondly, diversion through the revision of legal rules would result in much less interference in the private moral conduct of the citizen, leaving the resolution of many juvenile status problems— truancy, running away, drinking, dependency, and "incorrigibility" —to other institutions. If the labeling proponents are correct, then many forms of secondary deviance could also be prevented.

Thirdly, since many of the sources of income for organized crime come from the sale of such things as narcotics, gambling and illicit sex—activities around which there is no normative consensus in the populace—these sources would be dried up. The financial power of organized crime would be seriously hurt.

While these proposed changes have considerable appeal, it is clear that they would be devoted more to restructuring legal institutions, and eliminating harmful practices, than in indicating how legitimate identities are developed among the young. This is not to denigrate the importance of such changes, but to indicate the many dimensions and complexities of implementing the diversionary concept. Moreover, it is important to recognize that the removal of such acts as truancy, juvenile neglect, or "ungovernability" as delinquent offenses, while it may reduce the effects of legal stigma and the burdens on the juvenile justice system, would not really solve the problems of the youngsters in question. The point is that rule changes are but one of the kinds of steps needed for successful programs of diversion. Unless they are accompanied by additional forms of remediation—administered by schools, welfare agencies, and others—they may be little more than a sociological sleight-of-hand, a kind of social magic without lasting positive effect.

Another question to which little attention has been paid has to do with the extent to which, in a modern, impersonal and technological society, its members are dependent upon legislators and the courts to define basic norms for the society. The diversionary philosophy is based upon the assumption that individual morality has become functional and personal rather than sacred and universal in an older sense.

The problem with this assumption is in deciding what the moral and legal "minimum" should be for youth, and who should set it. Should society, for example, establish legal injunctions against the use of marijuana by the young? Should it attempt to regulate sexual behavior, or prostitution? Where should the society draw the legal line on these and a plethora of other issues? Such acts as robbery, murder, and assault are universally condemned, but who, if legislatures and courts do not, shall define other acts as unacceptable, or immoral?

In considering such questions it should not be forgotten that the juvenile court was originally set up to protect children from many problems that have now been eliminated—the exploiters of child labor, the sweat shop, an immoral servant class, cruel immigrant fathers, and traveling carnivals and circuses. Hence, Lemert suggests in a 1967 Crime Commission task force report that we have now entered into an era in which it has ". . . become more important to protect children from unanticipated and unwanted consequences of organized movements, programs and services in their behalf than from the unorganized, adventitious 'evils' which gave birth to the juvenile court."

As a method of trying to insure that reforms in legal rules and practices have a desirable effect, two suggestions have been made. First, Morris and Hawkins suggest that every legislature should have a standing law revision committee charged with the task of reviewing constantly the adequacy of existing rules, and the impact of any changes that are made. The task of reform, in other words, would not be a one-shot thing; rather the committee would act as a monitor over the legal system, and be charged with the responsibility of cleaning out the debris of useless laws and policies and seeing that new ones fulfill the purposes for which they were created.

Secondly, Rubin suggests that any alterations, either in basic legal rules, or in the administration of them, be tried on an experimental basis. Any time, for example, that new rules call for radical alterations in the services rendered by the justice-correctional system, an experimental design should be set up to see if the new social alternatives that are used are any better. Research would be conducted regularly to determine what the effects of legal changes actually are.

While these two suggestions are obviously debatable, they do represent ways for approaching the task of change in a reasonably systematic and rational way. If such steps are not taken, in fact, it will be difficult to build the necessary knowledge by which existing theory and practice can be tested, revised, and improved.

Diversion to Other Agencies—In addition to changes in the legal rules that define delinquency, a second major form of diversion would involve greater participation by other community agencies in dealing with youth problems. It is often assumed that the process by which a child becomes a delinquent involves only a simple act of arrest and adjudication by the court. It is much more complex than that, however, involving families, schools, neighbors, and police. In most cases, referral to court represents the cumulative effects of several kinds of experiences in several different contexts. The child may be neglected at home, a nuisance in the neighborhood, and a troublemaker at school. Any one of these groups may ask for intervention by the court, or if the police are called in for the commission of a specific act, they are often influenced negatively by a record of poor school adjustment or an angry and noncooperative family. The eventual act of adjudication, therefore, is likely to represent but the last in a long sequence of events, a sequence that might have been interrupted more profitably at some earlier point.

The diversionary philosophy is based upon the simple premise that intervention would be far more effective if, in lieu of detention and court action, it involved remedial action by one or more community agencies. Not only does a court appearance place the child's integrity and sense of moral worth in question, but intervention by community agencies may be much more central to the problems he faces. They can provide a more normal and less stigmatizing form of adjustment for him.

The basic intent is to find alternative methods of help and control that have been utilized most effectively in middle and upper class communities—suspended action by the police, referral to parents, and private placement in some remedial program. In recent years, efforts have been made to expand the availability of such resources in slum and lower class settings so that diversion can be made to work more effectively for the youth who live there. Youth from all strata and ethnic groups require equal opportunity.

In 1971, Lemert provided some much needed suggestions, out-lining not one but several models for diversion—a school, a welfare, a law-enforcement, and a community organization model. But it is only fair to say that, in terms of development, the diversionary movement is still in an embryonic phase. While such important bodies as the President's Commission on Law Enforcement and Administration of Justice have strongly endorsed it, few communities have organized themselves to implement it.

If there is one problem that has characterized most prevention and correction programs for delinquents, it has been their insular character. Rather than becoming an integral part of the community fabric, they are usually set apart from it. Lacking a strong institutional base in the community, they operate as a separate clinic, a recreation center, or a storefront hangout. Admittedly, some good can be accomplished in such settings, but that is not enough. Why not locate such programs in a setting where children with problems are not segregated from those whom we would prefer they emulate? How can they acquire the behavior patterns that are desired if they have no role models to follow?

Consider, for example, the possibility that more might be done to assist the school to play a central role in diversion. In our society, the young have become superfluous in the world of work. The unskilled, highly routine jobs once reserved for them have disappeared, and child labor laws, designed ironically to prevent their exploitation, now exclude them from satisfying work. Hence, the school has become a place of segregation for the young, and if legitimate identities are not acquired there, they may never materialize.

Not only is the school the one institution upon which employers and governments, as well as parents, rely for the preparation of the young for adulthood, but many cultural, recreational, and sports activities are funneled through it as well. Since such activities are of great importance for adolescents, it is not difficult to see why the school plays such an important role in the socialization of the young. Without it, they are denied access to the roles that establish them as legitimate, meaningful people.

In conclusion, the narrowing of the juvenile court mandate, and the diversion of many juveniles to other agencies, might do much to correct the overreach of the law that was instituted during the historical development of the juvenile court. Recognizing that many juvenile problems are rooted in the ongoing processes of the community, the existing needs of young people might be better served if these processes were altered in lieu of the extensive use of legal intervention.

DUE PROCESS

The provision of constitutional protections for the individual is such an important American tradition that it is difficult to see why children, of all people, have often been denied these protections. It is not merely that accepted safeguards have often been lacking, but that the juvenile court has been asked to play a game it cannot win. On one hand, it has been asked to deal with traditional forms of law breaking—robbery, burglary, assault, etc.—from which society requires protection, and for which legal procedures are clearly appropriate.

On the other hand, the court has also been asked to act as a social agency, not only for the purpose of controlling juvenile criminals and protecting the dependent and neglected, but for enforcing some unenforceable statutes. Consider some of the legal definitions of delinquency drawn from a number of different states. A delinquent is anyone "who habitually deports himself as to injure or endanger the morals or health of himself or others," or "who persistently or habitually refuses to obey the reasonable and proper orders or directives of his parents, guardian, custodian or school authorities, or who is beyond control of such persons," or "who from any cause is in danger of leading an idle, dissolute, lewd or immoral life."

To add insult to injury, attempts to enforce and to adjudicate such statutes as these have usually taken place in informal hearings, in the absence of legal defense counsel, in the absence of sworn testimony, and through the use of hearsay evidence. Not only would such procedures be totally unacceptable in most adult courts, but they could not be used as the basis for imposing severe sanctions. Yet, the juvenile court has been empowered to remove juveniles from their homes, to place them on probation, or to place them in a foster home, a private institution, or a state training school. Admittedly, it is not always possible to separate basic childhood problems from clear-cut violations of criminal law, but attempts to correct the latter scarcely justify the loss of constitutional safeguards for everyone. It is little wonder, then, that recommendations have been made to curtail the awesome powers of the juvenile court, and why, if juvenile problems are to be "corrected," such reforms are a necessity.

A mistaken assumption that is often made about those who advocate reforms of this type is that they do not view delinquency as a serious problem, and that they advocate a kind of permissiveness in which delinquency would be encouraged, not deterred. That is not true. Rather, it is being suggested that by screening out from the court's jurisdiction the preponderant majority of all juveniles who used to find themselves there for ill-defined and essentially noncriminal acts, greater justice could be served. Simultaneously, officials would be in a better position to deal more swiftly and effectively with juveniles who do commit criminal acts. Both society and the nation's youth would be better protected.

Due Process for Criminal Acts—With regard to the need for due process for the juvenile who does commit a criminal act, there must be certain prerequisites. First, as suggested above, there must be more consensus than at present on the deviant acts that are proscribed. For example, many authorities have suggested that a more narrowly circumscribed set of statutes concerned only with obvious harm to persons or property should be sought.

Secondly, the response of the juvenile justice system to predatory acts must be swift and efficient. Contrary to much public opinion, there is some evidence that the fear of punishment, as well as the anticipation of reward, has an influence on human behavior. A belief that the probability of punishment is high may directly deter the likelihood of criminal behavior among young people, especially if there is immediate response to their criminal acts.

Thirdly, the convicted person must learn from his experience, and be provided with a set of alternatives to delinquency. Effective learning is likely to be based upon two things: (a) the extent to which he is treated justly and fairly during the court experience, and (b) the extent to which correctional programs are able to assist him in adopting a legitimate identity and in achieving an acceptable nondelinquent role.

The existing evidence is overwhelmingly opposed to the notion that the juvenile justice system is now capable of realizing these three objectives. It is clogged and overburdened with cases of dependency and neglect, as well as cases of clear-cut law violation. Conditions are such as to question the system's effectiveness with the former, while the latter often escape the kinds of control they need. Hence, assuming that noncriminal acts by juveniles can be eliminated from court jurisdiction, the system might be able to insure due process and at the same time act more efficiently. Accompanied by appropriate correctional reforms, juvenile acts of criminal behavior might be addressed more effectively.

Insofar as the process of adjudication is concerned, the Supreme Court decisions mentioned earlier will require that several major steps be taken. At the time of arrest, the juvenile will have to be provided, at the very least, with the rights afforded adults: the right of both parents and child to be informed of the specific charges against the child; to be afforded the right to remain silent; to have counsel present during interrogation, if that is desired; and the right to be released into the custody of parents or on bond pending trial.

During the trial there are still many grounds for arguing that procedures should remain as informal as possible. Yet, during this period, there is special need for legal counsel. Traditionally, legal defense for the child has been extremely rare. The *Gault* decision, however, requires that counsel must be available. Not every child must have a lawyer, but every child has a right to one and must be so notified. Upon request, the court must secure the services of a lawyer if the family cannot afford one.

Procedures Pertinent to Juvenile Needs—There are many roles lawyers can play. In addition to insuring that methods of questioning, prior to trial, are proper or that a summons is properly served, the lawyer is needed to render judgments regarding the validity of the statute under which the child is charged, what his plea shall be, whether complaining witnesses are properly cross-examined, or whether evidence is admissible. In addition to these traditional court roles, he can assist in determining proper placement for the child; whether it is wise to remove him from his own home, or whether a mental health clinic or a private social agency would be preferable to the usual public agencies.

Paradoxically, it is not merely defense counsel that is needed, but reasonable and sound prosecution as well. In many jurisdictions, it has been customary for the investigating probation officer to act both as prosecutor and defense counsel and, then, if the court is small, to act as the correctional agent as well. This has led to all sorts of unimaginable difficulties and role conflicts, if for no other reason than that the probation officer is not a trained lawyer. Instead, his main obligation is to the court which employs him, not to the client or to the prosecution. Provision will have to be made, then, for a prosecutor who, as a member of the district attorney's staff, is a specialist in juvenile court law and procedure, and who is acquainted with, and promoting the need for, rehabilitation facilities in a community. While there is danger in the possibility that prosecution and defense counsel will become so locked in adversary proceedings that they overlook the needs of the child, there is no reason why they cannot be acquainted with these needs as well, and so conduct their business.

It comes as a surprise to many that in some states it has not been necessary for juvenile court judges to have legal training. This, coupled with the fact that lawyers and judges generally have little knowledge of childhood problems, means that much on-the-job as well as legal training is needed. The effective management of due process, especially for children, requires that judges be familiar with childhood needs and perspective, as well as the formalistic character of the law.

In sum, this short analysis has indicated that some traditional problems might be "corrected" (1) if many of the dependency, neglect, and moral problems of juveniles are left to other community agencies and do not become a matter of legalistic, court decision-making; (2) if the constitutional provisions of due process are extended to juveniles; and (3) if, in addition to adequate constitutional safeguards, legal personnel adopt court procedures pertinent to the unique needs of juveniles.

DEINSTITUTIONALIZTION

Efforts to deinstitutionalize correctional programs are based upon the growing belief that captivity for law violators does not successfully correct them. Beside such glaring examples in support of this trend as the riot at Attica State Prison in New York there are other signs.

Places of incarceration are what Goffman in 1961 called "total institutions." The total institution, he said, "is a social hybrid, part residential community, part formal organization . . ." which attempts both to punish and to reform the offender. It is so full of logical contradictions, therefore, that while it effectively suppresses the offender, it does little to change him.

The reasons are not difficult to discover. Conditions of imprisonment, even among such nondelinquents as prisoners-of-war or mental patients, almost inevitably seem to produce "anti" rather than "pro" organizational sentiments. Captivity, quite aside from one's delinquent or nondelinquent history, only seems to confirm negative perceptions of authority and to heighten resistances to change.

The reason is that places of confinement are typically caste systems. Inmates and authorities are divided into discrete groups, and even though the ostensible role of corrections is to help offenders to adopt the same perspectives, values and behaviors as their captors, the structural characteristics of a caste system make it difficult, if not impossible, for them to do so. In an effort to ease the pains of captivity, it is common for offenders to initiate their own illegal systems of barter and exchange, to engage in homosexual behavior—often raping unwilling inmates—to trade in illicit drugs, food or clothing and, in order to make all these things possible, to corrupt their guards in one way or another.

The impact of all this on the self-image of the young inmate is devastating. Membership in a place of incarceration places him in a kind of no-man's land where he is accepted neither by staff members as one of them, nor by the public as one of them. "Once an inmate, always an inmate." Consequently, the only place he has to turn for a sense of identity and definition of purpose is to his fellow inmates. Yet this is precisely what we do not want to happen. We would like the impressionable young person to identify with nondelinquents and with prosocial points of view, not the reverse.

In an effort to forestall such problems, special treatment institutions for juveniles have been built, but ironically, they seem to have perpetuated many of the same difficulties. Except for the protection of society in the most extreme cases, there is little evidence to support the notion that juvenile institutions are successful. Without some day-to-day contacts with normal people in normal surroundings, it is virtually impossible to devise organizational arrangements by which to encourage the offender to stop conceiving of himself as "delinquent," "inmate," or "patient" and to start thinking of himself as a self-determining and socially acceptable "nondelinquent," "student," or "employee." The problems inherent in trying to manage the total lives of an often large group of captives seem to preclude it.

Finally, perhaps the most devastating criticism of imprisonment is related to its separation of the offender from the community. The crux of any treatment program has ultimately to do with its ability to reintegrate the offender into the community, not to help him adjust to the atypical and stultifying routine of a reformatory. While it is true that he must discard delinquent beliefs and rationalizations, he must also have help in finding new and acceptable roles in society. It is in accomplishing this task that reformatories have little to contribute. Their efforts at rehabilitation do little, if anything, to change the social conditions that gave rise to the offender's problems in the first place.

Move to Community—It is for these reasons that most of the pressures in recent years have favored the deinstitutionalization of correctional programs and the improvement and enlargement of a number of community alternatives. As evidence of this, statistics reveal that in 1967 the ratio of delinquents in community versus institutional programs was four-to-one: two hundred eighty-five thousand were in the community while only sixty-three thousand were confined. The President's Crime Commission also popularized the notion of Youth Service Bureaus through which delinquents could be dealt with in their own communities. California instituted a probation subsidy program by which state funds are used to subsidize local counties for retaining many adults as well as juveniles who would otherwise be incarcerated. As a result, some institutions have been closed down, and new ones remain unopened. In Massachusetts recently, steps were taken to eliminate entirely all of the state's juvenile training schools and to substitute community programs for them. In short, the movement to deinstitutionalize correctional programs is growing.

Lack of Evaluation—While the movement reflects a growing climate of tolerance for juvenile offenders, the continuation of the movement will depend in the long run upon its ability to demonstrate some degree of success. Although the history of correctional movements has been characterized by an effort to make correctional programs more humane, it is clear that humane practices are not the same thing as the effective control of delinquency. Therefore, if the current movement is to be different, greater attention will have to be devoted to the conduct of scientific study.

To insure that such study is carried out is no mean task. As Stanton Wheeler and Leonard S. Cottrell point out in *Juvenile Delinquency: Its Prevention and Control:*

> No responsible business concern would operate with as little information regarding its success or failure as do nearly all of our delinquency prevention and control programs. It is almost possible to count on one hand the number of true experiments in which alternative techniques are compared; the number of systematic, though non-experimental evaluations is not a great deal larger. We spend millions of dollars a year in preventive and corrective efforts, with little other than guesswork to tell us whether we are getting the desired effects.

Hence, there is not a wealth of sound evidence upon which to justify the current effort to deinstitutionalize correctional programs.

In order to best understand the evidence that is available, however, it is useful to consider three types of community programs: *probation* which, as the oldest of community programs, involves only periodic supervision of the offender; *nonresidential programs* which provide more contact with the offender than probation, often on a daily basis while he continues to live at home; and *residential group homes* where offenders continue to live in the community, away from their families, but without the duress of guards and physical restraints on their movements. There are many variations on these three forms of community intervention, but they provide the most convenient, general framework for analysis.

PROBATION

Probation was introduced initially as a humanitarian measure, not as a scientific endeavor to discover more effective rehabilitative techniques. Early proponents wished simply to keep first offenders and minor recidivists from undergoing the corrupting effects of jail. Their orientation was social in nature.

During and after World War I, a marked change occurred in this orientation. As probation work continued to expand, there was an ever increasing demand for professionally educated people, especially trained social workers, to serve as probation officers. And the training of social workers, in turn, was profoundly influenced by the introduction of psychiatric and especially psychoanalytic theory. This theory was preoccupied with the individual and his emotional makeup, and the training of the professional caseworker reflected this concern.

More and more the offender was seen as a disturbed person in whom emotional healing was necessary, and the ability of the probation worker was judged in terms of his capacity to offer psychiatrically oriented therapy. Thus, both the philosophy and administration of probation became a highly complex admixture of psychotherapeutic theory and the older concern with helping the offender to adjust economically and socially to his environment. To some degree, it remains that way today. The ideology of probation is broad and amorphous, one of generalized beneficence. Ideally, it is supposed to help the offender with all phases of his life, as well as monitoring his capacity for discipline and self-control. Yet, in practice, the individual officer may be expected to maintain a caseload of from 75 to 200 probationers, to conduct presentence investigations, to maintain extensive paper work, and perhaps to carry out other functions as well. It is obvious, therefore, that ideology of beneficence has not been reconciled with probation in practice.

Despite these limitations, the research evidence relative to probation effectiveness is both surprising and revealing. In a summary analysis of fifteen probation studies conducted in a variety of jurisdictions, Ralph England reported success rates which varied between 60 and 90 percent. A survey by Max Grunhut of probation effectiveness in such states as Massachusetts, California, New York, and a variety of foreign countries provides similar reported results with the modal success rate at about 75 percent.

These findings are not totally valid because they were not obtained under experimental conditions nor were they supported by data which distinguished among the types of offenders who succeeded or the types of services that were rendered. Nevertheless, the success rates were rather uniform and relatively high and cannot, therefore, be discounted totally. They are the product of a variety of kinds of probation administered in different times and places.

Another key issue relative to the effectiveness of probation has to do with the potential danger to the community that probationers might pose. Is the community being adequately protected? The public commonly assumes that if offenders are not incarcerated, community safety will be endangered. This kind of question, for example, has been raised with respect to California's probation subsidy program in which the state has underwritten greater use of probation on a local level in lieu of incarceration by the state.

In a document released by the chief probation officer of Los Angeles County in 1972, the following evidence, drawn from the California State Bureau of Criminal Statistics, was cited:

1. In 1970, there were 123,716 individuals (both adults and juveniles) on probation in Los Angeles County. During that same period, only 682 of them, or 0.6 percent, were convicted of crimes agains persons. This meant that well over 99 percent were not found guilty of any delinquent act involving homicide, forcible rape, felony assault of any kind, robbery, or kidnapping.

2. Only 0.03 percent of the 123,716 probationers were convicted of homicide during 1970. Well over 99 percent were not involved in the most feared of all crimes. While this is a very low violation rate, the same would be true of the population at large. Very few people commit murders. Therefore, a basic question is whether the rate for probationers is higher. The report did not address this issue. Nevertheless, these are impressive findings which, contrary to prevailing opinion, suggest that offenders who have been found guilty of crime, but left on probation in the community, are not necessarily responsible for new crimes of violence. Such crimes, instead, are often committed by people who do not have prison records or are not on probation. Moreover, the chief probation officer's report indicates that the rate of revocation for people on probation has not gone up in Los Angeles County during the period of the probation subsidy program. Instead, it has remained at about the same rate (16 percent) for the past decade. Over eight out of ten persons did not violate the condition of their probation.

Even when evidence of this type is interpreted skeptically, some important issues are raised. But rather than suggesting that probation is of little utility, they suggest instead that steps should be taken to improve its functioning. Efforts to do so might not only be much less expensive than more complex programs, but also be more effective.

NONRESIDENTIAL COMMUNITY PROGRAMS

During the past decade, considerable effort has been expended on trying to develop nonresidential community programs that provide greater supervision for serious offenders than regular probation, but which stop short of total incarceration. Although the basic assumptions underlying these programs have differed widely, they have one thing in common. All tend to assume that, by working with the offender in the community, a more concerted attack can be made on his basic problems than if he were incarcerated.

Differential Treatment—One such program is the Community Treatment Program sponsored by the California Youth Authority and directed by Marguerite Q. Warren. This project, widely acclaimed for its promise, utilized randomly selected experimental and control groups as a means of determining effectiveness of programming in the community as contrasted to total incarceration in an institution.

The experimental group was released to the community where each individual was diagnosed according to his maturity level and, on the basis of that diagnosis, assigned to a parole agent skilled in working with that kind of delinquent. The control group was assigned to one of the institutions of the California Youth Authority where, after confinement, its members were released on regular parole. While in the community, the caseloads in the experimental program were small, from 9 to 10 offenders per agent, as compared to around 55 offenders per agent in the control program.

The published findings favored the community program. After a follow-up period of 15 months, 51 percent of the control group had violated parole, or had been unfavorably discharged, as contrasted to only 30 percent of the boys who were left in the community. After 24 months, the outcomes again favored the experimentals, 43 versus 63 percent.

Some questions have been raised about these findings, however, suggesting that differences may have been due, at least in part, to greater tolerance on the part of experimental staff to juvenile misconduct; that is, regular parole agents may have been more willing than experimental agents to revoke parole. This argument was countered by experimental staff who argued that, because of their more careful surveillance of offenders, they were not only more aware of violations by the juveniles under their care than were regular parole agents, but that juveniles should not have their paroles revoked for relatively minor incidents.

Until such issues are resolved, it will be difficult to be certain about the precise effects of the experimental program. Nevertheless, by taking a conservative stance, it would seem fair to say that the community program was doing at least as well as total incarceration without embodying all of the more subtle and negative effects of incarceration. This is not an insignificant achievement, and would certainly seem to argue for more experimentation.

Provo Experiment—The Provo Experiment, directed by this author, is a second experiment that has received rather wide attention. Like the Community Treatment Program, this one utilized experimental and control groups as a method of testing the effectiveness of intensive, nonresidential intervention for serious offenders, ages 15–18 years. This time, however, the experimental program was compared to two control programs: (1) regular probation and (2) total incarceration in a state training school.

Unlike the differential treatment model, however, an effort was made to give delinquents a greater say in what happened to them; i.e., to sponsor them in an active rather than passive role. This was done by using group techniques in which delinquents, along with staff, helped to solve problems, to extend controls, and to make decisions. Although boys lived in their own homes, these groups met daily, five days a week. In addition, an effort was made to open up conventional opportunities for them by providing a city work program, trying to keep them in school, and trying to find jobs after they were released.

In the book evaluating this experiment, the arrest rates of experimental and control subjects were compared both during and following intervention. An attempt was made as well to determine whether the effects of intervention were any more useful than no intervention at all. The results were these:

1. *Arrest rates during intervention.* An attempt was first made to discover whether serious offenders in the experimental program were a danger to the public while still under correctional supervision. It was discovered, however, that arrest rates for the experimental subjects were significantly lower than for those on regular probation. More intensive supervision for this group of serious delinquents, virtually all of whom had already failed on probation, seemed to pay off.

Of greater significance was the fact that arrest rates for the experimental subjects in the open community were almost as low as for those who were incarcerated. This seemed to be an impossible finding, but it was discovered that, despite institutional restrictions, some of the latter group committed new offenses while they were on furlough, or when they escaped from confinement. Moreover, it was this group, not the experimental boys or the boys on probation, who committed the most serious offenses. In fact, eight out of ten arrests of the community groups were for juvenile status offenses—truancy, "incorrigibility," drinking, curfew, etc.—not for criminal offenses. There was little evidence, then, that during the period of intervention, community programming was a danger to the community even though, under ordinary circumstances, many of these boys would have been incarcerated.

2. *Arrest rates following intervention.* All subjects were followed in the study for four years after release, until most of all of them had reached the legal age of adulthood. In comparing the relative effectiveness of experimental and control groups, it was found that the intensive experimental program did not seem to be greatly superior to regular probation. There was some evidence that the more intensive program resulted in fewer arrests during interven-vention, and fewer postrelease confinements, but its effects were not clearly superior in every circumstance.

By contrast, the experimental program was clearly superior to total incarceration. The boys who participated in it had significantly fewer arrests, their offenses were less serious, and far fewer of them were confined for adult crimes. For example, the findings showed that, after four years almost 40 percent of the boys who were confined had been arrested for highly serious offenses—assault, rape, kidnapping, grand larceny, burglary, and for two cases of homicide. If one wanted to locate a population of adult criminals, therefore, it would come from the incarcerated group, not the ones who remained in the community.

3. *Crime control.* Another way to evaluate programs like these is to evaluate their ability to reduce crime rates. This was done in the Provo Experiment by comparing the arrest rates of the various groups for the four years following the experiment with the rates for the four years preceding it. An attempt was made to determine whether boys were as delinquent after the experiment as before.

The findings reveal a surprising reduction in delinquent behavior, especially for the boys who remained in the community in the experimental program or on probation. For the probation experimental group, there was a 71 percent reduction; for the probation control group, a 66 percent reduction; and for the incarceration experimental group, a 49 percent reduction. Only in the case of the control group that was incarcerated was the reduction much smaller, 25 percent. Given the extent to which it is assumed that correctional programs have no effect, especially those in the community, these findings are provocative.

4. *Controlling for effects of intervention.* Given the fact that

crime rates tend to decelerate rapidly following adolescence, it is possible that the reductions just described were due not to the effects of intervention but to the effects of growing older, of maturing. Therefore, complex statistical procedures were used to control for the effects of age (and social class).

The analysis tended to confirm the notion that the experimental program had had clear and differential effects. While age did have an effect on the declining rates, the effects of the community programs, especially the experimental one, were positive while those of incarceration were highly negative. In other words, incarceration may have seriously impeded, rather than accelerated, desirable changes in delinquent boys. Just the opposite occurred in the experimental programs and, to a lesser degree, in the probation control program.

In conclusion, these two experiments, plus impressionistic findings from other studies, suggest that community programs may not only be of less danger to the community than is generally assumed, but may be far more effective in the long run than incarceration. For example, while only a handful of the boys in the community programs at Provo were ever confined in juvenile or adult institutions, 37 percent of the control boys who had been incarcerated were not only reconfined again in a juvenile institution, but 21 percent were eventually locked up in adult prison. Furthermore, the rates of reconfinement for this group coincide rather closely with those in other jurisdictions where delinquents have been confined: 40 percent reconfinement rates for the federal system; parole revocation rates of from 31 to 64 percent for the California system; reconfinement rates between 44 and 51 percent in Wisconsin; and a 26 percent rate for boys in Florida who were eventually confined in an adult institution. Although indirect, this evidence tends to confirm the idea that incarceration is not working effectively. At the very least, continued experimentation with community programming seems warranted.

RESIDENTIAL COMMUNITY PROGRAMS

Residential community programs are another alternative to total incarceration, because it is felt that the homes of some juveniles are so poor that they must be placed elsewhere. If greater use is made of diversionary programs for the neglected, the mentally disturbed, and the dependent, however, then one basic question is whether such homes are useful for the law-violating delinquent, either as an alternative to nonresidential programs or to total incarceration. The available evidence is mixed.

Highfields—The prototype for group-oriented but small residential centers is the Highfields Program, which was described by Lloyd W. McCorkle, Albert Elias, and F. Lovel Bixby. Highfields limits its population to 20 boys, ages 16 to 17, who are assigned directly from the juvenile court. Boys live informally in an old home without the usual institutional guards and detailed routine.

During the day, the boys work at a nearby mental hospital. In the evening, the total population is broken into two groups of ten, each of which then has a meeting. Formal rules are few. Control, instead, is exercised informally through the development of a group culture which presumably decreases distance between staff and offenders and sponsors the offender in a more active, reformation role. The idea is that individuals are best helped who themselves become capable of helping others. These are the principles which underlie Alcoholics Anonymous and Synanon, the private center run by and for drug addicts.

In order to test the effectiveness of the Highfields Program, its graduates were compared to a group of boys who had been committed to the New Jersey State Reformatory for males at Annandale. A lower percentage of Highfields than of Annandale boys recidivated (37 versus 53 percent). However, the results of the comparison have been debated because both groups were not randomly selected under experimental conditions such as they were in the Community Treatment Program or the Provo Experiment. Without such selection, there is some doubt as to whether the groups are comparable. For example, the Annandale boys tended to be a little older, perhaps more experienced in delinquency, and from poorer social backgrounds than the Highfields boys. As a consequence, the most appropriate conclusion is that Highfields has been proved neither less nor more successful than regular incarceration. What is significant, however, is that at least similar results were achieved at much less expense both in money and time saved in the lives of the delinquents. The stay at Highfields was only three or four months, and many of the negative aspects of institutionalization were avoided.

Silverlake Experiment—The Silverlake Experiment, conducted in Los Angeles, was modeled along the lines of the Provo Experiment, except that boys lived together rather than at home, and each one of them was required to attend school. These experimental boys were randomly selected and compared to a control group that was placed in a small noncustodial, educationally-oriented, private institution. The book describing this experiment notes several important findings.

After a one-year follow-up, it was found that the graduates of these two programs had almost identical arrest records. Six out of ten had no arrests, and eight out of ten had no more than one arrest. Very few of these arrests, moreover, involved serious offenses. Both groups had done well. Yet, what these outcome records for graduates does not reveal is that both of these residential, but noncustodial, programs had had high runaway and failure rates. Approximately half of the boys who started each program did not finish.

An analysis of the runaway rates seemed to indicate that many of the problems were due to forced involuntary residence. Even though neither of the programs was traditional in character, many of the problems associated with total institutions seemed to be present. It seemed likely that many, probably unnecessary, difficulties were being created that had little to do with delinquent acts, *per se*. Rather, like any other group of adolescents, these boys preferred to live at home, and when they could not, any small crisis seemed to precipitate runaway behavior.

There is some evidence in favor of this interpretation. First of all, high runaway and failure rates have been characteristic of most open, noncustodial programs. David Street *et al.* found in *Organization for Treatment* that two juvenile institutions that placed high emphasis upon control and containment had low runaway rates (16 and 20 percent), while those that emphasized "treatment" had high rates (50 and 29 percent). And in the Provo Experiment runaways were virtually nonexistent. Finally, the follow-up data at Silverlake revealed that, while the boys who did run away had higher arrest rates than those who graduated, almost 50 percent had no subsequent arrests and an additional 27 percent had only one. Clearly, they were not significantly more delinquent.

These findings suggest that, in devising new community programs for serious delinquents, consideration should be given to the relative merits of residential versus nonresidential programming. The analysis overall has implied that both probation and intensive programming may be preferable to incarceration in a reformatory, but it has not indicated clearly that forced residence in a community group home is superior to nonresidential programming. If special problems are created solely because delinquent youngsters are forced to leave their own homes, then care should be taken not to escalate the grounds whereby they might again be defined as delinquent. In many cases, runaway behavior is grounds for increased punitive sanctions.

RELATIVE COSTS OF COMMUNITY PROGRAMMING

It is useful to consider the relative costs of community versus institutional programs. Two examples will suffice.

In the Provo Experiment, the approximate cost per boy in each of the three programs was as follows: for probation, $200; for the intensive, experimental program, $609; and for incarceration, $2,015. Costs today would be greater. Nevertheless, the differentials are what are important.

If probation were used in lieu of incarceration, the savings would amount to about $1,800 per boy; or, if daily, nonresidential programming were used, the savings per boy would be about $1,400. Translated into larger terms, the savings would be great indeed, somewhere between $1.5 and $2 million per one thousand boys.

In the Silverlake Experiment the average cost per graduate in the community group home was $1,735 as contrasted to $4,594 in the control institution. Again, if the differentials were extended, a saving of nearly $3 million per one thousand boys would be realized.

Some of these differentials are due not merely to the extreme costs associated with complex institutional programs, but to the fact that boys remained in the community programs for much shorter periods. At Silverlake, for example, the average stay in the experimental program was approximately 6 months as contrasted to 13 in the institution.

Such findings are striking. Not only do they indicate that equal or better results were achieved in the community, and that delinquents were spared the negative effects of incarceration, but that without even enlarging existing correctional budgets, large sums would be freed for improving services and experimenting further. The grounds are compelling, in a humanitarian as well as a financial sense, for following such a course.

Conclusions

This chapter has pointed out that the juvenile justice system in the United States has not lived up to the idealistic and sometimes absolutistic expectations set for it. It has been characterized by a kind of authoritative overreach that has attempted to use legal means to solve a host of moral and nonlegal problems. As a consequence, the juvenile justice system has failed to grant young people the constitutional safeguards that any adult enjoys, it has attempted to correct a host of welfare, educational, and familial problems that might be better left to other institutions, and it has often imposed penal sanctions for essentially noncriminal acts. Many observers feel, therefore, that the system has tended to evoke and make worse many of the problems it was designed to correct. Expectations that it can both prevent delinquency and simultaneously correct almost every conceivable youth problem are unrealistic.

Invoking the truism that healthy and conformist self-concepts among the young are forged outside of, not within, the legal system, observers have recommended that reforms of three kinds be implemented:

1. *Diversion.* Steps should be taken to divert from the legal system many of the juveniles, and their problems, that heretofore it has been expected to correct. This would be accomplished by narrowing the legal mandate of the juvenile court, and by diverting juveniles who have familial, educational, social, and moral problems to community agencies more capable of addressing such problems. If this were done, the juvenile justice system could then focus its attention more effectively on the criminal behavior of the young, and upon the kinds of predatory acts that are now of such great concern to society.

2. *Due Process.* Greater effort should be made to insure constitutional safeguards for the young. Several Supreme Court cases have revealed that juveniles have been held to account for acts that clearly could not result in legal action if they were committed by adults; that the process of adjudication has denied them adequate legal counsel, adequate protections against self-incrimination, and adequate processual safeguards; and that severe penal sanctions have been invoked as the result of such unconstitutional procedures. As a result, steps should be taken to correct these glaring legal deficiencies. While some of the informal characteristics of the court should be retained, provision must be made to insure that informality does not become a cloak for proceedings reminiscent of the Star-Chamber.

3. *Deinstitutionalization.* For many reasons, places of captivity have not proven to be successful in their efforts to reform the young offender. A growing body of evidence suggests that a wide range of

community alternatives might be more successful, and far less costly to the taxpayer. Existing trends reflect the fact that it is in the community where the offender's problems lie and that it is in the community where they must be addressed. Community structures as well as offenders must be changed.

If, instead of setting up a system in which delinquents were either placed under limited supervision or probation or locked up entirely, use was made of a number of community alternatives, better results might be realized. The evidence has suggested that, for first-time or nonserious law violators, court adjudication alone might be enough. No formal supervision following a finding of guilty would be invoked. The next step might involve regular probation after adjudication. If that form of intervention did not work, or if greater supervision were required, a daily, but nonresidential program might be in order. Yet another community alternative might involve a group home for those who had no other place to live. Finally, as a step of last resort, serious offenders who are a clearcut danger to the community might be incarcerated. Rather than long periods of incarceration in a large institution, however, short periods of incarceration in a small institution would be preferable. Following that, the offender might be returned gradually to the community in one of the nonresidential daily programs or on parole. In that way, a more successful and humane correctional system might be devised.

Edith Elisabeth Flynn

2

Jails and Criminal Justice

Historical Perspective

Among any type of penal institution, the jail has the longest history. Paradoxically, it is the one institution about which we have the least knowledge. As a place of detention and safekeeping of the accused for trial, the jail can be traced to the earliest forms of civilization, when it made its debut in the form of murky dungeons, abysmal pits, unscalable precipices, strong poles or trees, and suspended cages in which hapless prisoners were kept.

The history of the American jail is firmly rooted in Anglo-Saxon society, from which we have derived most of our social institutions. The American jail is a curious hybrid between the tenth century gaol with its principal function being to detain arrested offenders until they were tried, and the fifteenth and sixteenth century houses of correction with their special function being punishment of minor offenders, debtors, vagrants, and beggars. From its beginning, how-

EDITH ELISABETH FLYNN *is associate director and assistant professor of sociology, National Clearinghouse for Criminal Justice Planning and Architecture, University of Illinois. She is also a member and consultant of the Task Force on Corrections of the National Advisory Commission on Criminal Justice Standards and Goals. Dr. Flynn has done extensive research and writing in her field. Her work in 1970 resulted in the publication of the federal* Guidelines for the Planning and Design of Regional and Community Correctional Centers for Adults.

The author expresses her gratitude to two persons instrumental in the development of her chapter: Professor Hans W. Mattick of the University of Illinois, Chicago Circle Campus; and William G. Nagel, executive director of the American Foundation, Inc., Philadelphia, Pennsylvania.

ever, the jail, as to its function, was broadly conceived. It included punishment and coercion as well as custody. In fact, the earliest source of information on incarceration documents a punitive intent and traces that intent to the written laws promulgated by Alfred the Great (871–899 A.D.), the greatest figure in Anglo-Saxon history.

The institution of the office of county sheriff coincides widely with the development of the gaol. Along with the ealdorman (later called the earl), the sheriff represented the king in the shire or county, the largest division of the kingdom in matters of local government. The sheriff's duties were to maintain the peace within the shire and to look after the king's revenues. Since rents from his vast estates constituted the king's principal income, the sheriff collected these rents and other payments, together with any fines assessed by the courts. Although earls became increasingly independent of the king, the sheriffs remained key representatives of royal authority and by the end of the Anglo-Saxon period had come to perform most of the administrative work in the counties. As a result, sheriffs had custody over suspected and arrested offenders and thereby had control over the county jail.

It is natural that the early American colonists brought with them the customs and institutions of their mother countries. Thus, they established the system of county government, built the first jails in America, and invested local sheriffs or marshals with the authority to keep the peace and to control the jails. The jails continued to serve chiefly as places of detention for pretrial detainees (to assure appearance for trial), and for those awaiting sentencing. Until the end of the eighteenth century, the predominant form of punishment was corporal, with death, physical mutilation, branding and whipping being decreed for the more serious offenses. Those found guilty of minor infractions were punished by public ridicule and humiliation—most effectively administered at the stocks, the pillory, and the ducking stool.

It was largely in reaction to the brutality of the harsh British penal codes and practices continued in the New World that the Quaker colony of Pennsylvania, founded by William Penn, attempted the first penal reform in America. For their religious convictions, Penn and many of his fellow Quakers had experienced at first hand the harshness of confinement during long periods of incarceration in England.

The Great Law of Pennsylvania, enacted in 1682, sought to eliminate to a considerable degree the stocks, the pillories, the branding iron, and the gallows. After winning its independence from England, the fledgling country followed the leadership of the Quakers and implemented criminal codes that reflected the classical legal philosophy of the enlightenment, and followed the recommendations of such great thinkers and social philosophers as Beccaria, Voltaire, Bentham, and Romilly. As a result, the number of crimes punishable by death—they had reached a staggering two hundred in early England—was greatly reduced. The predominant form of punishment for the vast majority of crimes became imprisonment or a fine.

With capital and corporal punishment eliminated as the principal sanction for the majority of serious crimes, a substitute form of punishment had to be found. The invention of the penitentiary served that purpose. Jails, however, remained untouched by penal reform and continued as the traditional dumping ground for the untried, the petty offender, the vagrant, the debtor and beggar, the promiscuous, and the mentally ill.

After the American county jail assumed its multiple functions of detention of arrestees, punishment and correction of convicted misdemeanants, and catchall for society's social and law enforcement problems, it experienced few changes, save for some minor variations in its clientele. The juvenile reformatory movement early in the nineteenth century and the appearance of hospitals for the criminally insane during the latter part of that century and the early part of the twentieth century siphoned off some of the population previously confined in jails. This movement was coupled with the development of adult reformatories and state farms. Finally, expanding use of the practice of probation as a court disposition served to divert an increasing number of misdemeanants from jail to community-based supervision. By and large, however, the overwhelming majority of accused offenders and sentenced misdemeanants continued to be sent to county jails.

The growth of cities and the development of city law-enforcement agencies brought about the development of yet another hybrid: the city jail. It emerged from the temporary police lockup and the need by the police for a place of temporary detention where the accused could be interrogated, detained for trial, and, upon conviction, await transportation to the county or state penal institution. More by default than by intent, city jails came under the jurisdiction of law-enforcement agencies and served in the dual function of custodial confinement of pretrial detainees and misdemeanant punishment.

Philosophical Considerations and Goals

Throughout its development, correctional philosophy has been dominated by theories of punishment which served as the guiding rationale for dealing with the adjudicated delinquent and the adult criminal. These theories have been epitomized by the key words: retribution, restraint, deterrence, and most recently, rehabilitation, resocialization, and reintegration.

Understanding the evolution of these concepts and their objectives is crucial because the heritage of earlier ideologies frequently conflicts with ideologies of today, thereby seriously impeding the development of an integrated theory needed for the implementation of a contemporary correctional system.

The concept of *retribution* and morally just punishment is deeply embedded in social thought. It is best codified in *lex talionis*—the principle of exacting compensation: "eye for an eye, tooth for a tooth." Although this view of justice is basically primitive and unworthy of an enlightened society, it is important to note that feelings of moral outrage do serve to enhance social cohesion and serve equally as measures of our regard for given social values. It would be irrational to ignore the pervasiveness and strength of natural feelings of revulsion toward particular criminal acts. However, legalizing severe punishments implies a societal retrogression in human dignity.

The concept of *restraint,* illustrated by long jail sentences, is best exemplified in statutory provisions for life imprisonment in penitentiaries, without the possibility of parole. Since it deters offenders from committing further crimes, at least for the duration of incarceration, it seems reasonable for society to detain those whose records of violent behavior are so pronounced that the safety of the community requires their detention. In view of the recognized inadequacies of our knowledge and treatment techniques, the detention of the particularly dangerous individual may be the only available resort at the present time. It should be quickly pointed out, however, that such drastic measures are needed only for a few, and certainly not for the convicted misdemeanant. Jails are full of people needlessly and inappropriately detained and incarcerated.

Similarly, detention decisions are weighted disproportionately toward the incarceration of minority groups, the unemployed, the undereducated, and the disenfranchised.

The concept of *deterrence* is firmly rooted in classical theory and in the utilitarian principle of crime prevention through fear of punishment. It is helpful to differentiate functionally between general and special deterrence. The effectiveness of general deterrence, which has as its object the public as a whole, seems more a function of certainty than of severity of punishment. These conditions are difficult, if not impossible, to achieve in view of the fact that only a small segment of offenders ever comes to trial and into the correctional process. Although there are practically no verified scientific studies to prove the theory of general deterrence, it is assumed that many persons are deterred by the threat of punishment and that this probably serves to reduce crimes requiring rational considerations as opposed to those involving intense passions. In contrast, the use of special deterrence directed toward the individual offender is frequently questioned because of the general lack of data as to the efficacy of this aspect of deterrence theory. Further research is needed on the role of deterrence in the administration of criminal justice, but there is growing evidence that casts doubt on the necessity of incarcerative punishment in the reducing of crime.

Rehabilitation, resocialization, and *reintegration* are today's objectives in corrections. Their theoretical base stems from the growing influence of psychology, psychiatry, and psychoanalysis in the early part of the twentieth century. Criminal behavior was attributed chiefly to factors within the individual, and the concept of treatment rather than punishment revolutionized correctional practices of that time. Undiminished crime and recidivism rates, however, have brought growing dissatisfaction with the individualized treatment approach. An impressive accumulation of studies points to the conclusion that favorable change seldom, if ever, occurs in correctional institutions. Whatever changes do occur are rarely translated to the community where the offender's adjustment is ultimately tested. This recognition, coupled with theoretical and conceptual advances linking crime chiefly to social factors, is instrumental in the formulation of a new correctional philosophy, the effect of which remains to be tested. The new philosophy is characterized by two main precepts.

The first precept is that society, in addition to human attitudes, needs changing. Secondly, more emphasis should be placed on the offender's social and cultural milieu if we are to obtain any substantial relief from recidivism. Individual differences and individual responsibility will still remain important factors in correction's response to criminal behavior, but they need to be considered within the setting of the offender's social group, the community, and the subcultural matrix. The new correctional thrust becomes clear: if the vexing pressures of an offender's social milieu contribute greatly to his criminal behavior, the social milieu itself must be changed. Successful adjustment, therefore, will require personal reformation and conditions within the community that are conducive to an offender's reintegration into it. Fundamentally, this is a community task. Communities must assume part of the responsibility for the problems they generate. Once they accept that responsibility, the correctional system will be removed from its splendid isolation and will become part of the larger social system.

There is another factor underwriting the urgent need for swift implementation of a new correctional approach. Continually escalating costs of confinement raise serious questions as to benefits received. For example, per capita annual costs at jails is roughly $2,000. In comparison, the annual cost of supervision of offenders on probation ranges from $250 to $400 per person. It should be noted that this spiraling of institutional costs is not to be attributed to significant increases in rehabilitation programs or to extravagant amenities. Far from it! As it will be seen in the subsequent discussion, incarceration requires large financial commitments in costly hardware, inmate subsistence, and custodial control. These are major items in any jail budget and are not open to significant economies.

In summary, correctional practice today is the product of diverse and frequently conflicting trends, interests, and reforms of the past. Most of these were guided by a basic philosophy of punishment as the primary objective in dealing with criminals, and by the thought that the most effective method with transgressors is to lock them behind bars for long periods of time.

Even though the public is beginning to recognize that the ultimate success of corrections depends on reintegrating the offender into the community and motivating him to refrain from breaking the law, the public's ambivalence as to reform and its lack of concern for the criminal offender seriously impede correctional reform. The situation is aggravated whenever change is resisted from within the system. In such instances, deliberate appeals may be made to public fears, in the interest of preserving traditional, locally controlled correctional practice with all its inequities and injustices.

Overview of Current Problems

The American jail has been traditionally held in low esteem by penologists and public officials. As a result, today it is the least studied and the least known penal institution in the country. There are few systematic and empirically verified studies on jails. Only rudimentary, statistical information is known about the "jail problem" on the national level.

The year 1970 saw the first national jail census. Conducted by the Law Enforcement Assistance Administration, it was coupled with a more elaborate survey of selected states. A total of 4,037 jails were found to meet LEAA's definition of "any facility operated by a unit of local government for the detention or correction of adults suspected or convicted of a crime and which has authority to detain longer than forty-eight hours." Although, for purposes of this discussion, we will adopt this definition, it is important to note that the count of 4,037 jails is an underestimate of the total number of jails existing in the country today. The count excludes police lockups, jails in municipalities reporting fewer than one thousand persons, and state-controlled facilities for convicted short-term offenders—facilities such as reformatories, state farms, and road camps.

In spite of a pervasive tendency to minimize the importance of jails and their impact on society, a brief analysis of statistical information quickly dispels such illusions. According to the LEAA census, American jails hold collectively, on an average day, a population of over one hundred sixty thousand—the equivalent of the entire population of North Dakota. But the real significance of jails does not emerge until one considers their turnover rate. According to the best available estimates, jails confine at least one and a half million and perhaps as many as five and a half million Americans during the course of a single year!

HETEROGENEOUS JAIL POPULATION

Typically, jails fall under the jurisdiction of county governments. They are locally administered and are characterized by a highly transient and heterogeneous population. As portico to the criminal justice system, jails hold those charged with or found guilty of minor offenses, as well as those accused or convicted of the most serious kinds of crime. Most legal distinctions categorize offenses according to their seriousness, in range from ordinance violations to misdemeanors and felonies. This difference is far from satisfatory, however, because current knowledge dictates that the type of offense is not a criterion for an index as to personal character, dangerousness of the offender, security requirements, or the offender's particular needs. Matters are further complicated by the fact that the specific offense for which a person is tried and convicted is often only partly related to the offense for which he was charged. For example, the typical charge against such "skid row" personalities as beggars, prostitutes, and drunks is "vagrancy," and the charge is less based upon their acts than upon their condition or status. Finally, during the process of plea bargaining, over 80 percent or more of the convictions in this country result from guilty pleas rather than from trials, and charges are frequently changed to ones of lesser magnitude. Specific charges filed by the police and the prosecuting attorney are often padded by a host of related charges, in anticipation of subsequent negotiations for a plea of guilty.

Beyond their formally acknowledged tasks of detention and correction, jails perform a variety of other functions: they provide social welfare service by accommodating homeless drunks and vagrants; they may furnish involuntary lodging for transients who may never be brought to trial but who are merely "helped" along to another jurisdiction. Because of this multiplicity of function, jails throw together a population, the heterogeneity of which is unsurpassed by any other correctional institution.

As a result, on an ordinary day, the typical jail may have among its population first offenders, situational offenders, occasional offenders, professional criminals, violent and predatory offenders prone to act out their hostilities, and hard-core multiple recidivists. It may include males, females, juveniles, and adults. According to the LEAA census of 1970, a little less than 5 percent, or 7,739 adult women, were located in jail on the date of the survey. An almost equal number of juveniles (7,800) were also detained, even though the majority of states explicitly prohibit their detention in jails. The jail may detain civil offenders, criminal offenders, and non-offenders—material witnesses, accused persons against whom complaints will be dropped, and many individuals entirely innocent. A growing majority of the population today is being held for trial or awaits some other disposition: an appeal or a transfer to another institution. The typical jail may contain persons serving out sentences or fines and may house parole violators en route back to the penitentiary, probation violators awaiting hearings, and persons awaiting transfer or extradition to other jurisdictions. Finally, it may hold sociomedical cases: the mentally ill, the alcoholic, and the drug addict, all of whose problems become simply exacerbated by the jail and who contribute disproportionately to the revolving-door syndrome so typical of this institution.

SIMILARITIES IN JAIL POPULATIONS

In spite of their highly diverse composition, jail populations are characterized by certain commonalities. With few exceptions, the people are poor, undereducated, unemployed, and they belong to minority groups. In 1970, 52 percent were unconvicted. Most were detained because they could not afford to post bail. Although the issue of bail and pretrial detention falls technically outside the jurisdiction of "corrections," it is clearly one of the most troublesome problems in the criminal justice process. This is true not only because of the sheer numbers of persons involved, but also because of the reverberating effect of pretrial detention on the outcome of the detained person's case. Detainees are unable to organize their own defense, arrange for witnesses, or prepare for trial. Detainees stand to lose their jobs at the same time that their families are losing their sources of income. Welfare rolls are increased. Most importantly, incarceration exerts a proved negative effect on the outcome of the detainee's case, mainly by increasing the probability of his subsequent conviction and imprisonment. Finally, in the absence of adequate physical separation of pretrial detainees from the convicted, there is damaging comingling of petty offenders with felons; first offenders with recidivists; and young, impressionable offenders with hard-core, predatory criminals.

In the light of these serious shortcomings, it is important to note that the majority of pretrial detainees are eventually released without any further incarceration. They are either released before trial or conviction—for want of evidence—or because the charges are dropped; or they may receive a suspended sentence or alternative to incarceration, such as probation. It is clear, therefore, that this particular segment of the jail population is needlessly made to suffer the hardships of pretrial detention and that, in contrast to current practice, a significantly larger proportion of pretrial detainees could easily be released without endangering the safety and welfare of the community.

For the most part, jails are not places of final disposition. The length of stay for detainees and for the convicted varies from a few hours, to a few weeks, to several months. On occasion, the duration of pretrial detention can stretch into years, largely by means of legal maneuvering by the defense, and frequently with the tacit cooperation of the prosecution. By and large, processing rates vary according to differences in local practice, availability of alternatives (detoxification centers, narcotic addiction treatment programs), and attitudes of the local community toward the problem of crime. Court practices exert a significant influence on the duration of pretrial detention. To judge from the vast delays and judicial backlogs, few seem to heed the advice of classical criminal law that in order for justice to be effective, it must be *swift*.

In summary, in terms of impact and sheer numbers, the jail is one of the most important social institutions in the criminal justice system. Its negative impact on the lives of those who pass through it is matched only by its rate of failure—as high as 60 to 75 percent, according to the best available estimates. Locally administered and controlled, it has successfully escaped study and reform for centuries, and thus presents society with one of the most vexing problems of the day.

Conditions and Practices

Although, in any general discussion, there are serious limitations of the essential characteristics of the American jail—largely because of the dearth of empirically verified studies available on the subject—there is sufficient consistency in the data we have to permit a description of the current state of the art. Among the principal and available sources of information on jails are the Jail Census that was conducted by the Law Enforcement Assistance Administration in 1970; a sample survey conducted by the National Council on Crime and Delinquency in 1966; some highly comprehensive surveys of the states of California in 1970; of Idaho in 1969; of Illinois in 1969; of New York in 1966; and of North Carolina in 1969. These surveys have been supplemented by less extensive research in other states, and by a number of pertinent publications on the subject.

ORGANIZATIONAL STRUCTURE

In terms of organizational structure, jails fall into two major categories. First, there is the relatively small rural jail, in a small town, in a county seat. Most of these jails are antiquated, having been built 50 to 80 years ago. The inmates are primarily sentenced misdemeanants, persons awaiting trial, or transients awaiting further disposition. Occasionally, some juveniles are there for pending adjudication. The majority of these jails are underutilized, dilapidated, and neglected. The second major type of jail is the large urban jail, such as New York City's festering Tombs, Chicago's badly congested Cook County Jail, and Los Angeles' incredibly large jail complex with its population approximating four thousand. Although urban jails are few in number, they hold over 50 percent of the country's jail population, and they are consistently and dangerously overcrowded. Their chief characteristics are crippling idleness, anonymous brutality, human degradation and repression. They represent the gravest obstacle to efforts for jail reform.

In addition to the typical city and county jails, there are a number of variations in their organizational structure. Some states assign pretrial detainees and sentenced misdemeanants to separate, locally administered institutions. Others may incarcerate sentenced minor offenders and even convicted felons for periods of up to five years in one and the same institution.

Operationally, the typical county jail comes under the control of the sheriff, the sheriff's duly appointed deputy or warden, or sometimes the chief of police. Financially, the jail is controlled by local county boards or similar governing bodies. It is precisely this phenomenon of autonomous, local control that has been consistently and invariably identified as the chief obstacle to jail reform. Local control invariably means involvement in local politics and patronage. Since most sheriffs are elected officials, they are frequently neither interested nor particularly experienced in matters of correction. They tend to view the jail as an adjunct to their law-enforcement activities and as a place for the temporary detention and warehousing of inmates. As a result, the majority of county jails suffer from a perennial lack of funding, from physical neglect, from the absence of any kind of program. Frequently, they fail to meet even the most rudimentary safety and health standards.

Although cost accounting is a prerequiste for the assessment of any enterprise, it is foreign to jail operations. Expenditures are frequently buried in the total operating cost of the sheriff's or the police department and hence are exceedingly difficult to extrapolate. In spite of the conspicuous absence of data, however, most serious students of jails agree that incarceration, whether in jail or in other penal institutions, is exceedingly costly in terms of dollars, social costs, and the overwhelming failure rate. Information obtained through the LEAA survey on jails confirmed the consensus: a total of $324,278,000 spent for the fiscal year of 1969 on 4,037 jails. This amounts to over $80,000 per jail per year—over $2,000 per inmate per year. Nothwithstanding these high expenditures, the major costs to society undoubtedly accrue from the destructive impact on the lives of those passing through the jails. Finally, expenditures for jails appear to be particularly high when compared to the operating costs of a host of community-based, noninstitutional alternatives. Early results on the effectiveness of such programs seem to indicate that alternatives to incarceration are at least as effective as traditional institutionalism, and that such alternatives are considerably less expensive in terms of money as well as in social costs.

Even though there is considerable discussion as to "regionalization," or the pooling of resources for establishing regional jails on a city-county or multiple-county basis, few such efforts have materialized. Predictably, the most common issue of contention centers around the question of control. Past efforts to regionalize have been largely unproductive, but currently there are serious planning efforts toward regionalizing jails in nearly half of the states.

The operational control of the typical city jail is generally under the authority of the city's chief of police. He, in turn, is responsible to the municipal government. The specific forms of that government may involve an almost infinite number of permutations. Large city jails tend to hold predominantly pretrial populations, with the exception of a small cadre of sentenced inmate "trusties" for janitorial and maintenance purposes. In addition to operating the jail, most cities manage separate institutions for sentenced misdemeanant offenders. Houses of correction are frequently under the auspices of a civilian authority—the Department of Social Services or the Department of Social Welfare. Finally, in our largest cities, there is a trend toward the formation of centralized departments of corrections. Such departments facilitate a unified approach to the major detention and corrections problems of the city.

INSPECTION AND STANDARDS

Jail inspection is another badly neglected area in administration and control. Although county grand juries are characteristically charged with this responsibility, few do more than pay occasional, perfunctory visits to their jails. The reasons for the neglect are simple. Grand jury members mirror the apathy of the general public and tend to support law-enforcement activities in preference to jail reform. Conditions are exacerbated by the fact that, in the past, most states have shown an extreme reluctance to assume an active role in jail inspection and in the development of jail standards.

But the picture is changing. A survey in 1972, conducted by the National Clearinghouse for Criminal Justice Planning and Architecture, at the University of Illinois, reveals that 25 states have established operational standards for local jails. Eighteen others administer standards for facility planning and construction.

Although the American Correctional Association for years has published minimum "standards" for detention facilities, it has consistently addressed itself to general principles rather than to specific standards. The most recent effort with regard to standards has come from the National Sheriffs' Association. Their document is characterized by considerable specificity and hence has increased utility. In addition, it incorporates a considerable number of advanced practices. Its overall direction, however, still stresses operational and custodial convenience over the necessity of meeting the vast physical, psychological, and social needs of detainees and convicted offenders.

Certainly, the development of uniform standards is an important step toward the improvement of jail programs, staffing, and facilities, but any effort is essentially an exercise in futility if it is not accompanied by the means to exact compliance. Few state agencies possess such powers. Improvement of jail conditions will doubtlessly require state inspection and, at the very least, full powers of enforcement. In recognition, however, of the pervasive evils of local jail administrations, significant changes in the system will no doubt have to await state operation of such facilities.

The role of the federal government in controlling jail standards has been equally insignificant. The federal system contracts with some eight hundred jails for the detention of federal prisoners awaiting trial or transportation to federal institutions. Contrary to popular belief, the federal system has no written standards of jail inspection. The existence of a federal contract with a local jail is frequently interpreted by local officials and by the public to mean that the jail is federally "approved." In reality, such jails are as disreputable as any in the United States. Actually, the existence of such contracts and the absence of written standards are operating to delay jail reform and to discourage litigation since they lend an aura of positive sanction to the jail in question.

PHYSICAL FACILITIES

In the absence of uniform standards and with perfunctory inspection practices, jails have managed to preserve admirably the "cagelike" atmosphere of their predecessors of over a century ago. The majority of jails are old and poorly maintained. They were constructed with custody as the principal and overriding concern. Archaic designs have produced inflexible cells, with equally inflexible dayrooms. Cells with single- and multiple-occupancy are the most frequent types of inmate housing. Inmates spend most of the day in large cages or "bullpens" adjacent to their cells, with food and drink passed to them through slotted doors or sally ports, thus preventing contact between staff and inmates as much as possible.

Although single-occupancy cells are vastly preferred by most jailers and are recommended by the American Correctional Association, by the National Jail Association, and by a number of state guidelines on jail construction, only few state legislatures have translated these preferences into law. Single-occupancy is clearly preferable in that it provides more flexibility in the separation of prisoners, reduces physical exploitation, aggressive behavior, and homosexual activity; and because it provides more privacy to the inmates, thus limiting the degree of physical and mental contamination between inmates, and affording security and greater protection to the jail staff.

Dormitories or open wards may range in occupancy from 12 to 60. Usually crowded, they contain both single- and double-deck beds. At best, they are storage bins. At the worst, they are jungles. Although the least expensive to build, they are indeed the most costly in terms of human values. Sexual exploitation, moral and physical contamination, and dehumanization are their principal characteristics. They are also highly dangerous to the staff.

Larger facilities, particularly city jails, have housing units constructed on multiple levels or tiers. Upper tiers are reached by long staircases and balconies into which cells open. The disadvantages of such arrangements are many: surveillance is difficult, cell blocks assume unmanageable proportions, heating and ventilating problems are intensified, and the din is insufferable.

By far the most insidious aspect of jails, largely a direct consequence of the abominable physical conditions, is the lack of sanitation and the general state of uncleanliness. Age alone does not offer a sufficient explanation, even though a third of the country's jails are over 50 years old. There are some relatively clean *old* jails as well as some festering *new* facilities. But as a rule, the majority of jails constitute a direct hazard to the staff and inmates alike, and to the community at large. Many jail cells lack toilets and washbasins altogether. Inmates have no access to such facilities for long periods of time and must use the infamous "honey bucket" system. Wherever sanitary facilities do exist, they are frequently in an advanced stage of disrepair. Those cells that do boast sanitary facilities tend to have an open "prison-type" toilet/basin combination perched between bunks and wall. Toilets may also be provided in the dayrooms so that inmates do not have to be returned to their cells during the day. For surveillance purposes, the toilets are left unscreened, thus contributing to the dehumanizing process.

Most jails are legally required to receive and hold persons with a wide range of medical, social, and behavioral pathologies: alcoholics, psychotics, drug abusers in various withdrawal stages, and potential suicides. Since few jails have access to medical services, the vast majority of such problem cases have to get along without any medical or psychiatric remedies. The unfortunates are put into drunk tanks or isolation cells. The former are usually unfurnished cubes of steel and concrete, with grilles. Floors generally slope to facilitate hosing and mopping. Most contain only one oriental type of floor toilet. Some may have the prison-type toilet with a remotely controlled flushing mechanism.

Space for programs in education, work, counseling, treatment, visiting, and recreation is virtually nonexistent. Only the larger urban facilities possess rudimentary libraries, some classroom space, and occasionally multipurpose rooms for religious and recreational activities. The acute absence of programs produces a daily routine of unbelievable and unrelieved idleness. Ubiquitous television viewing, card playing, perhaps ping-pong provide the only recreation and activity for the inmate.

In summary, the physical condition of most of the jails in this country is one of incipient decay. While many rural, county jails are suffering from underuse and neglect, urban jails are disintegrating because of overuse and overcrowding. As a result, they are ill equipped to meet even the most basic needs of their prisoners. They breed crime, they do not control it. They teach contempt of the law, they do not respect it. They spread depravity and disease among the residents and subsequently to the community rather than provide for their safekeeping.

JAIL STAFFING

Although decayed physical facilities decry most loudly the desperate straits of the American jail, the issue of jail staffing is even more crucial. Personnel are frequently the jetsam of the political patronage system. As the winds of political fortune change, so do the job-holders. This is particularly true of sheriffs who, in many jurisdictions, cannot succeed themselves. Since most sheriffs are elected to office, attention is seldom paid to their penological competence. Low job specifications are more often than not matched by the lowness of pay. Since local governments are frequently the most poverty-stricken of all echelons of government, they seldom provide jail administrators with the funding and staffing required to sustain either adequate custody or a modicum of treatment. Politically, there is no great incentive to invest in jail reform. Compared to the needs of the public schools, mental health, and hospitals, the jail has been traditionally characterized as being least eligible for budgetary support.

With the exception of a few large urban jails, the majority of jails are presently administered by law-enforcement officers. Police officers know little about the correctional role. Few consider themselves to be correctional officers, even when assigned in such a capacity to jails and lockups. As custodians of community values, they are primarily concerned with the detection and arrest of offenders and with the subsequent conviction and commitment to jail and other penal institutions. This places jailers in direct conflict with the goals of modern corrections that stress the reduced need for detention and incarceration and the earliest possible reintegration of offenders into society as productive and law-abiding citizens.

Recent developments, set in motion by the growth of urbanization, point to some important changes in the functional responsi-

bilities of jailers. On the county level, sheriffs are losing to municipal and city police departments a significant amount of their law-
enforcement responsibility. This process of gradual divestment
leaves them with the politically least desirable tasks of highway
traffic enforcement and jail administration. On the city level, some
large metropolitan jails are beginning to utilize personnel other
than police officers. Many of these, however, having been thwarted
in their aspirations to become policemen, are more interested in
exerting their authority than in helping to rehabilitate offenders.

Although, on the surface, staff-inmate ratios appear to be satisfactory, it is important to note that jails operate 24 hours a day,
365 days a year. As a result, a total of 28,053 full-time and 5,676
part-time employees, as determined by the LEAA survey in 1970,
boils down roughly to 1.6 full-time staff members per jail during
any one shift; these are in charge, on the average, of 40 inmates at
any one time. Averages, however, are misleading. Though the majority of full-time members are generally found in larger urban
facilities, many small county institutions do not have any full-time
employees. In such instances, staff may be present only during the
day and may frequently need to divide their attention to law enforcement or other activity. As a result, most jails fail to provide
even the most rudimentary kind of supervision to guarantee the
relative safety of their inmates. The way is open for homosexual
rape, robbery, extortion, and the many other kinds of violence of
inmate against inmate, so prevalent and characteristic of the American jail today.

The lack of professional workers in jails is even more acute.
Teachers, social workers, psychologists, and psychiatrists are con-
spicuously absent in the county jail and are only infrequently available to the larger urban jail. Access to medical services is equally
limited. Only the larger city facility provides such services, on a
highly limited basis. The majority of county prisoners must rely on
the varying "diagnostic" abilities of their jailers, who determine
the relative seriousness of the symptoms and the validity of the
complaint. This occurs in spite of the fact that jails contain a dis-
proportionate number of residents afflicted with contagious diseases
and infections—venereal disease, tuberculosis, infectious hepatitis,
etc.—all defying diagnosis by lay persons.

In summary, the majority of jails in this country are dangerously
understaffed. Jail personnel are characteristically untrained and
preoccupied with matters of law enforcement, security, and custody.

Staff wear uniforms and bear appropriate military titles. The strong identification with the military unduly influences the entire jail operation. It exacerbates the deep chasm between the keepers and the kept. Selection of staff occurs more often on the basis of political affiliation than on educational attainment. Few come under any form of civil service or merit system. Personal standards are either nonexistent or stress the wrong requirements. Low salaries, coupled with the stigma surrounding jails, make jobs unattractive. As a result, jail work becomes the second, third, or last career choice for many and is characterized by high turnover rates and low performance. The real crisis, however, is the lack of education and staff development programs. According to a survey by the Joint Commission on Correctional Manpower and Training, released in 1969, less than 14 percent of any category of workers in corrections were participating in an in-service training program. It follows that staff development is a far more important issue in jail reform than physical plant renovation or replacement.

Major Administrative and Operational Issues

SECURITY AND CUSTODIAL CONVENIENCE

In both the administration and the reform of the criminal justice system, jails continue to occupy a twilight zone. This is attributable, to a large degree, to public apathy regarding matters of jail reform, and to the ambivalence concerning the function of jails in particular and the goals of corrections in general. The result is a welter of paradox: underbudgeting and waste, overcrowding, underutilization, understaffing, and irrationality. Amidst all of these contradictions, only two common and related principles emerge: security considerations and custodial convenience. As much as possible, jails are geared to the fullest possible supervision, control, and surveillance of inmates. Physical structures, program choices—if any—and operational policies optimize security and administration convenience and restrict the inmate's movement to the point of removing all of his control over his environment. Technological developments and custodial artifacts have long since outpaced our ability to reach the inmate and to respond to his individual or social needs.

Most jails are maximum-security facilities. Lack of programs and lack of staff lead to the standard practice of viewing all inmates as maximum-security risks, with the exception of the inmate "trusties," who not only enjoy considerable freedom but who, for all intents and purposes, operate the jail. The corruptive influence of such arrangements on staff and inmates alike is well known and leads directly to the illicit exchange of goods and services and to the subsequent exploitation and abuse of inmates by other inmates. The situation is aggravated by the fact that trusties comprise the most criminalized segment of any jail population. Even though the evils of the trusty system are decried by the majority of administrators, the acute need for housekeeping and maintenance functions, coupled with the lack of funding for the purchase of such services, prevents discontinuance of the system.

At the same time that some smaller county facilities, with crumbling walls and lax operating procedures, may actually constitute a serious danger to the safety of the community, the majority of larger jails are frequently obsessed with issues of security. Such jails tend to pursue a policy of harassment of inmates through a barrage of excessive lock-ins, head counts, strip searches, and incessant shakedowns—night and day.

Judging from the experience of some innovators in the field, we know that the need for maximum-security detention at the local governmental level has been vastly exaggerated. For example, roughly 50 percent of most jail populations do not even belong in jail. They should be afforded more appropriate services in accordance with their clearly identifiable sociomedical needs. Moreover, the majority of convicted misdemeanants could easily be accommodated under minimum-security arrangements without unduly endangering the safety of the public. By definition, they have been found guilty of less severe crimes and are primary candidates for more innovative programs: educational or work releases, or weekend sentences. In contrast to the convicted inmate population, pretrial detainees require more security considerations. But even portions of this population can safely be assigned, without undue increase in security risks, to medium- and minimum-security environments, provided that the environment is properly classified according to custody and supervision requirements.

Custodial convenience dominates every aspect of administrative and operational procedures of jails. It is expressed succinctly in one of the more recent documents on jail standards and assures the reader that those running the system had not only been consulted in production of the document but had also helped to produce a plan they could all live with. Though no one will dispute the right for administrators to determine operating procedures, such a process tends to exclude systematically the consideration of the needs and concerns of the inmate population. In view of the emerging body of laws on the rights, status, and privileges of those under correctional control, operational procedures must change substantially. As a result, administrative convenience and unlimited discretion will have to yield to a consideration of the exigencies and rights of offenders and to the requirements of sound penological practice and humane treatment.

THE INTAKE PROCESS

Being received and processed as a prisoner into jail is for many the first and only contact with the criminal justice system. The intake procedure becomes one of the most critical events in the entire process. It is here that a person first loses contact with his family, employer, friends, personal belongings and clothes, and with every other symbol of his individuality and humanity. The stripping and frisking are symbolic of his new and exposed status. Whether innocent or guilty, the new inmate is now a nonperson, a number, an item to be processed.

In spite of the recognition of the necessity to separate and classify prisoners according to their legal status, security needs, and treatment requirements, the vast majority of jails tend to mix prisoners indiscriminately—with the exception of separating males from females. As a result, adults are mixed with juveniles, alcoholics and suicide-prone with the general population, and pretrial detainees with the convicted. Only the very large urban jails afford a separation of the last two categories. Records lack uniformity and are sporadically kept. Access to medical service is frequently nonexistent. Inmates are exposed to one another's contagious diseases and vermin. In the absence of programs, the opportunity to acquire at least some modicum of skills, counseling, or job placement is lost, at the same time that family ties and economic opportunities deteriorate. Insufficient staffing and perennial lack of funding leave inmates to work out their own internal order. Aggravated by a general absence of written rules, an informal social system emerges, wherein the stronger and more manipulative inmates control the weaker and more vulnerable. Though kangaroo courts appear to be less prevalent today, the barn-boss system continues, largely unchanged.

There is no question but that imaginative administrative procedure and creative reallocation of resources could significantly alter this process. Sufficient staffing and the opportunity to make a reasonable number of phone calls could undoubtedly speed up procedures and affect pretrial release programs, as well as reduce the need for holding inmates in bullpens or intake tanks. The provision of partitions could humanize search and examination procedures. Access to medical examinations could eliminate the dangers of infections and disease. Appropriate record-keeping could facilitate classification and the assessment of security requirements and at the same time provide the rudimentary information for subsequent program assignments. Finally, the availability of counselors, social workers, or other staff members for an intake interview could provide a humanizing element to the intake process for individual needs to be determined.

FOOD AND HEALTH

The majority of jails fall notoriously short of meeting the basic needs of their inmates. The poor quality of both food and medical service is matched only by the general inadequacy of the jail's social and physical environment. Nutritionally satisfying, good food is a basic right of inmates. It is also one of the most important factors in morale and discipline. Unpalatable, contaminated, and insufficient food is consistently identified as one of many legitimate grievances in inmate riots. Three meals a day may be standard practice for the rest of society, but many jails serve only twice a day. There is a tendency on the part of the staff to telescope the timing of meals for administrative convenience in order to complete the process during the day shift. Most meals are given between 7 o'clock in the morning and 4 o'clock in the evening. As a result, 15 hours or more may elapse between meals. This enforced period of abstinence is usually aggravated by prohibited storage of food in cells or dormitories.

The preparation of food in small facilities is generally handled by the sheriff's wife. Contractual arrangements with catering firms appear on the increase. Larger jails with kitchen facilities prepare their own meals with labor by the trusties. With few exceptions, such facilities are characterized by unsanitary conditions and health-endangering practices. The distribution of food from steam carts, more often cold than hot, is invariably handled by trusties. Their supervision is either insufficient or nonexistent and leads to favoritism, illicit exchange of goods for services, and contraband.

There are a number of ways in which food preparation and dining can be improved. As a governing principle, inmates should not eat in their cells. Though the use of dayrooms is far from ideal, dayrooms may be adequate if they are subdivided to accommodate dining.

The acute lack of adequate medical services—about half the number of jails surveyed by LEAA had none—has already been discussed. Jails are breeding grounds for infection and serve as vectors of diseases to inmates, staff, and community alike.

The spread of disease is further intensified through decaying or inadequate sanitary facilities, a perennial lack of basic, personal hygiene commodities (soap, toothbrushes and paste, clean bedding and towels, toilet tissue and safety razors), by an abundance of rodents and vermin, and by conditions of overcrowding.

It is axiomatic that provisions for health, cleanliness, and personal hygiene are vital for the individual well-being and should therefore be viewed as a basic human right. Though the total number of inmates requiring medical services will vary to some degree, it is essential that health care, including treatment, preventive medical, and mental health services, should be available to all.

WORK, TRAINING, AND TREATMENT

No other correctional institution matches the jail in enforced idleness, languor, and sheer boredom. With few exceptions, jails are devoid of work activities, rehabilitative and structured recreational programs. Although recent efforts at reform have served to spread the rhetoric of "enlightened" penology and reform to the jail level, very little of what is being said is reflected in practice. Institutional maintenance and housekeeping tasks, most of which can be completed easily by a few trusties in a few hours per day, constitute, in most instances, a facility's total "rehabilitation" program. Such work is wasteful, at best, and demoralizing, at worst. Larger institutions use inmate labor for laundry, kitchen and yard work. None of these activities require much skill or manual dexterity but merely represent the same kind of "busy work" so characteristic of correctional institutions.

Though nearly a total absence of programs constitutes the rule, there are the beginnings of some exceptions. However, work programs are generally available to misdemeanants only. Persons in pretrial detention must be presumed innocent until they are proved guilty in court. Hence, they cannot be forced to participate in what may be essentially termed "rehabilitative programs." A closer look at the issue reveals that many pretrial detainees participate voluntarily in such programs, if offered. Some seek relief from boredom, others hope to obtain favorable recommendations to the judiciary. It appears that those administrators who wish to provide programs to pretrial detainees do so successfully on a voluntary basis, whereas those who do not will hide under the smokescreen of constitutional questions. There is no reason why, as is presently the case, the status of a detained person needs to be generally worse than that of the convicted person confined in the same facility, and far worse than the condition of a felony offender confined in a state institution. Probably the easiest solution to the dilemma would be to adopt a policy of service concerning the varied needs of detainees and sentenced offenders alike, rather than emphasizing issues of "treatment" and "rehabilitation." Such a development appears all the more prudent in view of the questionable value of coerced treatment programs as a means to reducing crime.

The uncertain length of detention and the brevity of sentences aggravate the difficulties of establishing any semblance of programs. Most inmates are of relatively low educational attainment, having finished, on the average, the eighth or ninth grades. Mastery of school subjects is usually around the sixth grade. Because of accumulated failures within the normal school setting, the inmate's lack of motivation presents special challenges to the educational planner. Only the largest urban jails feature some type of academic training: elementary or high school classes.

Whereas few educational programs can be completed in jail, it becomes important for inmates to pursue programs that can be continued after their discharge. As a result, cooperation of the jails with local school districts is essential. Particular emphasis should be given to self-pacing programs and packaged instructional materials. In view of the general scarcity of funding, the use of volunteers and para-professionals as instructors should be stressed. Vocational training in jail is mostly a misnomer. It is either janitorial, housekeeping, or other work responding to institutional needs and rationalized as vocational education. Correlation between this type of work and marketable skills is usually lacking.

Much more promising than "in-house" programs are community-based activities, such as work release and educational release programs that permit eligible inmates to leave the jail during the day to seek or work at a job or attend school. Even though most programs operating today are designed for offenders who have been sentenced, the same rationales may technically be applied to pretrial release programs with the same advantages of uninterrupted work, family support, and maintenance of social contacts. Work release stands out as being one of the more successful correctional activities for misdemeanants, but it is important to note that work release is still the exception rather than the rule. Most jails offer more rhetoric and tokenism than actual practice.

RIGHTS AND STATUS OF INMATES

Until very recently, convicted misdemeanants had only such rights as were granted them either by statute or correctional authority. Hence, most institutional policies reflect the belief that virtually anything short of extreme torture or excessive physical punishment can be done with an inmate in the name of "treatment and rehabilitation." Thus, inmates are literally at the mercy of their keepers, and jails, which account by far for most incarceration in the United States, have permitted pervasive inhumane conditions, frequently laced with brutality, to become the norm.

The issue of pretrial detainee rights is even more thorny. By tradition, detention falls outside the jurisdiction of corrections. But similar disclaimers can be made by the judiciary and the law-enforcement branch. The net effect of these abrogations is to relegate the pretrial process into a veritable no-man's-land of the criminal justice system. This explains, to a considerable degree, why the problem of pretrial detention has assumed such Sisyphean proportions and why the prospects for reform are so bleak.

Gross physical abuse of inmates and dehumanizing conditions in many institutions have finally brought judicial involvement after decades of a "hands off" doctrine. As a result, the emerging body of law on the rights of accused and convicted offenders is one of the most active and promising areas of legal and constitutional development today.

Improved protection will first require statutory changes to provide the necessary legal norms; and secondly, implementation of appropriate administrative policy changes. The latter is of particular importance because neither statute nor judicial edict will be realized without the understanding and cooperation of the correctional official implementing it. Recent court decisions guarantee, from the Bill of Rights, protections to offenders and express the view that detainees and offenders retain essentially all the rights that citizens enjoy except for those rights that may need to be limited in order to carry out criminal sanctions or administer a correctional institution. In view of these developments, jail administrators will need to substantially redefine their operational procedures and approaches or face accelerating litigation before courts that are increasingly less inclined to put administrative convenience before basic human rights.

Proposals and Prospects for Reform

If past efforts at reform are any indication, the prospects for jail reform are gloomy, indeed. From their very inception, jails have been described by astute practitioners and thoughtful scholars alike as cesspools and schools of crime. With few exceptions, they violate every standard of human decency, destroy the spirit, and threaten the sanity of those imprisoned within. Yet despite decades of indictments, jails have remained essentially unchanged and continue to be the most irrational element in the entire criminal justice system. The reasons for this phenomenon are as varied as they are complex.

First, local administration is invariably identified as the central stumbling block to reform. It facilitates political opportunism and perpetuates the evils of the patronage system. Second, limited local financing virtually assures the perpetuation of archaic methods of operation and thereby systematically precludes the implementation of reform. Third, and most importantly, jails represent a myopic but highly expedient solution to the problems of crime for an apathetic and indifferent public. Not even periodic explosions, touched off by scandals and riots that reveal the shocking and debasing conditions of jails, have managed to bring the public out of its complacency and inertia. As a result, it is becoming increasingly clear that the "patchwork approach," which has characterized past efforts at jail reform, is incapable of solving the jail's perplexing and pervasive problems. Palliatives and eclecticism must give way to a more systematic planning approach. The jail, as we know it, must be replaced by a more rationally functioning system.

Although there is considerable variation regarding specific aspects and details of implementation, current thinking in jail reform appears united on the following issues. First, there is the recognition that the total problem is not the jail alone but the entire official response to the problems of delinquency and crime, otherwise known as the correctional system. There is agreement that only systematic and coordinated efforts on the part of legislative bodies, the courts, law enforcement, and corrections will produce the necessary changes to transform the jail from an infectious liability to a potential asset within the correctional armamentarium.

Recommended plans of action vary in comprehensiveness and range from procedural changes to dramatic calls for realignment of policies, resources, and practices. The most basic approach to jail reform calls for relatively simple shifts in administrative procedures and the establishment of alternative practices already existing in many jurisdictions. That approach is epitomized by the words decriminalization, diversion, minimum penetration into the system, and alternatives to incarceration. It rests on the premise that criminal law is grossly overused and is totally ineffective in dealing with sociomedical problems, certain types of individual and social deviance, and a host of moralistic "victimless" crimes. The call is for a comprehensive review of criminal law in an effort to "decriminalize" types of behavior clearly beyond the competence of corrections in order to control and to facilitate the diversion of such problem cases to human service agencies much better equipped to handle them. The recommendation of minimum penetration into the system rests on an increasing body of knowledge pointing to the criminogenic influence of the system and the recognition that it is neither desirable nor necessary to incarcerate certain types of offenders for the protection of the community. In such instances, noninstitutional dispositions provide viable and much more economical alternatives to incarceration. If implemented, the recommendations of this approach would go far to alleviate some of the more fundamental problems of the jail. However, since this reform does not strike at the basic evil of the jail, namely, local control and local administration, the probability of substantial change and long-range reform is greatly reduced.

The second approach to jail reform addresses itself to the goal of increasing local accountability and improving system performance by means of state-administered regulatory procedures and the introduction of standards. Though the provision of uniform guidelines and state inspection services are certainly steps in the right direction, such practices will need to go beyond the customary statements of general principles and platitudes to more precise definitions of standards and statements with "teeth" for legal enforcement.

The third and by far the most dramatic approach to jail reform advocates the abolition of local jail control and the elimination of jails in their present form. This view encourages the development of regional or community-based correctional centers as part of an integrated correctional system under state control. Functionally, such centers would continue to give some of the traditional services of jails but would assume new responsibilities. The primary focus would be on the delivery of service to the convicted as well as to the accused. In considering the pervasiveness of the jail problem and its remarkable capacity to resist all efforts at reform, it is reasonable to state that fundamental reform of the system is contingent upon the implementation of this alternative.

ALTERNATIVE PRACTICES

The pursuit of alternative practices has been described previously as the most basic approach to jail reform. It is the least radical approach since it does not propose to change local governmental control over jails and could be implemented in many jurisdictions with relative ease. A key component is the proposal to review criminal law statutes, to determine whether certain types of criminal sanctions could be repealed or "decriminalized" without jeopardizing the safety of the public. Other aspects would include suggestions for the implementation of a host of programs designed to divert, through noncriminal procedures, certain segments of the jail population into other service agencies, or to place them in pretrial release programs in lieu of pretrial detention. Finally, the reform encourages the implementation of an array of postconviction correctional and early release programs for the sentenced offender, each program being designed to reduce, as much as possible, the deleterious effects of jails.

Decriminalization—Corrections is characterized by an historic tendency to overload the jail with sociomedical and social welfare cases. It is clearly beyond the scope of jails to deal effectively with the mentally ill, alcoholics, and drug addicts. In fact, applying criminal sanctions simply exacerbates the problems of these individuals. Also our propensity for outlawing private behavior, because private behavior is found to be morally objectionable, has resulted in too many laws proscribing too many kinds of behavior. The effect has been to sidetrack the system from its mission of protecting society against really serious crime to assuming the dubious role of policing private morality. The behavior categories involved here are "victimless" crimes, defined as crimes without an effective complainant other than the official authority. These behaviors include gambling, homosexuality between consenting adults, prostitution, abortion, and a wide range of noncriminal activities by juveniles. The control of such actions by criminal sanction and jailing is singularly ineffective and corrupting. The need, therefore, for substantive criminal law reform is great in order to facilitate the systematic exclusion of such problem cases from the system. Rather than to ignore these problems, alternative dispositions must be developed at the local level to permit the diversion of sociomedical problem cases to other agencies and better-equipped facilities outside the criminal justice system.

Diversion from the System—Diversion of persons accused or found guilty of crimes is equally recommended in view of the jail's shocking record of failure. There is overwhelming evidence that jails create crime rather than prevent it. Their very nature insures failure.

Diversion can occur at all points of the traditional criminal justice process. It refers to all mechanisms, formal and informal, that lessen the chances of criminal processing and labeling, and to organized efforts at minimizing penetration into the system. Diversion programs are essentially community-based and provide either direct assistance or referral service to a host of individuals subject to criminal sanction but who are referred to such programs in lieu of official processing.

Early diversion techniques at the arrest and pretrial level appear to be particularly promising since they are ideally suited to lighten the burden of the jail by keeping sociomedical and morals problem cases out of the criminal justice system. For example, if police were granted more discretion in handling alleged offenders, public intoxicants and other alcohol-related offenders could be diverted into detoxification or alcoholic-treatment programs. Depending on the prevalence of alcoholism in a specific area, such diversion techniques could conceivably account for as much as a decrease of 40 to 50 percent in the number of commitments to jails. Similarly, if the offenses of public drunkenness, disorderly conduct, vagrancy, and related victimless crimes were eliminated from the criminal statutes, this nation's arrest rate could be cut in half without adding risks to the public safety.

Community-based crisis intervention centers are another promising method of early diversion. They provide information, advice, emergency assistance or referral services in communities with high crime rates. Functioning as resource centers for people in crisis, they constitute a direct effort at primary prevention.

Pretrial Release Programs—Commercial money bail and cash bail are the most commonly practiced release programs today. One of the many disadvantages of the practice is that it systematically discriminates against the poor. Only a few defendants are able to raise even relatively small amounts of bail—$100 or $500. Pretrial detention appears to increase significantly the likelihood that, if he is convicted, an offender will receive a sentence of imprisonment as against any other type of sentence. Sentences are also likely to be longer.

In an effort to overcome some of the inequities of the present bail bond system and to reduce cost and space requirements for pretrial detention, a number of innovative bail programs have become significant alternatives to pretrial diversion, such as the cash bail system, release on own recognizance, and the community bail program under which a man's release is backed financially by private citizens.

Quick diversion can also be attained if magistrates or bail commissioners are available on a 24-hour basis. Of similar value is the attempt on the part of some states to speed up court procedures by linking them to legislatively predetermined time limits. Prosecution must take a case to trial or else drop the charges.

Conditional release and summons release programs are the remaining pretrial diversion measures well-suited for indigent defendants accused of a host of minor offenses. Unfortunately, their potential for reducing jail populations remains largely unexplored.

Many of the reform programs we have considered have become meaningful alternatives to commercial bail. In spite of the demonstrated success of these programs, full-fledged bail reform has yet to become a reality—for several reasons. Many programs are experimental in nature and are characterized by short-term federal or private funding. Since few jurisdictions are willing to support these activities with permanent funding, the programs rarely survive a year or two. Further, selection criteria applied too conservatively result in the release of candidates who could have bailed out under conventional procedures. On the other hand, carelessly administered programs have led to substantial increases in the default rate. As a result, administrative procedures will have to be improved before characteristic bureaucratic inertia is overcome.

Postconviction Correctional Programs—Sentencing dispositions for misdemeanants are also characterized by disparity, lack of options, and a predilection for institutionalization. Since misdemeanants generally are less dangerous than felons, they would appear to be excellent candidates for alternatives to incarceration. In spite of this, the application of such readily available dispositions as the suspended sentence, probation, and fines has experienced little use.

In the vast majority of jurisdictions, misdemeanants are sentenced to incarceration without any information given to the judge other than the offender's name and the crime with which he is charged. This complete lack of information for sentencing decisions is identified today as the principal reason for judicial reluctance to utilize noninstitutional correctional dispositions for misdemeanants. To alleviate the situation, the use of presentence reports should be extended to misdemeanants and should be presented to the court in every case where there is a potential sentencing disposition that involves incarceration. Since, in many simple cases, extensive presentence reports are clearly a waste of resources, gradations of presentence reports should be developed between full and short-form reports in order to meet the variation of offender needs. To reduce incarceration to a minimum, presentence reports should be prepared prior to adjudication, whenever defendants are incarcerated pending trial and have given their consent; on the advice of counsel.

Extended use of presentence reports will no doubt place added burdens on the system. However, such information is essential if sentencing decisions are to be based on a correct evaluation and with dispositions conducive to reform. The availability of sufficient information should facilitate rapid expansion of existing alternatives to incarceration: *discharge following conviction, suspended sentence, informal or summary probation,* and *probation without verdict.* The latter alternatives represent a range of informal and quasi-formal methods of supervision by the court and offer considerable latitude and flexibility in sentencing. Under such provisions, offenders are generally required to meet conditions such as attending school, seeking work, or holding jobs for specified periods of time. Satisfactory performance may result in nullification of their conviction, expunging of their records, or discharge from supervision. On the other hand, failure to perform may lead to the offender's reactivation of formal adjudication proceedings or to incarceration.

One of the most promising quasi-formal methods of disposition for misdemeanants is the *deferred adjudication* program. This is chronologically at the earliest stage of the judicial process. The objective is to provide a misdemeanant with an opportunity to prove to the court that he can function successfully in the community without further intervention on the part of the criminal justice system.

Probation as a court disposition for misdemeanants is grossly underused. Even though misdemeanants outnumber felons by far, the number on probation is astonishingly small. To judge from reports of some of the larger misdemeanant jurisdictions, probation is used in less than 2 percent of all dispositions. The neglect of probation as an alternative to incarceration is all the more reprehensible since it offers the best returns on the correctional dollar. Probation is not only more effective in reducing recidivism, but it is also less costly than any other available correctional service.

The infrequent use of probation for misdemeanants is partly to be attributed to the fact that such service is not as well established in minor courts of general criminal jurisdiction. The major reason, however, apparently lies in the wide variation in the method in which probation is organized and placed within the government framework. The average program is one that evolved more by default than by design. The service is to be found in the judicial branch, although in some states it is in the executive branch or under combined sponsorship. There is no more logic in probation being a part of the judiciary than in the judicial system administering the jail or the penitentiary. Courts are clearly adjudicatory and regulatory bodies—they are not service-oriented organizations. As a result, probation is much more appropriately placed within the executive branch of the government. Since all other subsystems for offender dispositions are located within that branch, it is irrational to exclude probation from it. Surely, accidents of history should not be permitted to interfere with a more rational allocation of staff or the provision of a continuum of service.

In view of the fact that an expansion of correctional services to misdemeanants is contingent upon the development of a vastly improved information service, a more innovative approach is needed. Recent proposals calling for implementation of evaluative and diagnostic components at local and regional correctional facilities have been stressed. Under such an arrangement, properly trained personnel outside the adjudicatory process would be able to divert

sociomedical problem cases into more appropriate alternative programs: to public welfare agencies, mental health services, youth
service bureaus, or similar public or private agencies. Finally, agencies would conduct evaluative assessment services and presentence
investigations on the basis of which appropriate recommendations
for programs and services could be made in the courts.

Among many variations in probation programs, probation subsidy
plans seem to be particularly successful. Patterned after a program
initially developed in California, these programs involve state payments to participating counties of up to $4,000 per case. The pay-
ment provides for intensive care and treatment in the community
to selected probationers who otherwise would have been committed to state institutions. In California, the program produced
substantial savings to the taxpayers and led to the cancellation of
planned jail and prison construction, the closing of existing institutions, and even to the abandonment of new facilities that had
been constructed. Most importantly, the wider probation dispositions apparently did not increase the number of crimes in the participating counties.

Fines are by far the most common dispositions for the misdemeanant. This is primarily because traffic violations, in which fines
are consistently used, have been increasing. Unlike other penalties,
fines bring revenue! However, if for any reason an imposed fine is
not paid, the customary alternative is time in jail. Since many of
those affected are unable to pay the fine, the system is clearly discriminatory against the poor. Rulings from the Supreme Court have
interdicted the practice of imposing jail terms in lieu of payment
of fines, but the effect of the rulings remains to be seen. The use
of fines should undoubtedly be expanded. An effective system requires assessment of a person's ability to pay and suitable arrangements to facilitate payment of fines in installments.

Having discussed some of the more conventional postconviction
programs for misdemeanants, we are now ready to examine some
of the more innovative ones in the field. Among these, community
services, job placement, nonresidential treatment, and residential
probation treatment stand out.

A program of *community services* is particularly well suited for
first offenders and for cases where fines or incarceration would bring
increased hardship. Once a presentence investigation has established
eligibility, the court sentences the individual to a definite number
of hours of community service. After a successful performance by

an offender, the court expunges the record. The advantages are many: the public good is served, the misdemeanant stays in the community instead of becoming a drain on public funds while he is in jail, and his family and community ties remain intact.

Job placement programs are aimed at changing the normal course of delinquent careers. They are designed to help the young, the poorly educated, the unemployed, and the unskilled members of a particular target area who characteristically comprise the bulk of the area's official arrest statistics. An adjournment of trial is granted for several months. During that period, the defendant receives counseling, social service referrals, job counseling, and help to get a job. Successful performance results in the dismissal of charges. This kind of program offers an almost infinite number of advantages over a jail sentence: it emphasizes crime prevention, reduces the need for incarceration, interrupts the development of delinquent careers, and reduces unemployment in the community.

Nonresidential treatment programs are well suited for offenders who do not qualify for full probation but who can nevertheless safely remain in the community, but with intensive supervision. Qualifying offenders are permitted to live at home but are required to participate daily in a variety of correctional programs at a nonresidential treatment center.

Residential probation programs provide a more structured alternative to incarceration for both adult and juvenile offenders. They are particularly good alternatives to institutionalization in jail or penitentiaries and are recommended for those individuals who would not ordinarily qualify for probation, either because of a prior history of failure in a previous correctional program or because the protection of the public requires a more structured supervision.

A brief examination of early release activities reveals that work and educational release programs are among the most promising correctional programs offered today for the convicted misdemeanant. They rest on the premise that certain offenders, though they may require more intensive supervision than probation officers can actually give them, do not require full institutionalization in a jail. Although legislation facilitating work release exists in most states, there is much diversity in terms of statutes, implementation, program requirements, and eligibility of offenders. Work release permits the offender to maintain a job or to work on a new job while he continues to support his family without resorting to welfare. It enhances a man's employability at the same time that it eliminates idleness. A portion of the money he earns can be used to make restitution, to pay off debts or fines, and to pay room and board at the jail. Remarkable success rates and savings to taxpayers have helped to make work release one of the most popular correctional programs ever designed. Earnings run into the hundreds and thousands of dollars, failure rates remain outstandingly low. Educational or study release programs are also gaining favor. They utilize specialized community resources and thus avoid the necessity of duplicating such services within the jail.

In conclusion, it should be noted that with the exception of work release, most of the nontraditional programs and services for misdemeanants are still experimental in nature. Most lack validating research as to whether they result in a verified reduction of recidivism. However, they do represent a considerable advance in the treatment of misdemeanants, particularly when compared with practices of only a decade ago. Finally, there are sufficient indications pointing to their utility not only in terms of reduced cost, especially when compared with more conventional methods, but also because they reduce the isolating effect of institutions and focus on reintegration of offenders into their communities. This, after all, is the ultimate testing ground of the effectiveness of the correctional process.

STATE INTERVENTION

The second major approach to jail reform seeks to increase local accountability and to improve local jails by means of state-administered regulatory procedures along with the formulation of state standards and their enforcement through state inspection services. This approach is based on the recognition that the present condition and effectiveness of most jails are seriously deficient—a fact directly to be attributed to their local administration. Most jail studies reveal that state control of local corrections is needed to substantially alleviate the problems of jails and to provide the coordination of services and resources necessary for more effective program implementation. However, the objective of state operation and control of local jails is a long-range goal, at best, in view of the known reluctance of local jurisdictions to relinquish control over any function in their domain. As a result, interim measures need to be devised to improve jail performance. Formulation of state standards and a system of state inspection, with strong measures for enforcement, are promising ways to stimulate improvement. Further, increasing state and federal participation in funding, in return for meeting certain requirements and standards, seems an equally favorable method to speed up the transition. For example, in 1970, under Part E of the Amendment to the Omnibus Crime Control and Safe Streets Act of 1968, federal funding became available to states and local governments to finance correctional programs and facilities. To assist state and local governments in the planning of innovative, community-based correctional programs and facilities, the Law Enforcement Assistance Administration of the United States Department of Justice in 1971 established the National Clearinghouse for Criminal Justice Planning and Architecture, at the University of Illinois. Under federal contract, guidelines were developed at Illinois to accompany the administration of Part E funding by an LEAA network of state planning agencies from every state. The guidelines assist correctional administrators in the processes of identifying correctional problems, in developing alternatives to incarceration, in implementing correctional treatment programs in the community, and in correlating these processes with the design of innovative facilities.

Even though state and federal involvement in local corrections increased considerably in the preceding decade, change has been agonizingly slow. Where standards exist, they are frequently vague and hence difficult to enforce. Finally, standards set up for conditions in individual jails do not provide for the large complex of agencies and processes to which jails must relate. As a result, change continues at a snail's pace and perpetuates not only a haphazard approach to jail reform but also to an obviously bad system.

ABOLITION OF LOCAL CONTROL

The third and most radical approach to jail reform calls for the abolition of local control over jails and the elimination of jails in their present form. This has been the consistent recommendation of those knowledgeable on the subject and is based on the following considerations.

The delivery of correctional services to the misdemeanant has been seriously neglected, at best, or noticeably absent, at worst. The concepts of pretrial screening and diversion of sociomedical problem cases from the criminal justice system into human service agencies are barely known at the local level, let alone are they put into practice! As a result, local county and, particularly, city jails are burgeoning with people, most of whom could be safely released into alternative programs without endangering the public. In view of the documented history of the failure of the American jail—its inefficiency and waste, its neglect and indifference, its partisan politics and inhumanity to man, the time is ripe for fundamental change.

Only state control of local corrections could facilitate the approach needed to produce that change. Through the establishment of state-controlled, local and regional detention and community correctional centers (rather than jails), the law-enforcement branch could be relieved of its custodial responsibilities and utilize its resources for the real protection of the public. At the same time, detention and correctional functions, including intake assessment, diversion and referrals, could be more effectively administered by a coordinated state correctional system. It would facilitate uniform, statewide planning and a systematic approach to what is currently an inefficient and unproductive maze—a maze inextricably entwined with a melange of interagency jealousies, interpersonal rivalries, and duplication of services. It would facilitate coordinated staff training, the development of merit and civil service systems, interdepartmental career opportunities, and aid the growth of professionalism in areas long lacking all of these. Total system planning, defined as the process of determining, analyzing, and developing responses to problems of specific service areas, is needed if the problems of the jail are to be solved.

Whereas uniform state planning is the *sine qua non* for optimal planning results, regional, and occasionally, local level planning will undoubtedly continue, at least until more coordinated services are established. Irrespective of the administrative structure of the planning unit involved, planning should encompass a total system philosophy, taking into consideration both the full range of crime control needs and the ultimate goal of crime prevention. Under this concept of total planning, it would be ill advised to construct a single jail without fully assessing the total service needs of the planning area. Planning should always include a thorough assessment of current practices, an evaluation of resources, an analysis of trends based on sufficient statistical information, and an exploration of community-based alternatives to current dispositions. Basic to this consideration is the need to emphasize the development of service delivery systems, with specific programs and institutions to be determined within the framework of the larger system.

Dependent on population density, two overall planning concepts emerge: *a regional system* in which programs and facilities are centralized for a multicounty or city-county area; and *a network system* in which programs and facilities are dispersed to accommodate the vastly different needs of major metropolitan areas. Among the many benefits to be gained by systematized planning and regional re-organization of local detention and correctional institutions under state control are economic savings, improved system performance, and a high potential for a sizeable reduction in crime.

Daniel Glaser

3

Correction of Adult Offenders in the Community

Because criminals are rehabilitated only if they refrain from crime while free, instead of just when incarcerated, correctional programs to deal with offenders in the community have developed as alternatives or supplements to confinement. These programs have a diversity of organization, procedure and nomenclature, but they are most frequently designated by such terms as *probation, parole, work release, education release, furlough,* and *halfway house.*

All of these activities *graduate* the transition from confinement to freedom. All also modify at least three aspects of traditional sentencing and confinement procedure: *assessment of appropriate time for release, control of convicted persons,* and *assistance to releasees.* The manner in which this modification occurs, and the principles directing it, highlight important distinctions among the various forms of community correction for adults, and are related to current controversies in their administration.

Assessment of Appropriate Time for Release

In criminal courts, traditionally, the assessment of an offender in order to determine the optimum sentence was done exclusively

DANIEL GLASER *is professor of sociology at the University of Southern California. Among other positions in a varied career, he has been sociologist-actuary of the Illinois Parole and Pardon Board at Pontiac and Joliet-Stateville Prisons. Dr. Glaser has written widely in his field; his most recent books are* Social Deviance *and* Adult Crime and Social Policy.

by the judge, within limitations imposed on his discretion by statute. Soon after finding an accused person guilty, the judge imposed a specific term of confinement—for example, ten years—and often issued instructions on its implementation—for example, specifying hard labor or solitary confinement—in addition to, in many cases, imposing fines or other penalties. These hastily decided penalties were unalterable, except by pardons from the governor or the President, which rarely were granted. By contrast, all community correctional operations *defer* at least part of the penalty-fixing decision, and *delegate* some of the former purely judicial responsibility for it. The ways in which such diversion of the judge's assessment function occur determine key differences among the major forms of community correction.

PROBATION

Probation evolved mainly from the suspended sentence, whereby a judge waives a penalty after he imposes it, but only on condition that the convicted person conform forever, or for a designated period, to specific behavioral requirements. These requirements frequently include making restitution to the victim of the crime, being sober, working, paying court costs, and committing no further offenses. The suspended sentence usually has been called *probation* wherever a court appointee—voluntary or paid—has been officially designated as "probation officer." This officer's functions include advising the judge on whom to release conditionally, assisting the releasee, and checking that his behavior conforms to the requirements imposed by the court.

The United States claims credit for originating probation, tracing this practice to a Boston shoemaker named John Augustus, who in 1841 volunteered to employ misdemeanants if the judge would suspend their sentences and release them to his care. He soon recruited other volunteers to assist and supervise releasees, and they are reported to have had an impressive success record with their charges. In 1878 Massachusetts legislation established the position of probation officer in the criminal court. While Britain and other countries report the functioning of volunteers in roles analogous to that of Augustus before this period, British authorization of government-employed probation officers did not occur until 1907. The practice has since spread to most of the world.

Today the distinctive function of the probation officer is his presentence investigation of convicted offenders. In most courts such inquiry is routinely required by the judge for all persons eligible for probation, and often for any other convicted persons for whom the court may choose among alternative sentences, such as different maximum terms of imprisonment. When a person is found guilty, the judge normally defers sentencing sufficiently to permit him to receive and study a presentence report from his probation staff. This report summarizes and assesses the life history of the convicted person, describing and interpreting the circumstances of the current offense as well as any prior delinquent and criminal activity, appraising educational and employment performance, analyzing family relationships, noting the military service record, inferring character and personality traits, and providing other commentary relevant to the determination of an appropriate sentence. Information for this report is procured by the probation officer from interviews with the convicted person, as well as interviews and correspondence with this person's family, neighbors, employers, teachers or others, and by a search of official records. The thoroughness of this inquiry varies from one probation office to another and sometimes from one case to another. Usually the presentence report ends with a recommendation on sentencing, and studies indicate that most judges follow these recommendations in a majority of their decisions.

In addition to advising the judge on granting probation, the probation officer may recommend later that probation be revoked, and be replaced by a jail or prison term, because the probationer fails to conform to the rules and regulations imposed as a condition of probation. The officer may also suggest to the judge, or may order on his own authority, that changes be made in these conditions, such as altering work or residence requirements. The officer may also recommend early discharge from probation when the probationer's conduct is exemplary. Because of this continuous modifiability, probation clearly involves deferral of the court's traditional penalty determination functions, but final decision and authority on the sentence still rest exclusively with the judge.

PAROLE

In parole the delegation and deferral of responsibility for determining the offender's penalty is much more complete than in probation, for parole is a conditional release from the last portion of a confinement sentence. Such release of a sentenced criminal is ordered by a parole board, an administrative agency completely independent of the courts.

The term *parole* is traced to a convention of ancient military chivalry whereby a knight or other member of the upper classes captured in combat might be released on his word of honor, which in French is *parole d'honneur,* not to escape or not to resume combat. In the penal practice of English-speaking countries parole generally is traced to nineteenth century innovations in Australia and Ireland whereby prisoners earned credits for good behavior for which the warden might grant them a "ticket-of-leave" to initiate their freedom before the end of their sentence. The leave was given on their promise to be law-abiding, and was revocable if they were charged with misbehavior during their period of freedom. In Ireland such releasees had to report regularly to the nearest police station, which advised the prison of the releasee's conduct. This type of procedure was authorized by law in England in 1857, where it was called "conditional release on license," a label still predominant in most of Europe. A similar procedure was called "parole" when initiated in the United States in 1874 at the Elmira Reformatory in New York. This system spread to almost all the other states during the half-century ensuing, but early in this period state employees known as *parole agents* or *parole officers* largely took over from the police the primary responsibility for checking on the behavior of parolees.

Assessment of whether a prisoner should be released is made by a parole board, which employs diverse sources of information, especially:

1. Admission Summaries and Progress Reports. These are prepared by the staff of penal institutions, usually by a person trained in one of the behavioral sciences and having a title such as *Classification Officer, Parole Officer, Caseworker,* or *Counselor.* They update the presentence report by describing the prisoner's behavior during confinement, his current family relationships, and his asserted plans and arrangements for postrelease residence and employment.

2. Hearings. A more or less formal interview with the prisoner, and sometimes with his relatives or other interested parties, is conducted by one or more of the board's members, or sometimes by one of its employees with a title such as *Hearing Officer.* This interview usually is transcribed or summarized for all board members to study. A right to such a hearing often is claimed for prisoners, to assure that the board hears the prisoners' own arguments for release on parole, as well as their own accounts of past events and their plans, rather than just the reports of their views conveyed in the institution's Admission Summary and Progress Reports.

3. *Communications.* Parole boards sometimes solicit, and frequently receive unsolicited, a large variety of letters, telegrams, and phone calls exhorting them to grant or to deny parole to particular prisoners.

4. *Preparole Investigation Reports.* Usually in only a fraction of the cases, but in some jurisdictions routinely for almost every case, the parole board defers its final decision until a field investigation is made of the prisoner's prospective residential and employment arrangements. Most often this inquiry is conducted by the parole officers or agents. Usually the board reaches a decision approving parole without such an investigation, but stipulates that the parole may begin only when a favorable report is received on home and job arrangements. Under such procedure many prisoners without relatives or friends able to assist them may languish in prison for many months "overdue" on their parole, since they cannot obtain a job by correspondence from prison. Others have former employers, friends, or relatives who promise them a job. In many of the latter cases, however, the job actually cannot be provided for long or at all, but is offered as a favor, to facilitate release. As a consequence, research has demonstrated little or no relationship between parole outcome and promise of a job at the time of parole. Therefore many boards have become less rigid about a satisfactory job arrangement in the community before qualifying a prisoner for parole.

THE INDETERMINATE SENTENCE CONTROVERSY

In many states the introduction of parole was combined with a change in the sentencing law whereby the judge no longer imposed what was called a *definite sentence.* This traditional penalty—specifying a particular number of years to be served—was replaced by the *indeterminate sentence,* the minimum number of years before the prisoner can be considered for parole, and a maximum duration of sentence if parole is denied or revoked. Thus, where a person convicted of armed robbery might previously have received a definite sentence of ten years, under an indeterminate sentence law the court might impose a minimum term of five years before parole eligibility and a maximum of fifteen years imprisonment, usually referred to as a "five-to-fifteen-year" sentence. Here the judge is delegating a portion of his penalty-fixing authority to the parole board. Often the court is permitted to vary this delegation from case to case, so that it might give a one-to-ten year sentence to one armed robber, presumably a first offender about whom the judge feels uncertain, while it imposes a twelve-to-fifteen-year sentence on another armed robber whom the judge regards as a professional and vicious predator.

A few states, notably California and Washington, have an extreme form of indeterminate sentencing sometimes called an *indefinite* sentence. Here the court appears to have no sentencing power apart from granting probation, and for the most serious offenses this is barred. Every person sent to prison receives the maximum term prescribed by the legislature for his offense. The parole board investigates and provides a hearing for each prisoner during the first six months or year of confinement, after which it announces the minimum term which the prisoner must serve before parole will be considered. (For some offenses, however, the law restricts how low the minimum can be.) Appropriately, Washington officially designates its paroling agency as the "Board of Prison Terms and Paroles."

Interstate Comparison—There has been increasing argument, on a variety of grounds, over the alleged advantages of the indeterminate over the definite sentence. Perhaps the most questionable critique is that which simply presents evidence that in most states having indeterminate sentence laws, the average length of confinement in prison is greater than in most states which still have definite sentencing. This is, first of all, a semantically muddled argument, for when a state has definite sentences but the parole board is authorized to order a prisoner's release after he has served a fraction of his term, the state, in effect, has sentences which are indeterminate, with a minimum of this fraction (usually one-third, but sometimes less) and a maximum of the definite sentence.

Secondly, any comparison of durations of prison confinement in different states will be misleading unless the comparison is made for offenders sentenced for the same types of offenses and with similar prior criminal records. Many of the states making most use of the definite sentence are states making least use of probation, so that terms of confinement are briefer in these definite-sentence states because they imprison people who in most indeterminate-sentence states would receive probation. Some of the extreme indeterminate-sentence states, notably California and Washington, now imprison only a small percentage of the persons convicted of felonies in their courts; the rest receive jail and probation terms under programs of state subsidy to counties for these local correctional functions. Therefore, the average term of imprisonment in these states should not be compared to that in states imprisoning a much larger percentage of persons convicted of felonies.

Thirdly, one may well question whether a briefer duration of imprisonment is an adequate basis for considering one state's sentencing system superior to another, even for comparable types of offenders, unless there are data on the rates of recidivism for such offenders with different durations of imprisonment. In the absence of adequate knowledge on the optimum term of confinement, if any, for reduction of a particular type of offender's prospects of continuing in crime, one might well argue for a high degree of indeterminacy. This permits a very early experimental release if there is no clear evidence that the parolee will be dangerous, but reconfinement if he or she reverts to crime.

Parole Board Discretion—A persuasive criticism of the indeterminacy of sentences in some states is that parole boards have too much unchecked power over a convict's freedom and life circumstances. Evidence can be marshaled that some boards or board members have been incompetent, callous, arbitrary, prejudiced, or careless in their exercise of power. Also, the parole system acquires a major function of helping to maintain order in prisons, since boards tend to stress conformity to prison rules as a basis for release. With this stress, a highly indeterminate sentence may result in some prisoners serving years for petty misconduct in prison, often without fair trial and under unconscionable provocation from staff or from other inmates.

In opposition to criticism of parole board discretion, one may point out that if the length of confinement is not determined by the parole board it will be fixed by persons who may well be no more conscientious and capable. For example, in states where every judge has a large amount of discretion in determining sentence, there is great disparity of sentencing from one court to the next, and often from one judge to the next within a multijudge court. Indeed, sometimes little consistency is evident in the sentencing by a single judge. One of the less-heralded contributions of many boards is to reduce the effects of disparity of sentencing in their state, and this also occurs in the federal system of criminal justice. Having a board instead of a single individual fix or review the penalty, having a single such board for the entire correctional system, and permitting them more time for deliberation and investigation than most judges have, may make for more reasonable and consistent penalties than result from the traditional high autonomy of judges.

Uncertainty—Another argument against indeterminacy in sentences rests on humanitarian grounds. It is contended that the uncertain duration of confinement under highly indeterminate sentences and the prisoner's frequent inability to make it more certain render such penalties unusually cruel. When there is less indeterminacy because there is no parole, or because parole is granted on the basis of explicit rules, prisoners suffer less anxiety over when they will be released. An additional argument against indeterminacy contends that the most predictable penalties have the greatest deterrent effect, both in reducing further crime by those imprisoned, and as general deterrence against crimes by others.

These arguments have validity, but it should not be assumed that making sentences highly definite offers an easy solution to the problems of making penalties more protective of society, more humane, or more consistent. In the first place, it should be noted that any formal sentencing procedure will not necessarily freeze in a predictable manner the amount of penalty-fixing authority shifted from the courts to the parole board, or vice-versa. Informal procedures in the negotiation of judicial decisions often largely offset the intended effects of formal directives. With 80 to 95 percent of criminal cases settled by plea bargaining rather than by completed trials in most metropolitan courts, many guilty pleas are offered and accepted which have as their objectives the subversion of sentencing legislation.

Division of Authority—The particular informal procedure which develops in the courts to determine sentences depends largely on the division of authority in setting penalties, under the criminal statutes, between the legislature, the courts, and the parole board. If the legislature endeavors to control sentencing by restricting the discretion of the courts and the parole board, it does this by specifying a definite penalty for each type of offense, usually making many distinctions among crimes, such as having a first, second and third degree of burglary or robbery, with a different sentence prescribed for each. Under such legislation the defense will regularly offer to plead guilty to an offense having a lesser penalty, and will make the outcome of most trials prolonged and uncertain unless the prosecution drops the more serious charges in exchange for a plea of guilty to charges carrying lesser penalties. When the legislature wishes to give the parole board much discretion it prescribes a highly indeterminate sentence for each major category of crime, such as an automatic one-year-to-life sentence for all burglary and armed robbery and one to ten years for grand theft. Then, however, one commonly has burglars and armed robbers bargaining successfully to be allowed to plead guilty to grand theft; in the parlance of the court corridors, the prosecutor is often happy to let an armed robber "swallow his gun" if he will plead guilty to grand theft, thus maintaining the prosecutor's conviction rate and expediting court business. When the judge has great discretion in determining sentences there is usually more involvement of the judge in the bargaining process, with the prosecutor and public defenders, or "courthouse regulars" among defense lawyers, since all share much interest in making their collective work agreeable and frequently they are political or social cronies.

The discrepancy between the sentencing intent of lawmakers and actual penalties in the courts is not uniform from one judge to the next under any sentencing system, but is extensive in most urban courts. Furthermore, the discrepancy usually appears most striking when one compares the penalties received by indigent and unsophisticated offenders with those imposed on more experienced and professional predators. The offender with few resources and little astuteness at negotiation, especially if he cannot pay bail and thus is held in jail pending trial, pleads guilty much more readily to almost all relevant charges than the offender arrested for the same crimes who has resources to gain freedom on bail and to hire counsel that will delay proceedings.

Depoliticizing judges, prosecutors, and parole boards by making them all civil servants with high entrance and promotion standards (as in Europe), having checks on sentencing such as a sentence review and appeals board, and having limits to discretion and possibly a review process in parole—all would probably alleviate complaints aroused by indeterminacy in sentences more than would the complete or near elimination of indeterminacy. Other developments, however, such as the administrative release of prisoners to work and to halfway houses, probably can do more to alleviate these complaints than has generally been realized.

WORK OR EDUCATION RELEASE AND FURLOUGHS

Work release refers to programs whereby prisoners depart from a penal institution daily to hold jobs in the free community, usually returning at the end of each workday. Education release is analogous, except that the prisoner goes to school outside the correctional facility for instruction not available inside. Occasionally these are combined, in that inmates may hold jobs in the community and go to school there. Sometimes these releases are extended by permission to stay out longer for shopping, recreation, or family visiting. The latter, however, is more often handled by brief furloughs. Most frequently they are for a few days, and are for travel to a job interview or to make postrelease housing arrangements. Sometimes, quite confusingly, work release is called "work furlough" or "day parole."

Work release in essentially its current form in the United States has long existed in some local jails, notably in Wisconsin under its Huber Act of 1913. A boom in this system of release began when North Carolina initiated it in 1957, received favorable publicity for it in national mass media, and more than doubled the number thus released during each of the next three years. Work and education release were both introduced into the federal prisons in 1965, and grew rapidly there, nearly four thousand federal prisoners being released in this fashion by the end of 1967. During the 1970s these forms of community correction became firmly established in most state prison systems. One major limitation is the rural location of most penal institutions, far from extensive employment or schooling opportunities.

Assessment Value—Justifications stated in promoting work or educational release seldom stress, and often completely omit, their value as assessment procedures, but this may be one of their most important contributions. Behavior on work release provides evidence for decisions on parole presumably much more relevant to the assessment of the public's risk in a parole than the convict's record of adjustment to prison conditions. A decision to grant work or education release may thus be thought of as preliminary to a decision on more complete release.

Because of this appreciable grant of freedom, compared with traditional confinement, many states allow work or education release only with specific approval by the parole board for each case. In other states and in the federal prisons, however, assignment to such forms of release is authorized exclusively by prison officials rather than by the parole board, although each case sometimes must be approved by the penal system's central office instead of being authorized by a warden.

Effect on Parole Board—Whenever the parole board is not consulted in advance on these forms of release, it may be confronted at its parole decision date by a sort of *fait accompli*—the prospective parolee has already been conditionally released, to a large extent, through the work or education program.

Wherever a work or education release or a furlough is granted by prison staff without consulting the parole board, and especially when this is done before the board has even considered parole eligibility, some of the board's former authority to assess the optimum time of release has been delegated to the prison officials. This delegation is restricted with furloughs in many states, where prison officials may only grant short releases when the board has authorized parole at a specific future date. Furloughs are then given, in most cases, specifically to look for a job or to arrange other requirements of postrelease life. Sometimes, if an opportunity to start employment immediately is procured while the prisoner is out on such a furlough, the releasee may contact a parole officer who, after verification, may arrange by telephone that parole begin immediately. These arrangements, of course, constitute further graduation of the release process and further delegation of authority in assessment of the optimum time for release.

HALFWAY HOUSES

This term applies to residences provided for adult offenders. When not used voluntarily by their occupants they are regarded as custody intermediate between the confinement in a jail or prison and release by probation, parole, or complete discharge. At the end of a period of incarceration, these establishments are thought of as placing their residents "halfway out" of prison; when employed as an alternative both to release on probation and to incarceration, such abodes are viewed as placing their occupants "halfway in" confinement. They have sometimes been called *prerelease guidance centers, community correction centers,* and *community-based correctional facilities,* but these terms also denote offices for the assistance or control of released offenders who reside in their own homes.

Halfway houses were originally established privately by religious organizations and by philanthropic individuals, nondenominational groups, and foundations concerned with assisting homeless men upon their release from jails, mental institutions, or prisons. These privately-operated homes still exist, especially in the mental health field, along with government-operated establishments for the same purpose. The privately run residences generally are restricted to occupants who seek housing there voluntarily. Somewhat coerced "volunteering" occurs at times, however, when people from these establishments actively recruit volunteers in courts, jails, and prisons, most commonly with "skid row" alcoholics and, in New York, with drug addicts; regardless of recruiting, residence in these places is clearly somewhat coerced whenever it is a requirement imposed by a court or a board in granting probation or parole.

The distinctive feature of halfway houses is that the convicted persons there come and go freely most of the time. There may be curfew or bedcheck hours, individual appointments with staff, group counseling or temporary restrictions on individuals, when they are expected to stay at the home, but during most of the average day a majority of the residents are on their own. In addition, these houses usually are located in or near the community from which their residents come, or in which they wish to live when more free.

Halfway houses for persons still serving prison sentences test readiness for parole more fully than work or education release because the residents in these places control more of their own schedules than do prisoners in other forms of graduated release. They are relatively free to do as they please where they please during their leisure hours.

A markedly new delegation of decision-making is created when prison administrators are permitted to transfer inmates to halfway houses. Some parole board members object to such delegation of power, asserting that prison administrators thus usurp the board's authority. Some prison officials, however, maintain that their ability to graduate the release process by means of community centers makes parole boards obsolete. Frequently a compromise occurs where the board fixes a parole date six months to a year in advance, for then the prison officials are permitted to transfer inmates to the halfway houses only during the last four to six months before the parole date.

Control of Convicted Persons

Rehabilitative measures are important aspects of control, rather than just features of assistance, since the most effective controls for keeping all of us conforming to the law may well be the informal social influences of home, job, and other group settings. The concern of people with their obligations to specific individuals and with their reputations among persons whose good will they value seem to regulate their behavior much more than do the formal threats, restrictions, or surveillance of government agencies. This may become evident if we again consider each form of community correction separately, but this time from the standpoint of control. Such an examination will highlight controversies in the administration of community corrections. It will also demonstrate that assessment and control are as closely interrelated as are assistance and control.

PROBATION

Perhaps the most important argument for probation is that with minimal disturbance it permits control of any anticriminal activities and commitments in which the offender is involved. If he or she is employed and has good family relationships and helpful noncriminal friendships or group memberships, probation permits continued residence in the community and preservation of these ties, as well as the continuation of self-support and support for dependents. When incarcerated, a lawbreaker suffers loss of job and strain in family relationships and in anticriminal friendships, while at the same time undergoing criminalizing experiences through confinement in relative idleness in the company of criminals.

Probation can be criticized if it leaves undisturbed the circumstances and relationships which caused the criminality, and if it permits the probationer little loss of the material or psychological benefits gained from criminal activity. Requiring payment to the victims of crime where possible, or public service work as restitutive acts, and promoting the probationer's avoidance of situations or activities contributing to lawbreaking, may be controls of a rehabilitative nature in particular cases. Indeed, probation can be clearly justified only if it seems likely to assist in the preservation or development of anticriminal influences, and in the reduction of criminogenic conditions.

In the actual administration of probation too little attention is given to supervision, in this writer's opinion, and hence both assistance and control are neglected. In many jurisdictions, procedures and policies severely limit probation's effectiveness. Four major controversies as to the best method of implementing probation will especially concern us here, and several lesser ones will also be mentioned.

Question of a Right to Probation—In many courts the probation officers each handle hundreds of cases, despite optimum workload standards set at 50 cases or fewer under supervision, with each presentence investigation per month counted as the equivalent of four supervision cases. A workload of hundreds of cases is far too great to permit adequate investigation for assessment or control purposes, let alone for appreciable assistance.

It is especially in these crowded courts with overworked staff that probation tends to be regarded as a right in most cases of first conviction, and is granted without any field investigation. There is no appreciable control or assistance, except that the probationer is expected to report weekly or monthly, usually a matter of completing a form which clerical employees receive and simply file. Essentially, a suspended sentence is granted in such cases. This practice is referred to in the court as "a pass" for the first offense.

Probation in many courts has thus become almost automatic for all lesser felonies and all misdemeanors on the first conviction, but usually it is granted only if the accused pleads guilty instead of being found guilty by trial. Claims of innocence are thus discouraged, on the assumption that without such discouragement the court would be overburdened with trials, and that there usually is sound basis for police charges. The courts also presume that anyone who denies guilt but is found guilty must be too evil to warrant probation. Appellate courts have reprimanded lower courts for automatically denying probation to those who plead not guilty, but this practice is still widespread even though not officially proclaimed as policy, and it seldom is appealed.

In defense of an automatic right to probation on the first offense, the criminalizing consequences of incarceration are cited. Certainly, if any sentence should be automatic for the first conviction it is preferable that it be one of probation. Nevertheless, if an investigation can be conducted, a more valid case for probation can be made. Also, probation may then be planned with more adequate provision for control and assistance than when little or no presentence investigation occurs and the accused receives just "a pass," the equivalent of a suspended sentence.

Investigation often reveals that the so-called first offender is not that, even though never before convicted. Perhaps the first question to answer when investigating the risks in granting probation following conviction for a property offense—the most frequent type of felony in urban areas—is how the accused has been supporting himself at the time of his arrest. If he or she has a standard of living and net worth that cannot be accounted for by legitimate income, crime can be assumed to have been the source of livelihood. This is well accepted in income tax prosecutions, as a method of proving unreported income, and it is highly relevant to assessing criminality in other cases. If the convicted person's character may properly be considered in determining a sentence, probation might justifiably be denied when long reliance on illegal income is evident, or probation may be linked to a rigid requirement that there be legitimate employment or vocational training or both, and a disengagement from what are presumed to be the sources of illegal income.

One objection to the above approach contends that to deny probation because of an inference that the accused is guilty of additional crimes, rather than prosecuting him for additional crimes, is to punish for alleged offenses without formally charging and convicting in court. This is rebutted by the inescapable fact that no matter whether the legislature, the court, or the parole board, or all three, determine the penalty, there cannot be as rigorous a basis for proving the wisdom of decisions on optimum sentences as for reaching a decision on guilt. Inferences on character will be implicit in all penalty-fixing, even where the penalties are assigned without discretion purely on the basis of the offenses for which convictions occur, and even if plea-bargaining does not affect senences.

Another issue in probation is that defense attorneys cannot question in court the persons who supply the information in the presentence report. In many jurisdictions, presentence investigations are regarded as confidential, and only the conclusions are reported in open court. Increasingly, however, judges allow the defense to examine all findings in the report, although not the sources, and to present evidence and argument against these findings. Probation officers object to nonconfidentiality for their reports because their information comes from interviews with neighbors, relatives, and others who would not speak about the character of the accused if not assured of confidentiality. Critics insist that in most cases the probation officer should be able to present only verifiable evidence rather than accounts and opinions that may be mere gossip. They urge that information in presentence reports never be kept confidential, and that names of informants be kept confidential only in exceptional circumstances.

In crimes involving assaultive or harassing behavior, rather than property offenses, a presentence investigation rather than an automatic probation might suggest more reformative sentences than either probation or confinement. Fines have been especially effective in such cases, when their dimension takes into account the convicted person's resources. Requiring that a peace bond be posted is often similarly effective, with the bond forfeited if the accused molests or even approaches his victim without the court's permission. Such a bond is, in effect, a suspended fine sentence; if it is enforced by the probation officer's periodically checking on whether the victim has been molested, it becomes equivalent to probation.

Question of Pretrial Probation Services—Our traditional principle of separating power in government resulted originally in a sharp segmentation of responsibility for processing alleged offenders through the criminal justice system. Only police and sheriff staff handled them pretrial, and only correctional agencies dealt with them after they were convicted. Probation staff only contacted the accused who were found guilty.

When criticism of the bail system in the United States grew during the 1950s, there was increasing recognition that the penalizing and criminalizing consequences of arrest begin not just when a sentence of confinement is imposed, but are in many respects most damaging when the accused is held pretrial in our terrible jails. Furthermore, pretrial confinement occurs mainly because of poverty; except for a few cases, primarily involving capital offenses, those who can pay bail are released pending trial, and sometimes pending sentencing and pending appeals. This led to expansion of Release on Recognizance (commonly called ROR—or even OR—in the courts). Under ROR an accused who has had stable residence and employment in the community is released merely on his pledge to appear in court when his next hearing is scheduled or suffer a contempt of court penalty. Research has shown that rates of appearance at trial under well-screened ROR equal or exceed those with bail.

The primary barriers to growth of ROR in most states appear to be the political contributions and pressures of bail bonding firms. These businesses guarantee the appearance of the accused by posting his bail, for which they charge him or his friends and family a nonreturnable fee of about 5 percent. It is in their interest to encourage high bail even for persons whom research demonstrates would appear as certainly with ROR as with bail, and who can ill afford the bonding fee.

Another impediment to ROR has been disagreement as to who

should make the pretrial investigation and administer it. Regular probation staff have resisted assuming these tasks in many areas, feeling that such detective work is incompatible with their conception of themselves as psychiatric social workers, the same grounds on which they have in many localities resisted operating as a collection agency for restitution and nonsupport payments. In a few courts, however, notably those of New York City, special branches of the probation office have been established for all of these tasks. They provide types of service which should also be available in other locales.

For those whose employment has been too meager or unstable to make them a good risk for ROR, even when it is clear that they are not professional or dangerous criminals, a few specially-funded experiments in the early 1970s suggested an extremely constructive pretrial function that could well be institutionalized in probation agencies. In the Manhattan Court Employment Project of the Vera Foundation in New York and in Project Crossroads of the National Committee for Children and Youth in Washington, D.C., pretrial prisoners without employment were granted ROR on condition that they report regularly to an employment training or placement service, with modest stipends for those in training (in United States Manpower Administration programs). By the time of their hearings, not only were almost all present in court, but the probation officers involved in the administration of these enterprises could report to the judge that most had participated regularly in the programs, and many seemed to be securely employed. Thus people who initially were poor risks for both ROR and probation, who would have become progressively poorer risks had they stayed in jail pending trial, became good risks. Follow-up of the Crossroads group demonstrated clearly that those in the program had less recidivism than a control group without these services, and the economic savings to society from this nonrecidivism and nonjailing more than paid for the project.

Increasingly it has become evident that correctional potentialities exist from the moment a suspect is arrested, and that the earlier these opportunities are utilized the more effective the rehabilitative services may be. Of course, when an accused is not proved guilty he cannot be forced to participate in any program, but almost all such programs are most effective with a volunteer clientele. It is appropriate to offer employment, training, counseling, or other services deemed useful at a time when the prospective recipient is most likely to be receptive to them, and this time is often at the crisis of being apprehended, before becoming inured to confinement.

Question of Separating Investigative from Supervisory Functions —Efficiency and closer relationships with the client and his family are the benefits claimed for the customary practice of having a person who receives probation supervised by the officer who conducted the presentence investigation. In practice, however, presentence efforts are more immediately, clearly, and definitely rewarding to the officers, most of the time, than the supervisory activities; therefore, investigative work and report writing are given priority and supervisory tasks tend to be neglected when the same officer must do both. This disparity in emphasis was demonstrated dramatically some years ago when federal probation officers questioned their caseload measurement formula, which equated one presentence investigation and report per month with four supervision cases. A national time study revealed that the officers spent as much time on one presentence study as on thirteen supervision cases. Similarly, time studies in the California Youth Authority to determine why a reduction in caseload had no apparent effect on supervision revealed that most of the extra time acquired by reduction of caseload was devoted to paperwork and office activities, rather than to fieldwork with the clientele.

Investigative work in probation produces a tangible product, the presentence report. It is these reports—rather than supervision—that the superiors of the probation officer regularly see, that they rely on for their decisions, that they question him on, and by which they most frequently evaluate him. Not only are the supervisory tasks of assistance or control largely invisible to superiors, but much of its value in personal influence is not always clear even to the officers, except in unusual situations. Understandably, therefore, when an officer must both advise the judge on sentencing and try to check on and assist those already on probation, the former activity has deadlines and gets priority, while the latter tends to be secondary.

The two largest probation systems in the country, those of New York City and Los Angeles, have long separated investigative from supervisory functions, with specialized staffs for each. The federal probation system has been a center of resistance to such separation, perhaps because each district court's probation staff is hired, promoted, and discharged at the discretion of its highly autonomous life-term judges. In psychological terms, that behavior which is reinforced most immediately and pronouncedly tends to become dominant; when investigative and supervisory functions are combined, it is difficult for the reinforcement of supervision tasks to compete with that which presentence investigation and reporting receives.

Probation Subsidy and the Question of Split Sentences—Traditionally the financial consequences of probation militated against its being granted by the courts, since courts usually are county-financed agencies; if offenders were sent to state correctional institutions their care cost the county nothing, but if kept on probation their supervision was paid for by the county. In 1965 California enacted a "Probation Subsidy Law" whereby counties receive up to $4,000 per case for replacing their previous commitments of juveniles and young adults to state facilities by granting them probation, with the proviso that improvements in supervision services be made for these cases. Other states have rapidly copied this program, to a greater or lesser extent, despite the complexity of its methods for determining subsidies and for appraising advances in probation services. Where subsidy programs have been adopted, probation has generally increased markedly and the population of state correctional institutions has declined.

One accompaniment of increased use of probation in many courts, particularly in dealing with adults, has been an increase in the use of the so-called "split sentence," whereby probation is granted for a period of one or more years, but with the requirement that the first part of it—frequently three or six months—be spent in the county jail. This mixture in a single sentence is justified by the judges as imposing some retribution for the crime, "giving a taste of jail" as a deterrent, while also conforming with the pressures for more use of probation. In effect, a split sentence is analogous to a confinement sentence with early parole promised, but the parole part—here probation—revocable if serious misbehavior is reported during the jail confinement.

In criticism of split sentences it should be pointed out that the jail confinement destroys some of the principal justifications for probation, such as: (a) preservation of the jobs or school enrollments of the convicted persons; (b) maintenance of contact between such persons and their spouses, children, parents, or friends considered anticriminal in influence; and (c) making restitution to victims. Also, the typical jail has little or no work, education, or other rehabilitative services, stores most of its inmates in idleness in dormitories where criminalistic cliques dominate, and has a small staff of poor quality. On these grounds it is argued that a sentence to a state correctional institution which has constructive programs and the possibility of early parole would be preferable to a split sentence involving a half year in a typical county jail. On the other hand, some counties have developed considerable employment and training, as well as work release for jail inmates, in relatively small camp units where visiting with family is much easier than at a remote state institution; in such locales, if a jail term or a state commitment were the only choices available to a judge, the jail term might be preferable.

Imaginative thinking about sentences enables some judges to impose much more constructive penalities than traditional jail terms. For example, when deterrence or even retribution is deemed necessary, probation sentences are imposed with a requirement that evenings and weekends be spent in jail at first. A schedule of frequent review by the probation officer and recommendation to the judge permits the confinement to be diminished if the offender behaves well in the community, or jailing is increased for misconduct, particularly for failure to work or to seek work or for failure to pay restitution or meet other obligations.

The fact that judges follow the recommendations of their probation officers on sentencing, in most cases, may well show not the influence of the officers on the judges, but the judge's domination of the officer. Studies have indicated that regardless of their prior training, probation officers tend to adopt the philosophy of the court by which they are employed. If this philosophy is repulsive to them, they probably either leave or hide their dissent from the judge in order to have their work favorably regarded by him, for the judges control career prospects in their court's probation office.

Perhaps more imaginative and resourceful sentencing than prevails in most courts would occur if the judge's role in sentencing were given to local sentencing boards, containing specialists of diverse disciplines, to whom all cases would be referred when found guilty by judge or jury. Such boards might not only decide all sentences, but could review their jail and probation sentences at regular intervals. This could bring more attention and competence to sentencing, which is now the lonely task of judges who have many other concerns and little or no feedback on the consequences of their sentences.

PAROLE

Lack of control over convicts is the standard complaint against parole by police and public whenever a parolee commits a new crime, but they rarely voice such complaints against judges or against legislatively-fixed sentences when a person who is denied parole commits a new crime after discharge at the end of his sentence. Also, even if parole boards demonstrate outstanding superior judgment in selecting for parole, they are likely to be vilified for any judgment that appears to be wrong and not praised for any judgment that is correct. Only parole failures come to public attention and not parole successes, for the person who commits further crimes receives headlines and the ex-convict who is law-abiding generally does not.

A basic rationale for parole is that it increases control, as well as assistance, for those who are released from prison. Parole replaces outright discharge from prison, in which there are no further controls on the offender, and no ready access to a parole officer who is supposed to be a source of assistance. Nobody can predict with a high degree of accuracy whether or not an individual will commit further crimes when released from prison, but for parolees any presumed "drifting into crime" by failure to work, by association with known criminals, or by other violations of parole rules can lead to immediate reimprisonment. The parole officers are expected to check regularly on conformity to the parole rules, to take prompt action to achieve conformity, and to reincarcerate whenever this seems warranted for crime prevention. Contrastingly, if convicts are discharged from their sentence on release from prison, there is no further check on their behavior and they are only reimprisoned if apprehended and reconvicted for a new crime.

Complaints about parole controls come from different sources. While persons concerned with law enforcement cite crimes committed by those who would still be in prison if denied parole, persons concerned with justice cite the frequently high-handed and arbitrary nature of much parole rule enforcement, the fact that there is little check on the validity of rule violation charges, and the fact that reimprisonment for violation of rules often imposes incarceration for acts which are not crimes.

Revocation—In either probation or parole violation, officers may secure an immediate warrant for the arrest of the subject. The request for a warrant usually is reviewed carefully only by their administrative superiors, although the warrant is issued in the name of the judge or the board. Revocation of probation usually requires a hearing by the judge, in which defense counsel may be present. The hearing is local, relatively prompt, and if charges are disputed, both sides can be heard. If the allegations are accepted by the judge, a new sentence may be imposed (for example, extending the duration of probation, increasing its behavioral requirements, or replacing it by a prison sentence). By contrast, when parole is revoked a report of violation is mailed by the parole officer to a distant parole board, but the board gives the parolee a hearing on the alleged violation only after reimprisonment is ordered because of the violation report, and only when the board makes its next scheduled visit to the prison. Participation in the hearings by counsel and witnessess for the parolee is discouraged either by offical policy, or by the location and schedule of the hearing.

In practice, most revocation of probation or parole is initiated only when the supervising officer learns of the client's arrest on serious charges, or when there is no report from the client for an appreciable period and the officer cannot locate him or her. The warrant is primarily a detainer, to have the subject held for probation or parole authorities after release from arrest on other charges. Supervisory activity usually is too minimal in adult probation, especially when the staff is assigned both presentence and supervision work, for the officer to learn much that is unfavorable about the client's activities unless an arrest report is received. Arrests for rule violations alone seem more common in adult parole, but it is in parole that arguments are being increasingly recognized by appellate courts for provision of more prompt and fair hearings when violations are alleged that do not involve conviction for new felonies. Parole boards are responding to such court decisions by discouraging the issuance of violation warrants following infractions of parole rules without evidence of serious new crimes, and increasingly, by holding hearings on alleged violations more promptly, sometimes in local jails rather than in the prisons.

It is contended that parole boards should not have a right to imprison on grounds other than conviction for a crime committed while on parole. The parolee clearly has fewer rights than other people in the community if he or she can be imprisoned for failure to seek or to persist in employment, for excessive use of alcohol or drugs, or for quarreling with or lying to the parole officer, to cite a few frequent grounds for revocation.

The question of how rigorous controls should be in parole raises all of the issues in the indeterminate sentence controversy that were discussed earlier. If the state has a right to deny liberty by imprisoning those who have committed serious crimes, why should it be forced to fix in advance the optimum duration of confinement, and why can it not during the course of imprisonment reduce controls gradually rather than abruptly? If callousness, prejudice, or simply poor judgment on the part of the parole board or parole officers is alleged, an effort should be made to correct these faults, but changing the system of decision-making will not suffice to eliminate such problems. After all, humans with faults will also be involved in making the decision if the legislatures, the courts, or anyone else takes over the parole board's discretion in fixing penalties or in altering these penalties after their range of severity is initially determined.

Parole Personnel—It is the writer's impression that the quality of parole boards is most regularly superior when they are manned by civil servants assigned to the board from other state employment, with a high level of training in the behavioral sciences, and preferably, after service in both institutional and community corrections. This is the system in Wisconsin and Michigan. Arguments for boards manned by political appointees stress the objective of representing public opinion, but presumably public opinion is represented in the legislature, which fixes the maximum duration of confinement. Also, a political appointee usually has political obligations for the fulfillment of which he is rewarded more directly and significantly than for the quality of his service to the parole board. Expertise rather than representative opinion is required on a parole board if it is to protect the public by sound assessment, control, and assistance in administering parole within the range of sentence indeterminacy which the legislature authorizes.

High standards of training and character for parole officers, with a nonpolitical but not excessively rigid civil service system, probably also provide the best guarantee of careful, fair, and correctionally prudent supervision. No selection system for a parole board or for the parole officers, however, can guarantee optimum performance by everyone, in all activities. The best additional guarantees are systems of checks and balances, including automatic review of major decisions, and channels of appeal to an independent investigatory agency. Appeals against any clearly illegal action now are possible through the courts, but more satisfactory service to complainants could be provided by an ombudsman's office. It could investigate any allegedly inconsiderate, unfair, or ill-advised action, and could deal with complaints much more quickly and cheaply than do the courts. Appeal through the courts, of course, would still be possible.

WORK OR EDUCATION RELEASE, FURLOUGHS, AND HALFWAY HOUSES

All of these newer forms of community correction impose controls intermediate between those of a prison or jail and those of probation or parole. These forms all give staff contact with the client more frequently than is usual in probation or parole, but less continously than in institutional confinement. That is why they were all described as increasing the extent to which release is graduated. If a probationer or parolee reports to his officer only once a month, as frequently is the case, and the officer seldom visits the client's home, the officer's knowledge of the client's nonconforming behavior, emotional instability, or criminal orientations is much less immediate and complete than that of a staff member at a place of residence to which the client returns daily or after an absence of just a few days.

Furloughs—One of the major problems in operation of any form of community correction is that controls intended to be flexible become rigid, sometimes rigidly looser than intended and sometimes more stringent. Furloughs, for example, were established in a number of states as authorizations for departure of prisoners from institutional confinement for up to 72 hours, when their parole or discharge date was imminent, to permit the prisoners to make postrelease job and housing arrangements. After their successful use in a few such cases, furloughs were used more liberally, and were increasingly thought of by prisoners and staff as a right to which all inmates were entitled, if they behaved well in prison, regardless of need for postrelease arrangements, and to some extent, regardless of imminence of parole or discharge. All were for 72 hours.

In California when this liberalization of furlough use occurred, the inevitable consequence was that inmates looked forward to the furloughs primarily as a means of satisfying in a short time all of their pent-up desires. A number were arrested on furloughs in an intoxicated condition, driving stolen automobiles, or committing other offenses. In two cases they committed murder, one of a police officer and one of an old woman, both killings apparently panicky efforts to escape apprehension for other crimes. Immediately, of course, there was a public furor and a demand by police leaders for cancellation of the furlough program. Fortunately, in this case, the governor pointed out that there had been thousands of successful furloughs with only a small percentage of failures, and that those released in this fashion were soon to be fully released anyhow. After an initial suspension of the entire program, it was reinstated as a leave only for the time needed to make specific postrelease arrangements, and sometimes also permitting visits with spouses or particular relatives under specified conditions.

Inevitably, when people are confined in one-sex institutions they lust for the pleasures of the outside world from which they are barred. A halfway house permits them to seek these satisfactions on a gradual basis, for a few hours at a time at first, with a haven of shelter and friendship to which they can return readily, rather than having an uninterrupted spree for several days. This reduces the prospect of their getting into financial or companionship crises in centers of debauchery, and reverting promptly to crime.

Halfway Houses—A number of halfway houses have had recurrent problems and high failure rates because they were either over-regimented, with staff and residents continually hostile to each other, or they were undercontrolled, so that they became centers of drug or alcohol use and of idleness and crime. An ideally operated halfway house has a minimum number of rules, but these are clear rules for which the justification is readily apparent.

It is especially evident in halfway houses that control is closely linked with assistance. Close personal ties between staff and residents, a hospitable atmosphere, and a sense of obligation and loyalty to the house administration are the strongest forces for conformity with reasonable behavior standards communicated by the staff. Indeed, good relationships of staff to clientele in every form of community correction depend, first, on staff assistance equaling or exceeding the expectations that have been engendered and, secondly, on a consensus existing among clients that rules and rule enforcement penalties are reasonable. Such consensus is reached, if at all, not by curt announcement of rules and of enforcement practices, but by their being agreed upon through calm discussion, with a maximum of orderly communication by the clientele, reasonable concessions by staff, but clientele attaining a sense of pride and responsibility from their contribution to the understanding of what standards will be sought in their conduct. All of this, of course, is not always readily attained, but it is an ideal that can be usefully pursued in every form of community correction that has been discussed in this chapter.

Assistance

The aid which community correction programs can provide for offenders may well be the greatest contribution these enterprises can make to the protection of society, but the full potentialities of such aid seldom are realized. This aid will be discussed separately for different forms of community correction.

PROBATION AND PAROLE

These two oldest forms of community correction, the first widely used procedures for graduating release and deferring a final decision on penalties, can be discussed together here because they are virtually identical in the methods of assistance they employ. For this reason, the same officers supervise probationers and parolees in the federal and a few state correctional systems.

Loans—A lack of money, plus poor money management practices, are perhaps the most frequently and readily evident serious problems of newly released adult offenders. Parolees have a large volume of accumulated material requirements, little or no prospect of a paycheck soon, and usually insufficient cash to meet the needs and desires that to them seem urgent. Follow-ups of federal parolees in two different studies, in seven major cities, indicate that about a third are unemployed a month after release from prison and a sixth are unemployed three months after release. Probationers more often have jobs, but they are likely to be strapped financially from the expenses of bail, lawyers' fees, court costs, and loss of wages due to time away from work for their trial.

Most adult parolees and probationers survive this economic distress primarily because they obtain room, board, and financial assistance from spouses, parents, or other relatives, although many have no such resources. Frequently, however, those who depend on their families have a history of strained family relationships, reaching a peak during adolescence, and their crimes express recurrent desperate desires to become financially independent of their family. Conflicts in their home relationships, therefore, tend to recur whenever they are unable to obtain economic autonomy by legitimate means. Much recidivism by adults has been ascribed to a recapitulation of adolescent struggles to assert independence from parental authority.

A few probation and parole offices have small loan funds available for their clientele, which can be issued immediately on the recommendation of the supervising officer. Loans often are provided not so much in cash as in credits for meals, room, work clothes, or tools. Such assistance frequently can eliminate economic desperation and move the client toward self-sufficiency. Where these loan funds exist it is anticipated that some disbursements will never be repaid, since they are given most often to the worst risk cases, many of whom will be rearrested or will abscond. Replenishment of such funds by regular budget appropriations is an economical public expenditure, however, since prevention by small loans of even a few new crimes, arrests, trials, and reimprisonments will save enough public costs to offset numerous losses from a loan fund, in addition to the humane value in preventing recidivism.

Referral—Referral to other agencies for assistance is more common than direct material aid to clients in probation or parole. These agencies usually prefer staff with social work training, emphasizing casework, to provide skills in diagnosis of client needs and familiarity with the public welfare or philanthropic agencies which can supply these needs.

The major limitation to referral, as a mode of assistance, is that it too often appears to the client to be a form of buck-passing, if not outright rejection, even if done well, and especially if done incompetently. The client views his or her needs as urgent, and offices or organizations as remote and impersonal. The latter views are often based on frustrating and humiliating experiences, especially when there are language, education, or social class barriers to communication between the subject and the personnel of the agencies to which he goes for assistance, including the probation or parole office. Indeed, the client often waits long, uncomfortably, and with trepidation at such a correctional office for an opportunity to talk to the officer to whom he is assigned, and he is especially disappointed if he then is only told to go to another agency.

It follows from the foregoing that there is a close linkage between the effectiveness of referral and modes of communication. Many probation and parole staff have been trained with an emphasis on psychiatric social work, and a presumption that offenders are mainly in need of psychotherapy. Research has failed to confirm that such therapy can effectively prevent crime in the bulk of our convicted felons, and in any case, it is not available for more than a few. What the psychiatrist Karl Menninger has called "the therapy of friendship," however, seems to be a prerequisite to personal influence on someone else's behavior and thought. Yet the different social, economic, and education background of most probation and parole staff from that of most offenders, and the power to control which they combine with their efforts to assist, limit their capacity to befriend, inspire, or even understand their clientele. A major solution to this problem, therefore, has been to acquire a new type of correctional staff.

Para-professionals—Communication is facilitated if staff are similar in ethnicity, neighborhood, and experience to those whom they are to assist. The concentration of felony arrests among poor people in urban slum areas, combined with the requirement of an educational background for probation and parole staff that is not common among the poor, makes inevitable considerable contrast between these personnel and their clientele. This difficulty has been largely overcome in several cities through the augmentation of staff by so-called "para-professionals." These are often ex-offenders, and in any case, they come from the same sociocultural groups and live in the same neighborhoods as do the probationers and parolees whom they help supervise.

With such titles as "probation aide" or "community worker," para-professional staff serve in supervision teams with regular probation or parole officers. The assistance which the para-professionals are expected to provide is diffuse, and it may be given not just to the probationer but to his family. A female client may be helped with her housework or childcare in an emergency, or assistance will be provided in getting medcial care for the client's childern. Simply transporting them when public transportation is inadequate often becomes important during crises. Referrals become more effective because staff goes with the client to the place to which they are referred, such as a hospital or a welfare office. Material aid is frequently indirect, by advice on shopping and budgeting, particularly when the para-professional was once on welfare and knows about stores that raise their prices when welfare checks are due. Friendship is generated, by both professionals and para-professionals, through acts that express concern above and beyond that called for by the routines of a job. This, plus the similarity of the para-professional and client in background, and the example of the para-professional's own conquest of handicaps, greatly increase the personal influence of staff. These "treatment teams" in high crime rate areas have been impressively successful with difficult cases.

Volunteers—A quite different approach to the augmentation of probation and parole staff is the use of volunteers. In many correctional systems parolees are each expected to have a sponsor or advisor, who must be approved by the parole board or by the parole supervisor. This is an unpaid person of good reputation, often a minister, a teacher, or a local businessman. The parolee is expected to maintain regular contact with the sponsor, and both are expected to sign the parolee's monthly report, to confirm the parolee's employment and conformity to parole rules. The sponsor agrees to counsel and assist the parolee, and to advise the parole officer on the parolee's problems.

Parole staffs differ on the utility of the sponsor system. In urban areas particularly, they can cite instances of corrupt or indifferent sponsors, sometimes overloaded with parolees. They also complain about the burden of investigating the character of sponsors or recruiting them for prisoners who can obtain no sponsor on their own. In the latter cases, the sponsor requirement is often waived. Contrastingly, numerous cases of exemplary assistance by sponsors can be cited. They are especially useful in areas which the officer cannot frequently visit.

A much more extensive utilization of volunteers has developed in numerous probation offices. Many of these programs were stimulated by Project Misdemeanant, a national movement begun in the 1960s by Judge Keith J. Leenhouts after national publicity was repeatedly given the volunteer organization that he developed at his municipal court in Royal Oak, Michigan. One of the movement's sponsors was the General Board of Christian Social Concerns of the Methodist Church, which in the 1970s widely disseminated manuals to church members on how to secure community support for misdemeanant probation services. While this movement seems centered in small cities and towns, Denver and Seattle are among the larger cities which have participated in it. Numerous other metropolitan counties have created permanent "volunteer coordinator" positions on their probation staff, or such positions are maintained in a county welfare office which provides service for probationers on request. Most of the volunteers become sponsors for individual probationers, but those with special tutoring, administrative, counseling, or other expertise may augment the main probation office staff. Retired persons have been a major source of recruits, which at times creates the problem of a generation gap between the voluntary staff and the clientele, but often provides dedicated and appreciated avuncular figures.

WORK AND EDUCATION RELEASE, FURLOUGHS, AND HALFWAY HOUSES

All of these newer modes of graduating release obviously reduce sharply the prevalence of acute financial distress when prisoners are first returned to society, especially if these programs are compared with traditional release by parole. The releasees in these newer programs have food and shelter guaranteed at the correctional facility to which they return daily or within a few days, and until they secure earnings of their own they are provided with pocket money for essentials while in the community.

Residents of halfway houses are particularly free to concentrate in their release time on such requirements of satisfying and law-abiding community life as the procurement of a secure job and the cultivation of friendships, including those with the opposite sex. Only when they secure employment are they charged for room and board. When they begin parole after several months in a halfway house, they usually have a job, wardrobe, firm postrelease housing arrangements, and some cash. Very frequently they also have developed some romantic friendships. In Southern California many prisoners on work release buy or lease an automobile, and most of those in halfway houses soon own cars, as such private transportation is a near necessity for employment and social life there.

Halfway houses in which parolees are required to live have been established in some places, but it is the author's impression from several cases that these are much less succesful than halfway houses for the last few months of imprisonment. Enforced residence in these houses and the curfew hours there are resented by parolee residents as restrictions not imposed on other parolees. Prisoners, on the other hand, welcome the halfway house as an increase in their freedom before parole. Also, restriction of parole residence to a halfway house has frequently been imposed only on problem cases, such as drug addicts, thus concentrating advocates of deviant behavior in one building. Making short-term emergency shelter available to parolees at halfway houses if they request it, however, is another matter; this has been a useful adjunct to the services at halfway houses designed primarily for persons still serving prison terms.

Efforts of correctional staff to communicate helpfully are most likely to be successful in reducing recidivism if they deal with the problems that prisoners experienced today or yesterday, or that they anticipate tomorrow or soon thereafter. The failure of most prison research to find any relationship between recidivism and participation in counseling, especially group counseling, probably reflects the fact that such communication in prison deals mainly with problems of adjustment to institutional life, or with speculation about a remote and largely unknowable future. In addition, most counseling in prison occurs in a setting where prisoners know that their utterances may affect the conditions of their prison life or even their release date, so that they feel on stage and compelled to play a role insincerely.

Before and after a furlough, on work or education release, or at a halfway house, a prisoner's concerns when talking with staff or with other residents at the correctional facility will be with such matters as making a favorable impression in a job interview, what happened on the job yesterday or will happen tomorrow, impressing the opposite sex, budgeting pay among competing needs, or the selection or maintenance of a used car. These are all immediate and sincere interests on which staff may frequently be helpful, and for which they sometimes secure expert volunteer counselors. Under these circumstances, in contrast to the setting of most prison counseling, persons in the newer forms of community correction can develop a sense of obligation to the staff because of practical things that are done for them.

In summary, from the standpoints of assessment, control, and assistance, but primarily through more timely and relevant assistance, community corrections for adults provide vast advances from traditional jailing or imprisonment. As has been indicated, these methods of graduating and deferring decision on confinement have numerous implications for the entire criminal justice system, beginning at arrest and pretrial processing. All of these implications can be consolidated well by the general maxim: never set apart from the community, any more than can possibly be avoided, those whom you wish someday to bring safely back into the community.

Donald R. Cressey

4

Adult Felons in Prison

In the last decade, over three-quarters of a million men and women entered the state and federal prisons and reformatories of the United States. They did not "end up" in prison. The vast majority have been discharged from the institution to which they were committed, so that fewer than two hundred thousand persons were confined in American prisons and reformatories at the end of the decade. Within the next ten years almost all the remainder will return to the free community.

These prisoners, and thousands who preceded them to confinement, were forcibly removed from the social relations in which they were participating and were locked behind walls of concrete and steel where, we are prone to say, they "served their time," "paid their debt to society," and, perhaps, "learned their lesson." But they did more than pay, and serve, and learn in their prisons. They *lived* in them. Each participated in a very complex set of social relations, including a wide variety of social contacts, associations, bonds, alliances, compromises, and conflicts between hundreds of prisoners, guards, administrators, teachers, tradesmen, and professional personnel like social workers, psychologists, and physicians.

DONALD R. CRESSEY *is professor of sociology at the University of California, Santa Barbara, where he was dean of the College of Arts and Sciences during the sixties. He has done research in a half dozen prisons, and was a consultant to the President's Commission on Law Enforcement and the Administration of Justice. Among other works, Dr. Cressey is co-author, with Edwin H. Sutherland, of* Principles of Criminology, *now in its eighth edition, and author of* Theft of the Nation: The Structure and Operations of Organized Crime in America.

These social relations are really what make up any individual convict's prison, but the fact is that we know very little about them.

It is possible that participation in a prison's social relationships is complex because it is so difficult to describe. We are inclined, of course, to say the reverse—that the interaction is difficult to describe because it is so complex. Prison life is made up of social interactions that are confused, entangled, complicated, and so subtle in their effects that any detailed attempt to tell what happens sounds like the mouthings of a crazy man. No man can report accurately on what shapes his life in prison.

Perhaps it is for this reason that we are inclined to speak of the effects of prison life in generalities. We say prisons reform men. We say prisons are schools of crime. We say locking men in cages creates emotional problems. We say prisons make timid souls into "confirmed" or "hardened" criminals. Some of us even say, as I am prone to do, that only rarely does the prison have any appreciable effect on either the subsequent criminality or the subsequent noncriminality of the men it cages.

All such generalities are inaccurate. Imprisonment, as such, does not do anything to men except hurt them. The prison, as such, does not do anything at all. It just sits there—upstate, across the bay, or on the edge of town—ugly, menacing. What counts is the subtle specifics of each prisoner's participation in prison *life*.

Generally speaking, the organization of prison life is more conducive to the retention and development of criminal attitudes than to reformation. Further, one can generalize that prison life—especially as it involves relationships between prisoners and authorities—isolates some long-term inmates from any intimate contact with anticriminal behavior models and teaches them, instead, that success is to be achieved by deception, manipulation, and crime. These generalities don't tell us much, but they point us in the right direction—toward looking at vague, indefinite, and subtle relationships among people.

Inmates learn criminal techniques from each other, just as college students and businessmen do. Inmates sometimes form friendships, partnerships, and alliances which are the basis of cooperation in crime both within the prison and after release. But retaining the criminal attitudes a man brings to prison with him is not merely a matter of contamination and individual tutelage of one convict by another. Instead, retention of a crook's life style occurs in response to participation in a community which has *collectively* developed traditions favorable to crime and to the repression of any tendency toward reformation. It is a bit like saying that businessmen do not pay all their taxes because businessmen do not pay all their taxes.

Writing in an inmate newspaper some years ago, a prisoner of the United States Penitentiary at Atlanta put it this way:

> It is not the possibility of a non-legitimate vocational training that makes the prison a man-perverting agency of great power and efficiency. It is the doleful fact that some nebulous something happens to a man between the time that he checks into and checks out of a prison; some inculcation of the essence of bitterness and social antagonism, an inculcation that is not merely a veneering process but a deep inoculation. And this "something" spawns a man who is invariably less desirable as a citizen than he was at the time he stood before the bar of justice.

I think the "nebulous something" which happens to an inmate is his participation in a convict subculture that has developed an *esprit de corps,* with crime, hustling, extortion, and violation of official prison rules as common interests. The net effect of lengthy interaction with members of a group organized around such interests is likely to be a definition of one's self as an elite, a leader of the group who has few obligations to outsiders who conform to the law. We shall see that this conception of self is both stimulated and reinforced by the attitudes and conduct of prison officials as well as by the attitudes and conduct of inmates. We also will see that there are variations in the extent to which inmates participate in the antireform and procriminal *esprit de corps* of a prison.

History

It was not always that way. At one point in the history of imprisonment, inmates were allowed to see no evil, hear no evil, and speak no evil. They were locked in solitary confinement cells, in almost complete isolation. They did not contaminate each other. They went crazy.

Imprisonment as a governmental system for inflicting pain and suffering on criminals is, by and large, an invention of the American and French revolutions. The revolutionaries had suffered under despots. After they had starved and bloodied themselves to secure freedom from tyranny, they concluded as a matter of course that criminals would suffer enough if their freedom were restricted. They invented imprisonment as a punishment for crime, and the history of imprisonment ever since has been a history of freedom. As notions of liberty have changed, so have ideas about what is, or should be, involved as criminals are deprived of their liberty.

The Quakers of Pennsylvania were extraordinarily active in developing the notion that criminals should be punished and reformed by deprivation of their liberty. The "Great Law of Pennsylvania," adopted by the colony in 1682, was William Penn's idea of a criminal code for free men. Penn was a religious ex-convict. His code abolished bloody tortures and stipulated that crimes were to be punished by imprisonment. Violent criminals were to be confined at hard labor in a house of correction; arsonists were to pay double restitution to the injured party, be imprisoned for a year, and suffer such corporal punishments as the court deemed appropriate; thieves and burglars were to make fourfold restitution and suffer three months' imprisonment—if the offender could not make restitution, he was to be imprisoned for seven years. In their *New Horizons in Criminology*, Harry Elmer Barnes and Negley K. Teeters editorialize as follows on the importance of this Great Law:

> The wide reliance upon imprisonment as a mode of punishment, evident throughout the separate enactments of Penn's unique code, was an epoch-making departure in criminal procedure. Excepting only for the laws in the closely related colony of West Jersey, this Pennsylvania code of 1682 is the first instance in criminal jurisprudence of prescribing imprisonment at hard labor as a punishment for a majority of the acts branded as crimes by the community.

The idealistic leaders of the new eighteenth- and nineteenth-century democracies were by no means confident about the reality of their unfamiliar freedom. They substituted confinement for hanging and flogging all right, but they were not entirely sure that "mere" deprivation of criminals' freedom was sufficiently painful. Pennsylvania's 1776 constitution directed that imprisonment *at hard labor* be substituted for capital punishment. After the war, a law implementing this directive said imprisonment, "with continued hard labor, publicly and disgracefully imposed," should be substituted for corporal punishment and (except in murder cases) capital punishment. The law was enforced by organizing convicts into chain gangs, tethering them on the streets like cattle. The result was degradation and misery.

Philadelphia citizens were outraged at this conception of "mere" deprivation of liberty, and the policy and practice were soon abandoned. Because there was no state prison to be used as a replacement for the labor gangs, arrangements were made to keep state prisoners in county jails. Prisoners were sentenced to the pain of incarceration in them, but on top of this pain the revolutionaries piled the pain of bodily suffering. Some prisoners were forced to perform tasks such as carrying a cannon ball back and forth along a corridor, walking treadmills, turning cranks, and smashing boulders with mauls and sledge hammers. Sometimes a quota of such labor had to be accomplished as payment for each day's meals and lodgings, but often it was purely punitive—in the sense that it was useless. Among the results were degradation and misery.

GROUP AND SOLITARY CONFINEMENT

Almost simultaneously, the radicals of the revolution took "mere" deprivation of liberty more literally. Imprisonment came to mean perimeter control only, with freedom to do almost anything within the restricting walls of stone and steel. Among the results were degradation and misery, plus corruption and debauchery.

For example, inside Philadelphia's Walnut Street Jail—a state prison that had been used as a military lock-up by the British during the war—there were no constraints on the freedom of the mad, the vicious, and the depraved. There was no labor, no separation of prisoners by age or sex, and no separation of convicted criminals from persons awaiting trial. Half-naked prisoners slept on the cold floor, with no bedding. Whiskey and rum abounded and indeed were sold at a bar operated by one of the officers. Women got themselves committed so they could practice prostitution.

Then the revolutionary innovators went to the opposite extreme. Believing that deprivation of the criminal's degree of freedom should be as great as possible, they pressed the prison walls against him. They locked each criminal within the stone walls of a compound, but within that perimeter they also locked him alone behind the walls of a dark and tiny cell. Interaction among prisoners, and between prisoners and others, was minimized. Among the results were degradation and misery.

The Western State Penitentiary at Pittsburgh, which opened in 1826, adopted the "separate and silent" system. Prisoners were not permitted to work, and when later they were allowed to do so, the work was made subordinate to reflection. But it was in the Eastern State Penitentiary, which opened in Philadelphia in 1829, that the "Pennsylvania system" of solitary confinement for all really developed. Solitary confinement, it was contended, not only prevented the disastrous association of criminals, but also had the positive virtue of forcing prisoners to reflect on their crime and therefore of producing reformation.

Barnes and Teeters point out that the Eastern Penitentiary "was not merely a prison, for it epitomized one of the most influential penal philosophies ever conceived by man." The entire institution was designed for solitude. Seven cell blocks, each with a center corridor, radiated out from a rotunda, like the spokes of a wheel. Each solid-walled cell was secured by a latticed door of iron or wood, but a wooden door of heavy planking closed over the latticed door, isolating the prisoner. A rear door led from the cell (about seven feet wide and twelve feet long) to a stone-walled exercise space, about eight by twenty feet. Each inmate was allotted a daily hour for exercise; inmates in adjoining cells were not permitted to exercise at the same time. Some prisoners devoted their daily exercise hour to tending the flowers and vegetables they planted in the tiny yard. Others kept a rabbit or a cat in the yard, and it is likely that they had long conversations with the animals. More prisoners became insane than became penitent.

New York also experimented with the solitary system. The prison at Auburn was designed to implement a policy of solitary confinement that had been borrowed from Pennsylvania. When it opened, in 1821, the "oldest and most heinous offenders" were kept in solitary confinement continuously, others were kept in their cells three days a week, and a third class one day a week. The cells were small and dark, and no work was done in them. Of 80 prisoners who were kept in solitary confinement continuously, all but 2 were out of prison within two years, as a result of death, insanity, or pardon. A legislative commission in 1824 investigated the institution and recommended that the policy of solitary confinement be abandoned at once, and this recommendation was followed.

LABOR AND EDUCATION

A compromise between the extremes of complete freedom within walls and complete solitude soon appeared. It was based on the realistic view that liberty lies somewhere between absolute freedom to exercise one's whims and absolute restriction of one's movements by state officials. At the Auburn institution, prisoners were released from solitary confinement, but they were not given unfettered freedom within the institution's boundaries. Instead, they were forced to work as slaves, in association but in silence, and under strict regimentation. Among the results were degradation, misery, and corruption.

The new rules at Auburn called for downcast eyes, lockstep marching, no prisoners ever face to face, no talking, and constant work when outside the cells, which were used only at night. Because the "Auburn system" or "congregate system"—as the compromise came to be called—enabled the state to use inmate labor more effectively than did the separate system, something more than concern for inmate rehabilitation and deprivation of freedom was behind the shift away from solitary cells. The punishment for rule infractions was the lash, and most of the whippings were for failure to do satisfactory work. Like all its forerunners and all its successors, the Auburn prison mostly manufactured misery.

Technically speaking, both the Pennsylvania system and the Auburn system were in the late nineteenth century superseded by a third system, known both as the "Irish system" and the "Elmira system." Actually, this was merely an extension of the Auburn-type program. Emphasis was placed on productive labor, but a prison school also was provided. In the early days of New York's Elmira Reformatory (1876) the work and educational programs were administered in conjunction with the indeterminate sentence, a "mark system" under which inmates could gain their freedom by earning a certain number of credits, and parole. Prisons have not changed much, really, in the hundred years since Elmira was conceived. While "marks" have been generally abandoned, the other features remain as characteristics of contemporary imprisonment. Various ineffective rehabilitation programs have been added, along with public relations departments that puff them up.

The Pennsylvania system was generally adopted in Europe, but in the United States this program was abandoned in favor of the congregate system. The principal motivation for the shift was neither humanitarianism nor concern for reformation. It was economic. The congregrate-type prison was cheaper to build. Moreover, even if a prison school was added, the system made possible more efficient exploitation of convict labor, and before long labor for production of wealth, rather than work "for its own sake" or for its punitive value alone became a prison goal. Prisons became factories and remained as such until the 1930s, when businessmen and labor leaders began perceiving them as unfair competition. Now, inmates engaged in productive occupations are few and far between.

Prisoners at Auburn and Elmira were allowed to congregate physically, but repressive measures kept them isolated psychologically. This trend continued, and it is proper to say that since 1824 the history of imprisonment in the United States has been a history of attempts to substitute psychological solitary confinement for the physical solitary confinement characterizing the early Pennsylvania and New York prisons. Over the years, as the perceived need for inmate labor has diminished, the degree of psychological isolation in prisons has gradually been reduced. Even now, however, most prison rules and routines—and even the "inmate code"—are designed to keep inmates from bunching up in ways that might endanger institutional security. Current discussions of prison discipline are really arguments about the kinds and degrees of freedom from caging and repression that should be granted to men living in the misery accompanying restriction within fenced, walled, and armed boundaries.

Disciplinary measures and regimentation continue to be justified on the ground that interaction among inmates must be restricted if reformation is to occur. Indeed, the common contemporary assertion that prisons and reformatories are "schools of crime" does not imply only that these institutions should be abolished. Unfortunately, this dandy declaration also implies that we should cut recidivism rates by centering prison life in cold and dark solitary cells like those of the early Pennsylvania prisons.

On the other hand, many contemporary reformers argue that for most criminals any deprivation of liberty is too much. As alternatives to imprisonment, we have invented suspended sentences, probation, and parole. We are busily trying to invent "community treatment services" also, and the proportion of all criminals sent to prison is being reduced by these services. Further, there is an increasing tendency to fine offenders, to name their felonies misdemeanors so they can be sent to county jails, and even to ignore their crimes, rather than committing them to prisons and reformatories. Despite an increasing crime rate, state and federal institutions received seventy-nine thousand prisoners in 1970, as compared to over ninety-three thousand in 1961.

Purposes

Most prison administrators now take the position that staff members should make every possible effort, within a restricting and punitive framework of security, to rehabilitate prisoners by nonpunitive treatment methods. "Treatment" does not mean just medical care. It is a residual program—what is left over in prisons when punitive and restrictive programs and practices are subtracted.

Treatment includes everything from group counseling and psychotherapy to the teaching of eighth-grade arithmetic, to putting TV sets in recreation rooms, to the kindness implied in the phrase "We treat them well here." These and similar practices do not have any positive thing in common. I can *hurt* people in a number of ways—for instance by whipping them, by starving them, or by restricting their freedom. But what is it, generally, that I do when I bind their wounds, share their problems, improve their minds, or smile at them a lot? It is not that all these things are attempts to help—after all, just relaxing, smiling, and being kind is not positive assistance.

The answer must be given in a negative way, in terms of the absence of something, not its presence. What is absent in prison programs and practices called treatment or rehabilitation is punishment: if a program or practice is punitive, it is not treatment.

Awareness of this negative notion of treatment helps make understandable the deluge of doubletalk that pours out of prison public relations offices. Prison officials are supposed to be punitive and restrictive. That is what prisons are all about, when it comes down to it. After all, the maximum number of escapes a warden is allowed is zero. Yet prison officials also are—in administering treatment—to be nonpunitive and nonrestrictive. A warden who argues that his program is punitive and nonpunitive at the same time must do some fast talking, and most "progressive" wardens, especially, talk a mile a minute.

SOCIETY'S ATTITUDES

The most severe impediments to treatment in a prison are not due to inefficient prison administration. They are rooted in social attitudes about crime and punishment. These attitudes get transformed into directives prison wardens are supposed to follow.

Like our forefathers, we contemporary Americans have a variety of attitudes about crime control. Not all of us share all the attitudes. But men of influence and power do share some of them, and these have become "societal" concerns about the control of crime. These concerns, in turn, have been transformed into the social policy inherent in the criminal law and its administration.

First of all, retribution is considered desirable and just. At least since the time of Hammurabi it has been accepted that the criminal deserves to suffer simply because he is a criminal. I have already pointed out that about two hundred years ago Western societies tried to abandon whips, knives, spikes, boiling water, and similar machines for manufacturing this misery. Now prison programs are supposed to make life unpleasant for men who, by their crimes, have made others' lives unpleasant.

Secondly, protection from the criminal is desired and demanded. Whether punished or not, the offender is to be isolated so that the community is safe from him. Once this was done by banishing, branding, or mutilating offenders.

Thirdly, a low crime rate is a desirable social objective. But rather than putting our money on the difficult job of smashing the economic, political, and social conditions that generate crime, we prefer to rely on fear. We inflict pain on criminals because we think doing so will terrorize others into conformity. In deterrence, the future effect of punishment on society, not its effect on the criminal, is what is considered important. Prison life is supposed to be so unpleasant that no one will dare commit a crime punishable by imprisonment.

Finally, we want criminals changed, so they will commit no more crimes. This, too, is a way of reducing crime rates. The Puritans used the dunking stool, the stocks, the pillory and the brank (a cagelike helmet with a spiked rod that went into the mouth) as instruments of reformation as well as of retribution and deterrence. Now it is prison life that is supposed to reform criminals.

In early American prisons, few organizational problems arose as wardens tried to accomplish the four tasks assigned—retribution, incapacitation, deterrence, and reformation. Each function could be achieved by an enterprise designed to inflict punishment—pain purposively imposed by the state because of some value it is assumed to have. Within the walls protecting society from criminals, a rigorous, monotonous, and unpleasant regime, spiced with floggings, met the other three social demands.

Even subsidiary programs, such as work and school, could easily be made to fit into the scheme of things. At Auburn and Elmira, for example, retribution was exacted and deterrence promoted by the labor program. It was clear to everyone except the prisoners that inmate employment to produce wealth should be toil, their labor weariness. Closely supervised and regimented congregate labor, performed in silence, kept inmates out of mischief, and for that reason was considered part of the prison's program of incapacitation. At the same time, punitive toil, like systems of rigid military discipline, was justified on the ground that it develops habits of industry, obedience, perseverance, and conformity, thus having a reformative effect. In Elmira's school, as in the public schools of the time, boys were made to study because it was more painful to learn than to loaf, because classroom confinement in silence kept them off the streets and out of trouble, and because their school habits of obeying the teacher could be taken as evidence of reform.

DOUBTS ABOUT PUNISHMENT

Gradually, organizational strain has crept into this harmonious if miserable setting, first as a consequence of doubts about the use of physical punishments within prisons, and more recently by doubts that reformation can be achieved by punishment of any kind, physical or psychological.

First came questioning of the idea that there is a need for retributive, deterrent, and reformative punishment more severe than "mere" deprivation of liberty. This questioning, transformed into positive action, asked wardens to reduce physical tortures. Take whipping, hanging in chains, baking, freezing, electric shock, squirting with a fire hose, forced walks in a squatting position (duck walk), and forced standing at rigid attention on a line for hours at end. These and other modern prison tortures still crop up on occasion, but they are not routine, as they were as recently as the 1940s. They were used with reference to inspiring conformity to prison rules as well as with reference to inspiring conformity to society's laws. That is, they were to exact retribution, inflict deterrent pain, incapacitate, and reform *prison rule violators* as well as doing these things as more general crime control measures.

As the tortures diminished, many wardens were confident that "disciplinary problems" would arise, and they did. But things did not turn out as badly as some old-time wardens predicted. Some feared that without the threat that nonconformists in the prison would be tortured, prisoners could not be made to obey staff rules. Consequently, criminals in prison would escape some of the pains the general prison regime was supposed to impose. They hardly would be incapacitated if they went over the wall, or if they killed each other, stabbed each other, stole from each other, and hit guards over the head with clubs. They hardly would suffer the pain necessary for retribution, deterrence and reformation if they could roam the yard at will, enjoying illicit booze, drugs, pornographic pictures, paper-bound stories of crime and violence, and sex. "Nothing" painful would result if discipline became "lax" and prisons accordingly became "country clubs," even if some semblance of perimeter control were maintained.

But something did result. For one thing, use of psychological punishments increased. Among them is imprisonment within the prison. Inmates are punished by limiting their movements (no "yard time," no movies), by confining them to their own cells, by placing them in "segregation" cells, and by committing them to a term in solitary confinement—the epitome of deprivation of liberty within the conditions of deprived liberty. I do not mean to imply that physical punishments do not still accompany such psychological punishments. They do—the smell in a solitary cell without a toilet, the cold floor, the windowless room, the reduced and bland food, and the pushing, shoving, slapping, and beating that one occasionally hears about. But now the word in prison, as outside, clearly is that "mere" deprivation of liberty is punishment enough.

Also in response to removal of physical tortures has come development of a system of internal control that boils down to a matter of divide and conquer. It will be described later. This system has been used since the day inmates were let out of the solitary confinement cells of the early Pennsylvania prisons, but the general trend toward the contemporary view that men are sent to prison *as* punishment rather than *for* punishment has increased its popularity.

What I have been discussing is a controversy about alternative kinds and degrees of punishment in prison. More important, and more recent, is a debate about the relative merits of punitive and nonpunitive prison programs. This is a controversy between alternative theories to be used as the basis of programs to reform criminals. Leave retribution and deterrence aside, the idea goes. The purpose of prisons is to reform criminals, and so far as that function is concerned, the pain of punishment can at most be neutral. It might not reinforce the criminal's attitudes and behavior, but it will not extinguish them either. Negative punishment is not enough. Positive, nonpunitive treatment programs must be administered, the idea continues, if the prison is to carry out its reformative function.

PUNISHMENT AND NONPUNATIVE TREATMENT

This is the idea which, when transformed into a directive for prison administrators, introduces organizational strain and really puts wardens and chairmen of prison boards on the spot. Because prisoners are to be changed, they are not to be punished. They are to be "corrected" or "rehabilitated" by nonpunitive "treatment." Yet there is no doubt that prisons also are to be punitive. Inflicting pain is still an unequivocal goal of prisons. The criminal law insists on it. Every criminal statute specifies that any person behaving in a stipulated way shall be punished. Then, for felonies, imprisonment is specified as the proper means of inflicting this pain. We offer accused persons the right to be tried by a jury, to confront witnesses, and to have counsel because we do not want the pain of imprisonment to be experienced by those who are not guilty. Put positively, we want guilty persons to experience pain. If the prison experience were not painful or if it were not *intended* to be painful—as is true of the pain experienced by mental hospital patients—then there would be no need for such rigid due process safeguards. After all, you do not ask for a lawyer and a jury trial when a doctor orders you to the hospital for treatment of your fractured leg. You ask for those things before you let a judge send you to prison because you know he is doing it to hurt you, even if he says that in the prison you will get treated for your criminality as well as injured for it.

Prisons, then, have not increasingly been viewed as places of treatment, like hospitals. They have come to be seen as places of punishment and nonpunitive treatment. We have not asked wardens to *replace* programs designed to promote reformation through punishment with programs implementing the theory of reformation through treatment. We have asked them to set the new programs alongside the old ones, or under them, or on top of them. We have not abandoned the notion that prisons must be punitive for retribution and deterrence purposes either.

In the good old days, punishment was assumed to do everything, but now our directives to prison administrators are inherently contradictory. They, and other prison workers, must work out some way of bringing happiness both to those of us who want them to be punitive and to those of us who want them to be nonpunitive. This, as I said earlier, leads to some fast talking on their part.

The most common form of fast talk involves the presentation of arguments—complete with dry statistics and eye-watering stories—showing that a rehabilitation program existing mostly on paper is dramatically changing the lives of lost souls. It is no longer permissible to say a prison program is doing what the criminal law says it should do—punish criminals. But pay raises, promotions, good relations with policemen and prosecutors, and fine friendships with "law and order" politicians are likely to come to him who implements such a program while at the same time giving frequent speeches about the dramatic rehabilitation job being done by the members of the Junior Chamber of Commerce who visit the prison once a month.

The psychiatrists, the social workers, the sociologists, the judges, the civil liberties lawyers, the Republicans, the members of prison reform societies, the critical ladies, the militant blacks, the Democrats, the hippies, the yippies, the gays, and the poor who advocate nonpunitive help for criminals—all these and other radicals of the modern revolution must be placated too. It is not wise to tell an enlightened Chief Justice of the United States, who both softly and loudly asks for prison reform, that real rehabilitation programs in prison are restricted by the very criminal law system he represents. It is best to present some statistics and stories suggesting that great advances have been made for some prisoners, some of the time, in some places, and that further advances surely will follow. The fast talk will slip smoothly by if some name changing accompanies it. Above all, the prison always should be called a "correctional facility," the chief of the prison board should be called "director of corrections," the guard should be called a "correctional officer," and the solitary confinement cells should be called an "adjustment center." It is still all right to call prisoners prisoners.

Staff Organization

A chart of a prison's administrative hierarchy, showing the lines of authority, does not begin to describe how the prison is organized, who is responsible to whom, or who influences whom. It is even difficult to draw a picture of the official parts of the organization in this way, and these are the least complex aspects of the system. In addition, there are unofficial, complicated, and usually unstated aspects. In fact, whether something in prison organization is "official" or "unofficial" depends on whether or not it is clear and observable. If a prison warden can do something about some situation or practice, he is dealing with official organization. If there is something going on, the nature of which he cannot clearly state and which, consequently, he cannot change by order, he is dealing with unofficial organization. As an administrator, he can only flounder around, and most prison administrators necessarily flounder around most of the time.

Efficient administration of prisons has been generally lacking. When personnel are selected on the basis of political patronage, as they still are in some states, it is difficult to secure efficiency even in routine matters, let alone in complex affairs like rehabilitation. Over a period of 50 years, the average tenure of 612 American wardens was 5.2 years—only 13 percent held their jobs for 10 years or more, and 22 percent were in office 1 year or less. In only 23 states are the chief administrative officers of prisons and reformatories covered by a civil service or merit system, and such a system for other institutional employees does not exist in 13 states.

Unqualified men obviously cannot, by reason of ignorance or sheer indifference, perform the duties necessary for prevention of waste and for efficient businesslike operation of an institution. But even well-qualified and well-trained prison personnel find it difficult to secure this kind of efficiency. The reason is that, in two principal respects, the organization that is a prison differs significantly from the organization of factories and other industrial organizations, from the organization of business sales forces, and from the organization of both private and public paper-processing bureaus.

MANAGERS OF MEN

First of all, the personnel hierarchies of prisons are organized down to the lowest level for the administration of the daily activities of men. In a factory or business there are separate hierarchies of management personnel and of workers. In contrast, the guard, who is the lowest-level employee in a prison, is both a manager and worker. He is managed in a system of regulations and controls from above, but he also manages, in a concordant system of regulations, the inmates who are in his charge. He is a low-status worker in interaction with the warden and other front-office personnel, but a higher-status manager in interaction with inmates. He has no real counterpart in the business and industrial world. Most guards have nothing to do but guard. They do not "use" inmates productively any more than they themselves are used productively. Guards manage and are managed in organizations where management is an end, not a means.

This fact makes the guard's job an extraordinarily difficult one. Unlike popular stereotypes picturing the guard as either a brutal sadist with a club or as a robot standing on a wall with a rifle, guards are managers of men. They are responsible for keeping convicted criminals quiet and for supervising groups of men who have no loyalty to the prison. Yet they do not have the help of ordinary "incentives" such as wages, promotions, threat of discharge, or even force. They are expected to exact compliance to rules and restrictive conditions that have been deliberately designed to make inmates' lives unpleasant, but at the same time they are to minimize friction between inmates and staff. They are to contribute to inmate rehabilitation by relaxing, being nondirective, and showing concern for personality problems, but they also are expected to act as policemen, protecting inmates from each other. On top of all this, they are to keep inmates busy at maintenance, housekeeping, and production tasks, to administer justice, and to insure that escapes do not occur.

The fact that guards are managers makes the prison administrator's job a difficult one too. He cannot order them to do things. Instead, he must share policy decisions with them, meaning that he must "sell" them or otherwise try to persuade them to work in ways he considers desirable and efficient.

By way of contrast, take a factory whose managers have decided its function is to manufacture airplanes and whose workers rivet, saw, drill, turn screws and bolts, and run turret lathes as part of the manufacturing process. If the managers then decide as a matter of policy to manufacture boats instead of planes, they do not have to consult the workers about implementing the decision. The workers will in the boat factory do basically what they have been doing all along. It is just a matter of setting up the machines differently.

But the relationship between a prison warden and prison guards is quite different. The warden's policy decisions are likely to change the very nature of the guards' work. Suppose, for example, that a prison warden wants guards who have been punitive and custodial to relax and be therapeutic. Or suppose he simply wants men who have stood guard in prison shops to supervise crews of inmate maintenance men. Implementing either desire will drastically change the guards' relationships with the inmates they manage. They must be asked to "go along" with any proposed change in policy because they, like the warden, are managers of men, a job that is fundamentally different from running the machines essential to the manufacture of airplanes or boats.

UNRELATED EMPLOYEE ROLES

Prison staff organization differs from the organization of factories and businesses in a second respect. This difference is related to the first one, but it more directly stems from the curious change process experienced by prisons in their two-hundred-year history. As prisons have grown in size and as concepts of good penology have changed, new services and roles have been added without regard for those already existing. This process seems different from that accompanying similar growth of other organizations, for the new roles have been organized around purposes that are little related to one another.

In all prisons there is a line organization of custodial ranks, ranging from warden to guard, and salary differentials and descriptive titles indicate that a chain of command is expected within this hierarchy. But there is no clear expectation that the institution shall consist *solely* of a hierarchy of custodial ranks, even if all employees are responsible to the warden. Systems of nonline positions, such as those of psychologists, social workers, and industrial foremen are essentially separate and have their own salaries and titles. They are not part of the custodial chain of command, and they are not staff organizations either.

The structure of any prison provides for three principal personnel hierarchies devoted, respectively, to *keeping, using,* and *serving* inmates, but not for integration of their divergent purposes. The separate organizations concerned with keeping and serving inmates, for example, are not merely overlapping. They have entirely different and partly contradictory purposes. Each has its own specific kind of relationship between employees and inmates, its own pattern of communication, authority, and decision-making, and its own system for distributing rewards and punishments. Much of any prison warden's life is devoted to trying to maintain some semblance of balance between these three subsidiary organizations or to promoting one of them at the expense of the other. His general, or overall, system for allocating rewards and punishments is necessarily the machinery for maintaining this balance, or for officially assigning priority to keeping, or using, or serving inmates.

Inmate Organization

Although prison guards and other officers have some control over much of an inmate's overt behavior, mostly in the form of authority and power to punish for deviation, their control is negligible compared to control by the prisoners themselves. In a system of friendships, mutual obligations, statutes, reciprocal relations, loyalties, intimidation, deception, and violence, inmates learn that conformity to prisoner expectations is just as important to their welfare as is conformity to the formal controls imposed by "outsiders."

Powerful prisoners insist that most inmates be orthodox in their statements and actions most of the time. And orthodoxy is more important in prisons than in outside life, because in outside life a person has freedom of mobility not possible in prisons. Conformity is promoted by rewards and punishments, with the latter emphasizing gossip and ridicule but also including beatings, knifings, and killings.

"THE CODE"

Informal control may be seen in the persistence of the fundamental principles of prisoner organization, called "the code." The chief tenets of the code can be classified roughly into five major categories.

First, there are those maxims that caution: *Don't interfere with inmate interests.* These center on the idea that inmates should serve the least possible time, while enjoying the greatest possible number of pleasures and privileges. Included are directives such as, *Never rat on a con; Don't be nosey; Don't have a loose lip; Keep off a man's back; Don't put a guy on the spot.* Put positively, *Be loyal to your class, the cons.*

A second set of behavioral rules asks inmates to refrain from quarrels or arguments with fellow prisoners: *Don't lose your head; Play it cool; Do your own time; Don't bring heat.*

Third, prisoners assert that inmates should not take advantage of one another by means of force, fraud, or chicanery: *Don't exploit inmates.* This injunction sums up several directives: *Don't break your word; Don't steal from cons; Don't sell favors; Don't be a racketeer; Don't welsh on debts. Be right.*

Fourth, some rules have as their central theme the maintenance of self: *Don't weaken; Don't whine; Don't cop out* (plead guilty). Stated positively: *Be tough; Be a man.*

Fifth, prisoners express a variety of maxims that forbid according prestige or respect to the guards or the world for which they stand: *Don't be a sucker; Skim it off the top; Never talk to a screw* (guard); *Have a connection; Be sharp.*

There is no question that the code is frequently violated, just as the formal legal code is violated. Nevertheless, its effects can be seen everywhere in the prison community. It helps inmates avoid some of the conditions of punitive deprivation which the prison is supposed to impose on them. Yet it should not be assumed that the code is "anti-administration" in emphasis as it seems to be. On the contrary, the code reflects important alliances between inmate leaders and prison officials, as we shall see in the next section.

THREE SUBCULTURES

Three principal categories of inmates can be found in any prison. Their ways of behaving—their subcultures—are quite different. The three kinds of inmates adjust to each other, and to the guards and other personnel, and the three subcultures mesh in various ways. The outcome of the adjusting and the meshing is the organizational character—the "inmate culture"—of a particular prison.

First, there is the subculture of the "thief." Prison "right guys" or "real men," as they are called, participate in this subculture, which thrives on the street as well as in institutions. These men have the highest status among the inmates in any prison. This is no accident, for the prisoner's code is really the code of the "right guys." They subscribe to the code and promote it because it is their benefit to do so. On the street, any man deserving of the title "thief" is a man known to be "right," "solid." The "right guy" in a prison is this thief locked behind walls and bars. Gresham Sykes and Sheldon Messinger a few years ago summarized the "right guy's" relations in prisons as follows:

> In his dealings with prison officials, the *right guy* is unmistakably against them, but he doesn't act foolishly. When he talks about the officials with other inmates, he's sure to say that even the hacks with the best intentions are stupid, incompetent, and not to be trusted; that the worst thing you can do is to give the hacks information—they'll only use it against you when the chips are down. A *right guy* sticks up for his rights, but he doesn't ask for pity: he can take all the lousy screws can hand out and more. . . . He realizes that there are just two kinds of people in the world. Those in the know skim it off the top. Suckers work.

Then there is the culture of the "convict." It is oriented to manipulating the conditions of prison life, not to an honorable and proud life as a thief. Prison argot identified some of the men participating in this subculture as "merchants," "peddlers," "shots," "politicians."

Nowadays prisoners tend to call them, simply, "convicts." Not all inmates are "convicts." Prisoners playing this role do favors for their fellow prisoners in direct exchange for favors from them, or for payment in cigarettes, the medium of exchange in most prisons. Many if not most of the favors involve distribution of goods and services which should go to inmates without cost—the "merchant" demands a price for dental care, laundry, food, library books, a good job assignment, etc. Their central value is utilitarianism, and the most manipulative and the most utilitarian individuals win the available wealth, privileges, and positions of influence.

Also oriented to the "convict" subculture and to manipulating prison life are men who exhibit highly aggressive behavior against other inmates or against officials. They are likely to be called "gorillas," "toughs," "hoods," "ballbusters," or some similar name, depending on the prison they are in. The terms are all synonyms, and they refer to men, likely to be diagnosed as "psychopaths" by psychiatrists, who hijack their fellow inmates when the latter are returning from the commissary, who attack guards and fellow inmates verbally and physically, who run any kangaroo court, who force incoming inmates to pay for cell and job assignments, who smash up the prison at the beginning of a riot. These "convicts" offer "protection" to weak inmates for a fee but, like the "merchants," they actually exploit other inmates while seeming to help make prison life easier for them.

A final category of inmates is oriented to legitimate subcultures. Prisoners with this orientation are called "straights," "square Johns," "do-rights," etc. When they enter prison they are not members of the thief subculture. Further, while they are in prison they reject both the values of the thieves ("right guys") and the values of the convicts ("merchants," "gorillas"). These men are oriented neither to crime nor to prison. They present few problems to prison administrators. Like "dings" (psychotic or highly eccentric inmates), they isolate themselves—or are isolated—from the thief and convict subcultures.

INTERRELATION OF SUBCULTURES

There are great differences in the prison behavior of men oriented to one or the other of the three subcultures. As indicated, the hardcore member of the convict subculture seeks status through means available in the prison. But it is important for an understanding of inmate conduct to note that the hard-core member of the thief subculture seeks status in the broader criminal world of which the prison is only part. Similarly, a man oriented to legitimate life is, by definition, committed to the values of persons outside the prison.

Numerous studies have documented the fact that "right guys," many of whom can be identified as leaders of the thieves, not of the convicts, exercise the greatest influences over the total prisoner population. The influence is the long-run kind stemming from the ability to define what is right and proper. The thief, after all, has the respect of many inmates who are not themselves thieves. He acts, forms opinions, and evaluates events in the prison according to the "right guy" values of the code, and in time he in this way determines the basic behavior patterns in the institution. In what the thief thinks of as "small matters"—getting job transfers, enforcing payment of gambling debts, making cell assignments, stealing and selling food, and acquiring symbols of status such as specially tailored clothing—members of the convict subculture run things.

Most inmates are under the influence of both the thief subculture and the convict subculture. Without realizing it, inmates who serve long prison terms are likely to move toward the middle, toward a compromise between the directives coming from the two sources of deviance. A convict may come to see that thieves are the men with the real prestige; a thief or even a do-right may lose his ability to sustain his status needs by outside criteria.

The thief subculture scarcely exists in institutions for women and some institutions for juveniles. In places of short-term confinement, the convict subculture is dominant, for the thief subculture involves status distinctions that are not readily noticeable or influential in the short run. At the other extreme, in prisons confining only long-term men, the distinctions between the two subcultures are likely to be blurred. Probably the two subcultures exist in their purest forms in institutions holding inmates in their twenties, with varying sentences for a variety of criminal offenses. Such institutions, of course, are the typical prisons of the United States.

Perceiving that the prison community is made up of three principal subcultures helps make sense of prisoners' behavior after they are released. Because "square Johns" are oriented to a "straight" life, we should expect them to have a low parole violation rate, and we should further expect this rate to remain low no matter how much time was served. We should expect "right guys" to have a high violation rate that decreases markedly as time in prison increases—the continued incarceration tending to sever the thief's connections with the thief subculture on the outside, thus increasing the probability of successful parole. Finally, we should expect "merchants" to have a low parole violation rate if their sentences are rather short, but to find the rate increasing systematically with time served—with continued incarceration they should learn to wheel, deal, exploit, and manipulate in ways that get them right back into prison. A number of sociological studies have found the violation rates of "straights," "thieves," and "convicts" to be almost exactly as expected.

Control

One of the most amazing things about prisons is that they work. Any American prison is made up of the synchronized actions of hundreds of people, some of whom hate and distrust each other, love each other, fight each other physically and psychologically, think of each other as stupid and mentally disturbed, "manage" and "control" each other, and vie with each other for favors, prestige, power, and money. Despite these conditions, the social system which is a prison does not degenerate into a chaotic mess of social relations that have no order and make no sense. Somehow the personnel, including the prisoners, are bound together so that most conflicts and misunderstandings are not crucial.

We observed earlier that humanitarian, political, and treatment considerations have limited the means available to prison administrators for keeping inmates quietly confined, yet these officials continue to be held responsible for the prisoners' orderly confinement. One solution is to keep inmates unorganized. Psychological solitary confinement permits inmates to work together and to participate in other group activities, but it minimizes the danger of escape or riot. It is achieved by offering rewards of various kinds—parole, good-time allowances, and special privileges (including the privilege of participating in treatment programs)—for those inmates who heed the administrators' admonition to "do your own time." It is also achieved by rewarding informers—rats, finks, stool pigeons— and by going slow on policing the prison community. "If they are fighting each other, they aren't fighting us," the saying goes. Individual prisoners are easier to control than are groups of prisoners.

Clearly, this policy has for many years kept most inmates ungrouped. The very first extended sociological study of an American prison community (done in the 1930s) estimated that in an Illinois prison about 40 percent of the prisoners were not in any way intimately integrated in groups in which strong social relationships existed, and that another 40 percent engaged in only some of the superficial practices of group life. Things have not changed much. Despite a new awareness, a new wisdom, a new militancy, and a new collective identity among prisoners—especially blacks—the high percentage of ungrouped inmates continues.

A second, and more complex, kind of solution to the problem of control without physical torture is to enlist the aid of some of the inmates. When prisons become huge sprawling monsters with far more prisoners than staff members, it is extremely difficult, if not impossible, to keep the inmates psychologically isolated. But control is facilitated if inmate elites develop and enforce norms and values which promote orthodoxy, conformity, and psychological isolation among the other inmates.

Interestingly enough, the inmate code which puts emphasis upon being an astute criminal, upon maintaining social distance from the guards, and upon inmate solidarity promotes all these things. Inmate leaders in both the thief subculture and the convict subculture wittingly and unwittingly help prison employees maintain a quiet, secure correctional facility marked by the conditions of peaceful coexistence. The values and type of organization which these inmate elites attempt to maintain are to a large degree systems for exploiting fellow captives, a condition attended by control and repression of inmates by inmates rather than by guards and other prison workers.

The advice thieves and convicts give to incoming inmates—and to each other—is the exact counterpart of the officials' admonitions to one and all. Be rational, self-disciplined, not wild. Don't bring "heat" to other inmates by antagonizing employees. Don't cause trouble by stealing from fellow inmates. Above all, and generally, "do your own time." In enforcing these directives, of course, the inmate elites necessarily violate them. When an inmate leader is insisting that inmates "do their own time," he is not doing his own time.

Since it seems obvious that inmate control of other inmates is valuable to prison workers, we should expect to find that, in any prison, power of various kinds will be unofficially (and maybe unintentionally) allocated to inmate leaders, rather than seized by them. Dozens of prison researchers, hundreds of prison workers, and a few inmates have all observed that this is the case. Judicious distribution of goods in short supply, including power, measures of freedom, and symbols of status, enables administrators to enlist the aid of some inmates in the task of controlling the others. In return for the scarce goods, usually called "favors," inmate elites lead the community in a movement for peace.

Big shots among the thieves and convicts are men who, like the administrators, have a vested interest in maintaining the status quo. A basic tenet in the code of the "right guy" and the "merchant" is that prisoners must stick together in all matters. They should not exploit each other. Most importantly, they should not cooperate with the officials as a means to gaining advantages over fellow captives. But such cooperation, paradoxically, is a principal chapter in the life story of a "right guy" or "merchant."

Officials insist that guards must not fraternize with inmates, and inmate elites insist that prisoners must not fraternize with guards. As a consequence, officials and elites share control of the channels of communication, an important source of power. Like administrators and "square Johns," some convicts and thieves insist that all inmates are equal. But by this they mean that "outside" criteria such as occupation, wealth, or criminal notoriety shall not be used to determine the power, prestige, and special privileges within the institution. "Your past was forgotten when you walked in that gate," it is said. "In here, you have a chance to start a new life."

Such rules and homilies protect the privileged positions of prisoner elites as well as of wardens and guard captains. They insure that few inmates can seriously threaten the power positions of their leaders. Such stability is of course valuable to any warden wanting peace. "Inmate rules," like "prison rules," function to keep the bulk of the inmates unorganized.

Consider an oversimplified example of administrative-inmate alliances. Suppose a guard allows an inmate to steal a little coffee from the kitchen. He does this, he is apt to say, because both men are good guys. They have worked in the kitchen together for years. The inmate is cooperative, works hard, discourages other inmates from violence, and, generally, makes the guard's job an easy one. But what happens, of course, is that the coffee-stealing privilege becomes an incentive for continuing to do all these things. Moreover, the coffee stealer now protects the coffee supply from criminals. Certainly he will take a dim view of other inmates who would steal coffee in such manner and measure that the guard and his superiors would put all coffee under strict control. He then makes the guard's job even easier, for *he* guards the coffee.

But he really does not have to guard it, literally. The "inmate code" takes care of that. Other inmates are prohibited from making inroads on his coffee-stealing privileges by a code stressing the importance of doing one's own time, not bringing heat, not interfering with another inmate's interests, sticking together against the administration, and not ratting. The guard and inmate, then, have joined together—and with others—in an alliance for peace. The inmate is allowed to exploit other inmates by stealing coffee allotted for their use because permitting him to do so enlists his aid in keeping the bulk of the inmates unorganized and, thus, under control.

Conflict

A prison riot, confrontation, or demonstration is likely to be much more than a mere conflict between the keepers and the kept. For about twenty years it has been an established fact—with reference to mental hospitals as well as to prisons—that disturbances among institutionalized inmates follow disturbances among staff members.

Riots make visible the contradictory and even conflicting orientations of the three principal prison staff organizations—the one for keeping inmates, the one for using them, and the one for serving them. They also shed light on the orientations of "right guys," "merchants," and "gorillas," and on the exploitative relationship between elite inmate leaders and their followers. And riots most dramatically reveal the principal control measure used to keep the peace during less tumultuous times—witting or unwitting cooperative alliances between staff members and inmates. Rarely do riot investigation commissions seeking the causes of riots look back to complex staff organization, complex inmate organization, and complex bonds between staff organization and inmate organization.

The explosion of a prison powder keg into a riot has potential benefits for guards as well as for inmates. Moreover, a riot's possible benefits are greater for the "old guard" among guards and inmates than for others. This is true because riots are, among other things, reactions to prison reform movements that would take power from the staff hierarchy dedicated to keeping inmates and give it to the hierarchy dedicated to serving them. The same reform movements would take power from inmate elites and distribute it more democratically in the inmate population.

OLD GUARD STAFF STAKE IN STATUS QUO

This is not the place for a detailed analysis of prison riots. I merely note that a working-class prison guard who has learned what is "right" and "proper" in the world is likely to implement in his work a strong moral code that stresses righteous indignation about crime, hatred of robbers and rapists, intolerance of slovenliness and laziness, disdain for acquisition except by the slow process of honest labor, and "self-discipline" rather than "self-expression." And, too, the politicians controlling prison budgets must be opposed to crime and criminals as well as to sin and man-eating sharks.

Any prison reformer who tries to implement a program at variance with such attitudes must expect resistance. Should he be a warden, his efforts will be resisted by old guard staff members who know their legal and moral duty is to cage bad men. Should the reformer be a director of an entire system of prisons, the wardens themselves might be members of the old guard.

I do not claim that the old guard "starts" or "stimulates" or "incites" or "instigates" an inmate riot in order to counter the revolution a reformer promotes and leads. There is no doubt, however, that past riots have functioned to produce the demotion or discharge of prison wardens and commissioners who introduced too many changes too fast. "We didn't have all this trouble when Old Joe was here," riot investigating committees have in essence concluded. "So let's replace this official with someone who, like Old Joe, knows how to control inmates."

Perhaps I can best make my point with an anecdote. Some years ago, a commissioner of corrections was trying to introduce and stimulate changes in an old-fashioned prison ruled by a wise and politically independent warden. After several months of thrusts and parries, he received a memorandum from the warden. It listed the changes being made, and then went on to say something like this: "I have noticed that the changes being introduced by you are very similar to the changes attempted by [an earlier commissioner]. A riot followed the changes he tried. Since I am not responsible for the changes you are introducing, I hereby absolve myself of responsibility for any riot that might occur as a result of them. I am placing a copy of this memorandum in my personal files."

No one can prove that the warden in this case intended his memorandum to be a veiled threat. But the commissioner receiving the memorandum interpreted it to mean, "Lay off my prison, Mister, or I'll give you a riot." That is what he told me, at least. Compare the tenor of the memorandum with the views of some of the men working in New York's Attica Correctional Facility when that prison experienced both a riot and a bloody massacre of prisoners. Writing in the September 15, 1971, *New York Times,* Michael T. Kaufman reported:

> What [an ex-convict] admires and what others—including guards and townspeople—deplore have been the attempts made in Mr. Oswald's tenure to use new approaches and recruit new personnel. In conversations around this village, people talk of the toughness that the system had under the former commissioner, Paul D. McGinnis, who, unlike Mr. Oswald, came up through the ranks. They view the new commissioner as too permissive, too lenient. . . . In less troubled times than these, Commissioner Oswald has frequently indicated the need to change the thinking of correctional officers, shifting away from "custodial aspects" to more training and rehabilitation.

Just after inmates in one prison had seized hostages, barricaded themselves in a cellblock, torn up the plumbing and heating system in their own cells, and wrecked whatever else was wreckable, an experienced warden professed himself baffled by the uprising: "This prison is their home," he said. "I don't know why they want to tear it up." Why, indeed, would the inmates destroy their own living quarters and, more generally, shake up the conditions of peaceful coexistence usually prevailing among inmates and guards in prisons? Perhaps because old guard inmates like old guard guards unwittingly anticipate that losing a battle might win a war—a war against "oppressive conditions" but also a war against reformers who would more permanently destroy the alliances that serve to maintain the peace and privileges of the old guard inmates' "home."

ELITE PRISONERS' STAKE IN STATUS QUO

In many prisons, "right guys" and "merchants" are allied with guards, as noted earlier. Any prison reformer whose program would break up these alliances—which give inmate leaders an undue share of a prison's scarce goods—must promise the involved inmates a substitute for their special privileges. Usually what is explicitly or implicitly promised in exchange for the good life "right guys" and "convicts" are living is a program of "rehabilitation" or, generally, "better living conditions." If the reformer cannot produce the promised change, "right guys" and "convicts" alike are in a position to withdraw their stabilizing influence and to flit around the edges of the kind of violent demonstration commonly called a "spontaneous riot."

Recall the prison "gorilla" who quite regularly violates both prison rules and the inmate code. He is even likely to hit a guard over the head with a club, knowing full well (if rationality is assumed) that the guard and the prison system he represents have more than enough power to crush the attacker and grind up his soul. Because "gorillas" bring heat (close surveillance), rather than playing it cool and acting like men, "right guys" and other inmates see them as losers. They know that one belief enforced by prison staff members and endorsed by the general public always has been that the prisoner who aggresses against the prison ought to remain in prison. "Gorilla" behavior and staff reaction to it, then, is viewed as undesirable because it makes prison life uncomfortable and also because it is likely to keep a man off the streets, where he can win by making a bit of money through criminal means. But at riot time "gorillas" and their tactics can be useful.

Although proposed prison reforms are not very threatening to "gorillas," they do, as indicated, threaten the peace and the status of "right guys." They also threaten "merchants" and "convicts" generally. These men have learned to adjust to prison life and they enjoy it, such as it is. Prison reform might break up their homosexual partnerships, deprive them of the starched and well-pressed uniforms they consider symbols of status, decrease their profits from gambling, cut off their sources of illegal alcohol and drugs, and so on.

Like the old guard among staff members, the inmate old guard—"right guys" and "merchants"—stand to reap certain benefits if "gorillas" initiate a riot that will stop or slow down a reformer's program. If reform has been progressing for some time, a riot might even restore the conditions of the good old days. For this reason, riots are—to some inmates as well as to some staff—more like anti-revisionist confrontations or even counterrevolutions than they are like revolutions.

RIOT BEHAVIOR PATTERN

The pattern of inmate conduct during riots has been uncannily uniform for about two decades. For a few days "gorillas" are in charge, and it is during these days that sex, alcohol and drug orgies occur, cells are wrecked and buildings burned, hostages are threatened and (on rare occasions) murdered, and inmates armed with knives and clubs settle old grudges among themselves. In days of calm, guards spend some of their time trying, with various degrees of efficiency and enthusiasm, to function as policemen who protect inmates from each other. But when, during a riot, this police force withdraws to the walls, the crime rate goes up.

Then the leadership changes. "Right guys" take over from "gorillas." They are assisted by leaders of the "convicts," many of whom aspire to "right guy" status. At this juncture there is likely to be additional maiming and even an inmate murder or two—byproducts of the fight for leadership—and the persons maimed or murdered are likely to be either "convicts" or "gorillas." At this juncture, also, "right guys" (who like to be called *men*) note for the ears of one and all that any half-baked revolutionary scheme or escape plot that might have existed early in the riot has been thoroughly squashed. No violent confrontation will succeed when *we* are sitting here as open targets in a burning prison and *they* have speckled the wall with machine gunners and flecked the sky with armed helicopters. But peaceful negotiation over inmate "demands" might now direct public attention to needed prison programs.

Not stated publicly is the "right guys'" assumption that their negotiations with prison administrators, politicians, and newsmen will surely produce no new prison programs that do not protect the privileged positions of the negotiators. What they want is improved living conditions but no shaking up of the inmate social structure or of the alliances between staff and inmate leaders. Generally speaking, the demands made by "right guy" negotiators during times of crisis—demands for better food, better parole practices, more trade training, and so forth—have only added up to requests that prison administrators be given the enlarged budgets they have been seeking for years.

POLITICALIZATION

Owing to what is commonly called the "politicalization" of prisoners, especially black ones, the proportion of "gorillas" in most prisons has increased in recent years, while the proportion of "right guys" has decreased. Because the prison now, as always, is a microcosm of the society in which it sits, militancy on the outside is bound to be reflected on the inside. Numerous observers of recent change in prisons have considered the new militancy a sign of new prisoner power. But prisoner power is nothing new. Inmates have dominated the internal affairs, and have had a strong voice in the external affairs, of prisons during most of their two-hundred-year history. What is new is the shift of inmate power from "right guys" to "gorillas."

The militant "politicalized" prisoner is likely to take the "gorilla" role. A black man who is convinced that he has been victimized by white society and then has been imprisoned only because he tried to undo some of the effects of that victimization is not likely to play it cool in the prison, as "right guys" and old guard staff members would have him do.

"No longer do black prisoners play the sychophant's game of 'pleasing the powers,' " said a former prisoner who served ten years in a California prison for armed robbery and murder. In an interview with a *New York Times* reporter, the warden of a California prison put the matter in a different way: "Our prisoners are consumed with bitterness and resentment and are ideal recruits for the more sophisticated radicals on the outside who cloak their real intentions with talk of humanitarian reform." The former inmate was saying, I think, that black prisoners are no longer going to be Uncle Toms, and the warden seemed to be saying that this admirable resolution is somehow nefarious.

But, in prison or elsewhere, one need not be a "gorilla," a "hero," or a loser in order to avoid being a sycophant or an Uncle Tom. Inmates of Swedish prisons are by no means happy prisoners, but at least a decade ago they won humane conditions and many rights denied to almost all American prisoners and just now becoming the subject of lawsuits and other legal actions. They won reductions in the degree of restriction placed on their liberty, and they did it by means of peaceful confrontations of a kind that is typical of neither Uncle Toms nor "gorillas." These nonviolent confrontations attracted public support and correlated political power for the inmates, who now are trying to use the political power to shed even more of the restrictions on their freedom. Perhaps the Swedish prisoners will exceed the limits of public tolerance and thus lose some of their power, as David A. Ward noted in a recent article appearing in the *Journal of Criminal Law and Criminology*. But they surely would lose it, and perhaps would not have it, if they used "hero" tactics in an attempt to avoid looking like blond Uncle Toms.

In the United States, "right guys" and almost all other inmates have long realized the impotence of a lone "gorilla" prisoner who in a fit of anger throws a drinking glass at a guard. They know such action will not improve prison conditions for "right guys" or anyone else. "Right guys" and other inmates have realized too, I think, that a primitively armed collectivity of "gorillas" that smashes a prison and then huddles miserably in a cell-block or prison yard has no power to produce progressive changes either. "Right guys" and "merchants" alike have manipulated such collective violence to stifle prison reforms that threaten their ability to live in prisons under conditions less painful than those experienced by the masses. But the recent shift of power from "right guys" to more militant inmates has done what prison reformers have rarely done—disrupted the privileged prison lives of "thieves" and their allies.

Unlike the old "gorillas," however, the new militants are getting wise—their leaders are trying to establish a racial-ethnic awareness and identity that is proudly anticriminal. Maybe now "right guys" will join with the "wise gorillas," and with prison reformers, "straight" inmates, and "merchants," in a collective but peaceful attempt to mitigate the miseries of all prisoners.

Success

The success or failure of imprisonment should be judged according to the four principal goals assigned to prisons—retribution, incapacitation, deterrence, and reformation.

As a retributive machine, the prison seems highly successful. Prisoners live miserable lives even in the minimum-security institutions likely to be called "country clubs" by those who want imprisonment to be even more painful than it is. We send men to prison because we want them hurt, and we succeed.

As a means of incapacitation, imprisonment has not been very successful. Very few crimes against outsiders are committed by prisoners during the period of incarceration, but the crime rate in prisons is high nevertheless. The crimes of prisoners are committed principally against other prisoners, but there also are a few crimes against prison guards and other officers, and many crimes against prison property.

The success of the prison in deterring the general public from crime is probably much less than its success in incapacitating criminals. Imprisonment certainly has some deterrent effect, but it is difficult to compare the deterrent effects of different prison policies or to isolate the effect of any prison policy from the effect of arrest and conviction. The deterrent effect of imprisonment probably increases slightly with the horrors of prison life, though this is likely to be offset by the difficulty of securing convictions if the public feels that the horrors of imprisonment are greater than the horrors of crime. Perhaps the fact of incarceration, regardless of conditions within prisons, is the most important factor in deterrence.

The success of imprisonment as a means of reformation is very slight. There is no need to review the numerous presentations of statistics showing high rates of recidivism among ex-convicts. The general rate runs from about 35 percent to as high as 80 or 90 percent, depending in part on how you calculate it.

OUTCOME DETERMINED ELSEWHERE

The high recidivism rates should not be regarded as the responsibility of the last institution to deal with the offenders. No institution receiving the men made "failures" by the rest of society should be expected to make "successes" of a very large proportion of them. Also, prisons cannot properly be given credit for those who commit no more crimes after imprisonment. Committing first offenses, persistence in crime, and desistance in crime are all determined principally by conditions other than institutional programs and policies. There is a tendency to believe a prison is a success if it does not make offenders worse.

Awareness that prisons hurt men but do not change their criminality is again making it fashionable to argue, as it was argued twenty years ago, that we should "break down the walls." More and more concerned citizens and correctional workers are saying that imprisonment should be regarded as a barbarian method of dealing with criminals, and that other methods should be substituted for it as rapidly as possible. As I said earlier, we have begun to listen, and to carry out these recommendations. The general tendency in the last generation has been to substitute probation for imprisonment. In many states probation is now used for more offenders than is imprisonment, although 50 years ago the ratio could not have been more than one to ten. Now "community treatment programs" are being developed to replace, or supplement, probation as well as prison.

REALISTIC LEGAL THEORY NEEDED

Nevertheless, the idea that criminals are dangerous and should be imprisoned has become deeply rooted in the last two centuries, and imprisonment will be with us for some time to come. What is needed is legal theory and practice which explicitly face the fact that in our present society prisons must, by definition, be abnormally restrictive, and thus, punitive.

In trying to keep the peace, the state centuries ago began to mediate and arbitrate in what we think of as criminal affairs, somewhat as it now does (through courts and judges) when in a tort case it orders a plaintiff to pay damages to a defendant. But in criminal affairs the same state that now rescues a criminal from, say, the vengeance of an irate victim, itself incapacitates him and wreaks vengeance on him. That is why we have prisons.

Because commitment to an institution is intended to render criminals powerless, the state—the political authority with power—reserves to itself the right to determine how much power will be restored to powerless prisoners, and at what time. Moreover, our prisons hold an undue proportion of citizens who have been quite openly and intentionally excluded from sharing in power even when they are not in prison. Youths and minority groups outside prisons have been, and still are, effectively excluded from a rightful share of the political decisions that affect their fate as well as the fate of other citizens. It is easy for the politically powerful to conclude, erroneously, that because these persons are excluded from power their participation in decisions about the distribution of power is not needed. It is even easy to conclude—compounding the error—that because they are excluded from power they—especially the poor ones—are not needed by the society or state at all. Accordingly, an undue proportion of them are locked in cages.

By definition, punishment imposed by the state is punishment imposed on the less powerful by the more powerful. For about 200 years the powerful have been inflicting pain on quite powerless lower-class criminals by intentionally depriving them of even the restricted liberty they possess as half-educated, half-employed, half-housed, half-clothed, and half-fed citizens in the land of the free. And all this punishing of the less powerful by the more powerful has been made easier by the idea that imprisonment is good for them, that it reforms them, rehabilitates them, resocializes them, educates them, trains them for work, and generally makes them into "decent men" and "upright citizens" who consequently can "take their rightful place in society."

When we say these things, we lie. Prison programs rarely rehabilitate anyone, and we know it. I think we keep reciting our faith in the rehabilitative ideal because believing in this ideal eases our consciences as we inflict pain and powerlessness on men already enduring much pain and holding little power. Perhaps if we called a spade a spade we would be better off, and criminals would be better off. Thus it might be wise to send persons to prison only for retribution, deterrence, and incapacitation. Rehabilitation programs would be located outside prison. Such a policy would smash to bits the rehabilitative ideal that now, like rose-colored glass, dims our view of the fact that we send men to prison for pain. Perhaps with our protective glass destroyed we would send fewer men to prison.

Elizabeth W. Vorenberg and James Vorenberg

5

Early Diversion from the Criminal Justice System:

Practice in Search of a Theory

Introduction

In the years since the President's Crime Commission began its work and reform of the criminal justice system became a major national goal, certain words and phrases have become the shorthand for improvements that all "reformers" in the field are deemed to accept. A few examples are "professionalization" and "community service" as applied to the police; "business management techniques" as applied to the courts; and "community treatment" and "collaborative model" as applied to corrections. In hundreds of the criminal justice plans required of the states by the block-grant formulation of the Law Enforcement Assistance Act and in the individual grant applications submitted pursuant to such plans, these and other slogans appear thousands of times, thereby wrapping a particular proposal in the flag of the Crime Commission and the massive subsequent literature. But no word has had quite the power

ELIZABETH W. VORENBERG *was assistant director of the Vera Manhattan Court Employment Project in 1967–68 and worked in the foundation field from 1968–70. After practicing law for a number of years,* JAMES VORENBERG *became professor of law at Harvard University in 1962. During the 1960s, he also served as director of the Office of Criminal Justice in the United States Department of Justice and executive director of the President's Commission on Law Enforcement and the Administration of Justice.*

of "diversion" (or, if real specificity is desired, "early diversion") which offers the promise of the best of all worlds: cost savings, rehabilitation, and more humane treatment.

The purpose of this chapter is to explore what we mean by diversion in the criminal justice system, what we have and have not learned from programs or approaches that can fairly use the label, and what the issues are that must be considered in reacting to the concept of diversion generally and to its application to particular situations.

"Diversion"—or "early diversion"—has no real meaning in relationship to the criminal justice system in the absence of a context that tells us (1) what the process is by which diversion takes place; (2) what the person is diverted from—i.e., what is diversion instead of? and (3) what he is diverted to. Thus, if we take the Perry Mason image of the criminal process by which every person apprehended in a criminal act is arrested, charged, tried, and, if convicted, sentenced to prison, any disposition short of serving the full prison term could fairly be regarded an early diversion. This would include a decision of a policeman to let a traffic violation offender go with a tongue-lashing; a district attorney to drop a shoplifting case against a first offender because the store fails to prosecute; a judge to give a convicted person probation or a suspended sentence; or a parole board to release a prisoner at his first parole hearing. These are all diversions from a more serious burden that would have been imposed but for the action taken.

But these early exits from the system are familiar and of long standing and may fairly be regarded as part of the system itself and will generally be so regarded in this chapter. What is usually meant by current calls for early diversion is, to put it simply, something that is *new*. This may consist of (1) recognition that some categories of offenders such as drunks, addicts and the mentally ill are special candidates for diversion; (2) new procedures or incentives to raise the number, the percentage or the seriousness-of-offense level of the offenders who leave the system early; (3) new screening devices to select those who will leave; or (4) new places, programs or opportunities for those who do leave. Many of the most important new programs are built on well-recognized early exit points in the system. Thus the California probation subsidy program is basically a financial and political device to get judges to put more offenders on probation, and the Manhattan Court Employment Project is an elaborate administrative mechanism to encourage and improve a practice long in use in many places—the suspension of prosecution on condition that the offender show the court he can and will hold down a job.

We will try not to agonize over what does and does not qualify as an early diversion program; the chapter will try to focus on issues raised by relatively recent programs.

Although this chapter is part of a book on corrections, it necessarily looks at diversion at earlier stages of the system. For one of the principal purposes of diversion is to offer an offender the kind of treatment which under certain correctional programs he would receive only after conviction, but without the delays, the pressure on the offender, or the costs of full processing through the system. Thus, in one sense, diversion is simply a way of starting correctional treatment sooner. More broadly, it has become clear that for many purposes the criminal justice system should be seen not as a line but as a closed loop that has as its starting point the offender at the time of the offense and as its closing point and its goal the return of the offender to responsibility for his own life. As discussed below there are strong arguments that for many offenders the trip around the circle is meaningless and damaging and costly—and that therefore we should consider whether and under what circumstances we should and can leave offenders where we find them.

Early diversion may be seen as a means of implementing a number of theories that underlie current efforts at correctional reform. Two of these deserve brief mention. Perhaps the most important for our purposes—and central to the Crime Commission's recommendations in the corrections area—is that every effort should be made to avoid relieving an offender of the responsibility and burdens of making decisions and managing his own life, since the goal is to return him to society better able to cope on his own. One manifestation of this theory is that if he must be institutionalized, the offender should have the privilege/burden of participating in decisions affecting him—thus the proposal for "collaborative institutions" that was at the heart of the commission's recommendations about prisons. Another manifestation was that the absence from society—necessitating under the best of circumstances a break in the sequence of responsibility—should be as slight as possible.

Also underlying early diversion is the so-called "labeling" theory. This theory hypothesizes that society's label may be accepted in part by the individual himself. Therefore, imposing the status and label of a convicted criminal makes recidivism more likely. Closely related is the recognition that the label limits or precludes opportunities an offender may have to be reintegrated into lawful society.

It is beyond the scope of this chapter to consider in depth the relation of early diversion to theories of corrections or crime causation, and therefore we have dealt only briefly with those issues. However, in addition to whatever theories may have contributed to the movement for diversion we have a strong sense that perhaps most important of all is the recognition that the system is hopelessly overloaded with cases; is brutal, corrupt and ineffective; and that therefore every case removed is a gain.

Hundreds of projects have been undertaken around the country which have early diversion as a component. Because of the fragmentation of the criminal justice operations among counties, cities, states, and the federal system, it is impossible to make even a rough quantitative assessment of the extent to which offenders are being diverted out of the system. The nation's sources of information about the operation of the conventional parts of the criminal justice system are limited. And since, as will be discussed below, early diversion takes place in many forms and involves many agencies which we normally do not consider to be part of the criminal justice system, we simply must accept that we do not know, except impressionistically, how much real change the movement toward diversion has made. It may be that notwithstanding all the money and all the writing about diversion, only a relatively few offenders are being treated differently than a decade earlier. (One example of how easy it is to be misled on the extent of actual change was the finding by a study at the Harvard Center for Criminal Justice that more than two years after the Crime Commission had recommended community residential facilities and at a time when much was being written and said about them, less than 2 percent of adult offenders in state custody were in residential facilities outside the walls of traditional prisons.)

Unfortunately, the slipshod handling of evaluation and reporting under the Law Enforcement Assistance Act makes it unlikely that even several years from now we will know what the extent of the shift toward early diversion has been or what impact it has had on crime, criminal justice costs, efficiency, morale, or rehabilitation. Despite the lack of any real quantitative information on the scope of early diversion or probing evaluation of its effects, it may be useful to describe briefly as a basis for discussion and analysis some of the major types of diversion projects—both by the points in the system at which diversion takes place (second part of this chapter) and by the type of offender for whom they are designed (third part). Much of the description of these projects draws on or paraphrases secondary literature. The bibliographical note at the end of this volume indicates the sources of such description.

Diversion Projects: Exit Points

There are hundreds of new diversion programs being undertaken in the United States. They result in the offender's leaving the traditional criminal justice system at various points from before arrest until after conviction. The way the offender's case is disposed of depends on where and by whom in the system diversion is considered, and the fact of diversion, in turn, has an impact on the various agencies in the system. To try to illuminate some of these issues, this second part of the chapter will consider examples of diversion projects at different points in the system. It needs emphasis that the projects listed here and in the third part are not necessarily the most important or the best of their kind. They are simply among those about which we have been able to obtain enough information to raise issues for consideration. It is also worth noting that the fact that the Vera Institute of Justice of New York City appears repeatedly in this paper is no accident. Vera has carried the concept of early diversion into practice at various stages of the criminal justice system. Because of its pragmatic approach and its record of success in setting up projects, it has provided an important incentive for the development of such projects nationally.

DIVERSION BY POLICE

In most jurisdictions, the statutory authority of the police to arrest is mandatory not discretionary. Nonetheless, the police everywhere have always exercised broad discretion to decide whether or not to arrest. Of course, if serious crimes or highly dangerous conduct is involved, the police will arrest and participate in an offender's prosecution. But crime connected with family arguments, such misdemeanors as public drunkenness, loitering and disorderly conduct, mildly destructive behavior by juveniles, and minor crimes generally will often lead to a decision not to arrest or take into custody. Thus at a pre-arrest stage of the process large numbers of potential offenders have already been diverted in the sense that they have been dropped from the system.

Even after an offender is brought into the station, police power (if not legal authority) to handle a case informally continues. In some cities substantial numbers of cases are dropped at the station-house in a completely invisible, informal, and nonlegal procedure. A case may be dropped unconditionally or on condition that the offender stay out of trouble or make restitution.

On the other hand, in some cities there are well structured hearing procedures for juveniles which are similar to intake hearings of juvenile courts. There are formal notices to parents and minors setting the time and place for a meeting with a "hearing officer." The police officer in charge of the hearing seeks to make a common-sense judgment on whether the juvenile should be sent to court. He takes into account such factors as the juvenile's prior record and his reputation with the police and the community as a troublemaker, the likelihood that the family will cooperate in keeping the juvenile out of trouble, and the extent to which the police may be criticized for being too lenient if the offense was serious or if there is further trouble. While the participation of the juvenile and his parents is voluntary in the sense they can opt for a court appearance, there is in fact great pressure to cooperate in order to stay out of court. Often the police will use this pressure and the juvenile's desire to avoid a police record to get a confession for their files that will enable them to treat the case as closed and which may have an *in terrorem* effect on the future misconduct of the juvenile.

Police Referral—A much broader role for the police is involved in proposals that the police become a referral agency to effect non-criminal disposition of arrested persons. Vera Institute's Manhattan Bowery project for handling drunks (discussed in third part below) is one example, although the police role is a limited one. The New York City Police Department announced in the fall of 1972 that addicts arrested for offenses or misdemeanors will be offered an opportunity to be sent to a drug treatment program with submission of their cases for prosecution held in abeyance. Addicts who agree to treatment and who are accepted by a treatment center would be paroled, with the court's approval, in the custody of the center. One possible role for the community service officer recommended by the President's Crime Commission would be to screen persons arrested for relatively minor crimes and dismiss or refer to social or health agencies those without a serious criminal record.

There is no way of knowing how many police departments are now engaged in such dismissal-referral programs. What is clear is that to the extent they become visible and acknowledged, such programs have an important bearing on the continuing debate about police participation in a social service role. That debate is usually in terms of how police resources should be allocated. But police responsibility for early diversion raises deeper questions as to whether it is inherently inappropriate for the police to make corrections-type decisions and whether the whole postarrest situation is simply too pressured to ensure that a suspect's decision to accept a particular form of treatment (such as participation in a methadone program) is truly voluntary. At least until more is known of the extent and content of diversion by the police in this country, one should probably be cautious about taking a general position about the appropriateness of police agencies undertaking this responsibility. There are undoubtedy some situations—particularly where the decision is not onerous—in which a police role would be generally acceptable. There are others where, without strong protections for the suspect including providing him with a lawyer, there would be general agreement that the police should not take responsibility for diversion. There is one point on which we believe there should be no disagreement. To the extent the police are making arrangements for the conditional dropping of cases, the practice should be openly acknowledged rather than hidden as it so often is.

British Practice—In considering formalized diversion by the police, the British experience may provide some guidance. Great Britain has proceeded further than the United States in formalizing police diversion practices by establishing in 1968 the Juvenile Bureaux within the Metropolitan Police in London. Up to that time the practice of the London police was to arrest and charge juvenile offenders in much the same way as adults. The changes included amending police procedure so that many young offenders would be brought in on a summons instead of a formal charge. But the heart of the new system is use of the "caution" by the police as a substitute for court proceedings.

Police Juvenile Bureaux personnel are responsible for gathering information from the Children's Departments, Probation and Education Services, and other revelant agencies about a young person brought to the station for an alleged offense. In most cases an officer will visit the juvenile's home. A background report is prepared which, together with the evidence relating to the offense, is considered by the chief inspector in charge of the Bureau who decides whether or not the young offender should be prosecuted. The cautioning procedure, which in 1970 was used for 39 percent of juveniles who committed offenses, is based on the following criteria:

a. The offender must admit the offense.
b. The parents must agree that the child be cautioned.
c. The person victimized must be willing to leave the matter to the police.

The caution is given under formal circumstances at the police station by a chief inspector in uniform. While a juvenile's record is relevant to whether he will have the benefit of the cautioning procedure, the fact that he has been cautioned previously does not necessarily mean that he will be prosecuted if he commits a subsequent offense.

At the outset, other social agencies responsible for juveniles were concerned that the police would not be adequately trained, that they would tend to pass judgment on the character of the juvenile, and that they might abuse confidential information. Representatives of the London Police say that care has been taken in the choice and training of personnel so as to eliminate grounds for such concern.

DIVERSION FROM PRETRIAL DETENTION

Programs to reduce the extent of pretrial detention have a dual importance in considering early diversion. It is true, of course, that neither the situation from which diversion takes place nor the alternative—release (with or without supervision)—is generally thought of as a correctional program. Nonetheless, diversion from this traditional stage of the criminal justice system is of great importance, because pretrial detention has an enormous and generally damaging impact on many arrested persons. Furthermore, as exemplified by the Des Moines project referred to below, such programs may facilitate subsequent diversion of the defendant after conviction.

The Vera Institute of Justice in New York City has pioneered in developing a "point" system for release on personal recognizance and subsequently adapted that system to enable the New York City Police Department to issue station-house summonses instead of detaining persons accused of minor crimes. If a desk officer in a station house can verify by telephone that an accused person has a sufficient number of points based on "roots in the community," the police can release him with a summons instead of taking him to arraignment court. The Vera summons is now used statewide in New York and is available for all crimes except felonies, unless the accused is under the influence of alcohol or drugs.

A similar program in California showed that more than 90 percent of those arrested persons whose community ties were investigated and who were released appeared for arraignment. Since 1969 police in California are required to consider station-house release of persons charged with misdemeanors.

Similar bail and summons projects based on the Vera experiments have been duplicated in many other cities and states. The Des Moines, Iowa, Model Neighborhood Corrections Project is an example of how pretrial release can be tied to correctional programs. Indeed, the purpose of the project was to permit an offender to show his reliability during his pretrial release period and thereby improve his chances for probation or some other nonprison sentence following trial. The project dealt with persons who did not qualify for release under the Vera-type criteria. After screening, those selected for release were supervised by staff of the project who linked the releasees with social agencies and other existing community resources. Follow-up studies have shown that those released in the project were as good risks as those released on money bail, and that, compared with a similar group of nonreleased defendants, they were less likely to be convicted if tried, less likely to be imprisoned if convicted, and likely to receive shorter sentences if imprisoned.

PRETRIAL DIVERSION: PROSECUTORIAL DISCRETION

A large percentage of cases is disposed of in the prosecutor's office. Many of these dispositions are the result of agreed-upon guilty pleas and generally they lead to further processing within the criminal justice system. Some cases are dropped unconditionally on the basis of the prosecutor's judgment that the case is not strong enough or the offense is not serious. In some cases the decision not to prosecute is based on an agreement between the prosecutor and the accused that the accused will seek some other form of treatment or change his life in other ways, such as seeking psychiatric care, getting a job, participating in an educational program, or making restitution to the victim. Generally there are no stated standards or guidelines as to how the prosecutor will act in different kinds of situations. District Attorney William Cahalan of Wayne County, Michigan, has experimented with formalizing the procedures for

pretrial conferences and plea negotiation with the aim of relieving
the court of the task of docketing criminal cases. During a two-year
span, his office reported that the average delay between arrest and
trial was reduced from fourteen months to four. Tentative Draft
No. 5 of the American Law Institute Model Code of Pre-Arraignment Procedure includes detailed procedures for a precharge
screening conference at which the prosecutor and the accused and
his lawyer may consider informal disposition of the case including
diversion. Section 320.1 of the draft also provides for regulations
regarding the conference which "to the extent the prosecutor be-
lieves feasible in the effective administration of justice shall include
guidelines concerning action which the prosecutor will consider
taking in certain types of cases or factual situations."

One interesting elaboration of the notion of a formalized pretrial conference to consider early diversion is a proposed Philadelphia program known as "Arbitration as an Alternative" which is
designed to get the parties in a criminal action together so that
disputes between them can be settled, all under the control of the
district attorney. Arbitration in the settlement of personal injury
suits has for some time been in use in Philadelphia, and the proposed experiment represents an extension of this model to criminal
proceedings.

One of the most important types of programs for early diversion
envisioned by the American Law Institute proposal is the so-called
"court employment" project, again based on a Vera Institute innovation, the Manhattan Court Employment Project. This project,
begun in 1968, has served as a model for a large number of similar
projects around the country and is one of the most promising types
of diversion projects at the prosecution stage. The Manhattan Court
Employment Project intervenes in the usual court process just after
arrest. Accused persons who meet the eligibility criteria are asked
if they wish to participate in the project in order to earn a recommendation to the court after 90 days that charges against them be
dismissed. In order to be recommended for a dismissal participants
must not be rearrested nor use narcotics. They must keep all appointments with project staff and prospective employers; they must
attend and become involved in counseling sessions; and they must
make satisfactory vocational adjustments.

During the 90 days, a participant works closely with two people
—his representative, who typically has served time in prison himself and serves as counselor, and a career developer, who advises and

refers the defendant to job opportunities. Most participants require more than one job placement. They are also encouraged to attend a group session every week, and they receive other appropriate referrals, such as to schools, drug treatment centers, hospitals, and welfare centers.

During the first year of operation, dismissal of charges was recommended and accepted for 39 percent of the participants; for the second year, 46 percent; and for the third year, 61 percent. For "dismissed" participants (those for whom dismissal of charges was successfully obtained) unemployment fourteen months after dismissal was 16.1 percent for a sample group as compared to 40 percent for terminated participants (those who failed in the project). The rearrest rate for "dismissed" participants was 15.8 percent; for participants terminated from the project, 30.8 percent; and for a comparison group drawn from the general court population, 46.1 percent.

In evaluating these figures, it should be noted that eligibility requirements have varied over the life of the project and that the comparison of those who stayed with the project and those who dropped out is necessarily not on a matched basis.

POSTCONVICTION DIVERSION

The problem of defining "diversion" is presented in its most difficult form in the postconviction stage. Probation and suspended sentences are established parts of criminal justice administration, so here it is particularly important to be clear as to what the new practices or programs are that are being considered. In fact we probably can find elements of most of the new postconviction programs in earlier probation programs. What is new may be a difference of degree: the greater numbers of offenders who have an opportunity to participate in the programs or more intensive supervision or services.

Three aspects of postconviction programs deserve discussion: (1) greater willingness now to return to the community offenders who have traditionally been incarcerated; (2) the need for special incentives to encourage the early return of offenders to the community; and (3) the development of new techniques of support or supervision in the community. Since another chapter deals with community treatment programs, we will only give a few examples of each of these developments in order to provide a basis for some observations and questions that bear on diversion at this stage.

Diversion to Community—Two of the most important examples of diverting to the community offenders who traditionally would have been confined are the Community Treatment Program of the California Youth Authority and the closing down of the juvenile institutions by the Massachusetts Department of Youth Services.

The California Community Treatment Program unquestionably was the most influential single source of encouragement for diversion to the community in the late 1960s and early 1970s. It had completed its first phase at the time the President's Crime Commission was in existence, and the commission's report provided a means for disseminating the message of the program: offenders treated in the community will be less dangerous than those incarcerated. Furthermore, this message had enormous influence on the commission's Corrections Task Force in encouraging a broad advocacy of community treatment—not only for juveniles but for adults as well. Although the program was carried on as a research project, the large numbers of offenders in the project and the long period of time over which it has operated entitle it to be regarded as a major treatment program.

Male and female Youth Authority wards from Sacramento, Stockton, San Francisco, and Modesto were randomly assigned during the first phase of the program to the intensive community program or to the usual Youth Authority traditional institutional structure. During the first two phases (1961–1969) almost 700 cases were studied with an additional 330 in the control group. The project's reports showed that those treated in the community had dramatically lower failure rates than those sent to the Youth Authority's regular institutions. The figures used in the Crime Commission report were 28 percent failure among the Community Treatment group, compared to 52 percent for the control group. However, some observers have suggested that at least part of the differential may be due to more lenient treatment by parole agents and other decision-making authorities of subsequent misconduct by those in the Community Treatment group. In response, it has been suggested that the very fact the Community Treatment group was seen as special may have resulted in its members being under closer surveillance than other youths and hence more likely to come to the attention of the authorities. This issue has not been resolved and may never be, but at least it appears that in terms of cost savings and personal and social adjustment those sent to the community did better.

The most dramatic example of releasing traditionally confined offenders is the closing down of the juvenile institutions in the state program undertaken by Massachusetts Youth Services Commissioner Jerome Miller. After a frustrating attempt to establish therapeutic communities in the institutions and further frustration in gradual closings, Miller in a matter of a few months simply closed down all but the short-term detention facility. He believed a system without juvenile institutions would have less crime, and, having made that judgment, he undertook to find alternatives in the community for the seven hundred juveniles previously held in his institutions. The Harvard Law School Center for Criminal Justice is making an intensive evaluation of this program, including a cohort study, and should over the next few years be able to document its effects.

Incentives for Diversion—The second issue referred to above—the need for incentives to encourage diversion—raises puzzling questions. If diversion is generally quicker, cheaper, and more humane and if there is doubt that it endangers public safety, why are so many offenders still going the traditional route? Part of the explanation is the lack of reliable data on the effects of diversion on an offender's dangerousness and on the deterrent message of criminal sanctions generally. In the face of this gap in our knowledge, presumably the slowness of change is explained by a degree of real or assumed punitiveness on the part of the public, the inherent conservatism of criminal justice officials, and the natural vested interest that everyone has to continue to do his job as he always has.

The money available under the Law Enforcement Assistance Administration program was designed to provide incentives for change, but the combination of the "block grant" approach in the legislation and weak administration at the federal and state levels has substantially reduced the federal program's effectiveness as an instrument of change. Thus to date it is hard to measure LEAA's impact on diversion. The most comprehensive attempt to provide an incentive for moving offenders to the community is the California Probation Subsidy. This program aims at encouraging counties to divert offenders from the state correctional institutions by offering a financial incentive proportionate to numbers diverted. The funds made available to the counties also enable them to offer better probation supervision and services. Experience during the first two years indicates that the counties can give improved service to five or six probationers with the subsidy saved on every new uncommitted case held at the county level. So far there are no data that would permit an evaluation of the impact of the subsidy program on crime in California or on the lives of those diverted. What does seem clear, however, is that the subsidy technique is an effective method for diverting many offenders from the prison population in a jurisdiction that has made the policy judgment that it wishes to do so.

Improved Supervision—The third aspect of postconviction projects referred to above—improvement of supervision or services in the community—is relevant to diversion at all stages. However, the further along the system an offender proceeds, the greater the pressure to show that the alternative to which he is diverted has real substance. Every postconviction diversion program seeks to justify its existence in large part by the substance of the services and/or supervision it provides to the offender as an alternative to incarceration. Since there is virtually no persuasive evaluation of the effectiveness of the new alternatives, policy-makers and funding agencies necessarily are forced to proceed on the basis of hunch, faith, or desperation about the traditional alternatives. One generalization that can be made about the alternatives offered is that most tend to combine in varying degrees three principal elements: (1) pressure or encouragement to the offender to take responsibility for his life in the community in which he will be living; (2) supportive services; (3) a relatively noncoercive form of supervision.

An example of an early experiment that appears to combine these features is the misdemeanant probation program in Royal Oak, Michigan, in which citizen volunteer sponsors are used on a one-to-one basis with misdemeanant probationers. Started in 1960 by Judge Keith J. Leenhouts, the program had around five hundred misdemeanants on some form of probation by the end of 1969. Twenty-four different treatment techniques are available in the program, including group therapy and assigned work detail projects whereby an offender can earn dismissal of his case and erasure of his record. The number of sponsors available in 1969 was about 250, with 100 awaiting assignments. This allows for considerable freedom in matching sponsors to probationers. An evaluative study of the program found that the recidivism rate for the program probationers was half that of probationers under a conventional misdemeanant probation system.

The Vera Institute has experimented more recently with diverting convicted misdemeanants to nonprison sentences, also using volunteer efforts. The Bronx Sentencing Project began operations in 1968 as an attempt to provide judges with short-form presentence reports. Using the experience of the Bail and Summons projects in developing reliable, verified information about defendants, the project hoped to change sentencing patterns by providing information on some of the 88 percent of convicted adult misdemeanants who were being sentenced by judges who did not have before them reports on the offenders' backgrounds and social histories.

The effect on the increase of nonprison sentences was slight until the project developed a referral capability. Failure rates had suggested that referral to a community agency rather than traditional probation might be more relevant for these offenders (who were indeed higher risks, having been taken from the defendant pool after the lower-risk candidates for probation had been identified). After experimenting with several community agencies, Vera decided to focus on referrals to one, Volunteer Opportunities, Inc. (VOI). And instead of recommending a sentence of conditional discharge for those cases it wished to refer to VOI, it recommended adjournment of the cases for one to six months, with sentencing to take place after the experience of working with VOI. For participants with satisfactory progress, the reward is avoiding a prison sentence. VOI's services include group and individual counseling; assistance on personal problems such as housing, health, job training, and employment; tutoring; and recreation.

The examples given above are necessarily arbitrarily selected from the hundreds of relatively new postconviction diversion programs. Other chapters describe other programs. No one today can have more than an impressionistic view of the extent to which community alternatives are replacing incarceration, and it will be years before we can know the answer to even this preliminary question which requires only a relatively simple "counting" type of research. And, of course, before judgment can be made about the relative effectiveness of diversion-type programs in reducing recidivism, the results of much deeper and more difficult evaluation must be done. Doubts such as those raised about the California Community Treatment project must be resolved. We must have the results of the few in-depth research projects now underway, and long-term and costly research on many existing projects must be undertaken.

Lest the current fashion in this country for diversion projects suggests that the United States is the leader in this movement, it is worth noting that we have probably been relatively slow to seek alternatives to incarceration. In Sweden noninstitutional treatment is used much more frequently than in the United States. A report of the Advisory Council on the Penal System on Non-Custodial and Semi-Custodial Penalties in Great Britain includes among its recommendations a suggestion that offenders should perform a specified number of hours of service to the community in their spare time in lieu of incarceration.

In Israel, a judge is able to sentence an offender to work in a police station by day and return to home at night. This is an outgrowth of a system that existed when Palestine was a British mandate, when the police themselves, not the judge, made the decision to assign prisoners to police station work. A number of prisoners in Israel are also diverted into the army. Those selected are put initially into a military scout program in the prisons, which is followed by three months of additional training under military supervision, then transfer to regular army units. For most participants prison terms are suspended at this point. To cite these examples is not to endorse them—merely to suggest that other nations have been and are grappling with the same issues as we are.

"Special Population" Diversion Programs

The second part of this chapter examined the criminal justice system chronologically with examples of diversion projects at particular points in the suspect's or offender's movement through the system. Another approach is to consider certain types of offenders whose personal difficulties or youth make them candidates for less punitive and more therapeutic treatment. This third part will consider briefly some examples of diversion programs for juveniles, drunks, narcotic addicts, and those in need of psychiatric treatment.

JUVENILES

In the earlier discussion of diversion at various stages of the criminal process, several programs involving juveniles were outlined. This section will analyze in greater depth some of the special issues relating to juvenile diversion programs, particularly those raised by the President's Crime Commission's recommended Youth Services Bureaus.

The creation of the juvenile court system in the United States was an attempt to treat the juvenile offender in a noncriminal, more therapeutic way. But over time most juvenile courts have become in essence criminal courts with criminal-type dispositions. One consequence has been the United States Supreme Court's imposition on juvenile courts of many of the due process protections required of adult courts. Another is the search for new means of meeting the original goals envisioned for the juvenile courts.

One of the most important recommendations of the 1967 report of the Crime Commission was that communities should establish new agencies as a means of diverting juveniles from the criminal system, including keeping them out of the juvenile court.

The commission suggested that such agencies—which it labeled Youth Services Bureaus—should be available for (1) youths who have not committed criminal acts but whose problems at home, in school, or in the community may lead them to do so if they do not receive help, and (2) delinquents whose misconduct is rooted in similar problems. The commission report states:

> Such an agency ideally would be located in a comprehensive community center and would serve both delinquent and nondelinquent youths. While some referrals to the Youth Services Bureau would normally originate with parents, schools, and other sources, the bulk of the referrals could be expected to come from the police and the juvenile court intake staff, and police and court referrals should have special status in that the Youth Services Bureau would be required to accept them all . . . These agencies would act as central coordinators of all community services for young people and would also provide services lacking in the community or neighborhood, especially ones designed for less seriously delinquent juveniles.

Because of the commission's recommendation and the availability of massive funding from the Law Enforcement Assistance Administration, there came into being agencies with an enormous number of programs bearing the Youth Services Bureau label but with widely differing forms and objectives. A seminar held at the University of Chicago Criminal Research Center in 1971 to collect and exchange information on the development of Youth Services Bureaus revealed how varied and conflicting the rationales of existing bureaus are. Some of those responsible for the new agencies sought to work with existing community agencies, while others wanted to have minimal contact with the existing system. Some found it difficult to distinguish between the limited aim of diverting children from the criminal justice system and the more general aim of delinquency prevention. Some believed bureaus should provide direct service; others believed that they should rely on mobilizing existing community resources. In one instance a teen-age drop-in center called itself a Youth Services Bureau in order to obtain support.

The general impression that emerged was that many local agencies had absorbed the name and the federal funds but felt no obligation to accept the commission's goals of creating comprehensive local diversion agencies.

The situation nationally was summarized by a request of the California Youth Authority for funds to conduct a national survey of Youth Services Bureaus in which it stated:

> Nationally we have no information regarding the total numbers of children served. . . . We do not even know where or how many Youth Services Bureaus exist. We lack information on the relative cost of the services provided. We lack information about the effectiveness of various types of models used for the delivery of services, and we lack specific information regarding whether or not justice agencies and youths themselves are using these new alternatives to the criminal justice system. In brief, we know little about a strongly supported idea that is commanding more and more federal dollars under the umbrella of prevention.

Massachusetts Experience—The differing form these agencies have taken is exemplified by the form in which they have developed in one state—Massachusetts—which has sought to evaluate their operations. The Governor's Committee on Law Enforcement and Administration of Criminal Justice has funded four bureaus (known as Youth Resources Bureaus to distinguish them from the Department of Youth Services, the state's juvenile correctional agency). Each is based on a different model:

1. Brockton Youth Resources Bureau: This bureau sees itself as a clearing-house for agency activity and information, positioning itself between sources of referrals (police, court, schools) and sources of community services.
2. Waltham Youth Resources Bureau: Its approach is clinical, relying on psychiatric and psychological evaluations, followed by an appropriate treatment plan, minimizing contact work with outside agencies.
3. Cambridge Youth Resources Bureau: It has concentrated on a detached worker model of delinquency prevention.
4. New Bedford Youth Resources Bureau: It is a broad juvenile delinquency prevention program based on maximum participation of community residents who are being trained by the program as apprentice social workers.

The fact that the bureaus have taken diverse forms is not necessarily bad. However, there is something peculiar about a decision-making and funding process that does not look beyond the label of an agency in deciding that it has merit. Furthermore, it is simply not clear yet whether the commission's recommendation of Youth Services Bureaus has succeeded in a major shift toward early diversion of juvenile offenders, or whether the concept has been distorted and the label misused to provide a means for funding a miscellaneous collection of pre-existing and newly devised programs for juveniles.

Vera Program—Even where they have sought to follow the Crime Commission's model, it appears that few of the bureaus have succeeded in producing an agency that will "go to bat" for delinquent and predelinquent youth who now tend to lose out in their access to needed services. The Neighborhood Youth Diversion Program begun early in 1971 by the Vera Institute of Justice in New York City appears to come close to meeting the Youth Services Bureau goals in design and execution. As described by Vera,

> Its aim is to divert young people in trouble with the law from the conventional police-probation-Family Court processes to a community-based program of assistance and mediation. It is designed to do so by drawing on and, where necessary, constructing new community resources that can help resolve the problems of troubled youths. . . . It is based on a concept that perceives of rising delinquency in terms of unstable social conditions and of cultural patterns rather than merely of disturbed personalities.

The program operates in a limited section of the Bronx, New York, an area that in a little more than five years moved from a predominantly Jewish community to one overwhelmingly black and Puerto Rican. Many religious and social organizations moved to other locations or dissolved, with the result that the schools and other public agencies were unable to meet the needs of the residents.

The program works with young persons between the ages of twelve and fifteen and is run by people living in the community. Of all the program's elements, the most innovative is a device called the Forum, a series of panels of community residents who receive training as mediators and conciliators. Forum members work out the problems surrounding minor offenses committed by neighborhood juveniles and deal with crises between parents and children which had often resulted in sending young people to the state training schools.

Cases are referred to the program from three sources—the Office of Probation, the Police Department's Youth Aid Division, and

Family Court. Referrals from agencies not involved in the juvenile justice system are not sought. (While this varies from the commission's Youth Services Bureau format, it may be the only way to ensure that those most in need of services do not come at the end of the line.)

Each case is assigned to an advocate, a person generally under 30 who also resides in the community. He acts as a counselor and a link to family, friends and schools, and provides assistance to outside referrals—especially for finding temporary homes, useful jobs, and education. All referrals are followed carefully to determine what is being done for the youth. The project has referral arrangements with more than 150 agencies, including boys' clubs, health centers, child welfare agencies, and drug programs. As described by Vera,

> Almost all cases go to a Forum hearing at some point during their participation in the program, usually early. Each Forum consists of three volunteer judges who live in the community and who agree to mediate. Usually two or three hearings are required. The Forum's task is not to make judgments and rulings, but to attempt to bring the disputing parties together to resolve their differences without reference to the formal criminal justice system. . . . During the first four months of the program, 21 cases were presented to Forums. All but one resolved the problems sufficiently to eliminate the necessity of Formal Court proceedings. One case was returned to Family Court.

An evaluation reported that the recidivism rate of those in the project was half that of a comparison group. It was also reported that between February and October 1971 the program was able to divert 36 percent of the delinquency cases and 21 percent of PINS (Persons in Need of Supervision) cases appearing in probation intake. The evaluation also indicated that the youths referred were not necessarily the more pliable and easy to work with. It was further reported that the program has had difficulty delivering services because (1) it lacked funds to purchase services, (2) there are few services in the area, (3) the indigenous staff is not part of the professional network that controls most of the social services in the city.

Sacramento County Project—Because so many serious criminal careers begin with truancy, running away from home, and other conduct not criminal for adults, the 601 Diversion Project of the Sacramento County Probation Department is worth noting. The project is testing whether juveniles charged with a 601 offense (a predelinquent offense) can be handled better through short-term family crisis therapy administered at intake by specially trained probation officers than through the traditional procedures of the juvenile court. Youths beyond control of their parents, runaways, truants, and others falling within section 601 of the Welfare and Institutions Code constitute over one-third of all juvenile court cases in Sacramento County.

In October of 1970, the project began receiving referrals on 601 matters from police, schools, parents, and other sources. Family sessions are held to discuss the problem, the first session usually within the first hour or two after referral. The counselor tries to have the family as a whole take responsibility for the problem. Locking up the youth is discouraged; what is sought is a return home with a commitment to work through the problem. If this seems impossible, an attempt is made to find a temporary place for the youth to stay. This is a voluntary procedure which requires the consent of both the parents and the youth.

Families are encouraged to return for subsequent discussions, although after the first session all sessions are essentially voluntary. Normally the maximum number of sessions is five, based on recent evidence that crisis counseling and short-term casework are one of the most effective ways of dealing with problems arising out of family situations and that extended casework is much more expensive and seems no more successful. In many cases counselors are in contact with the family by phone whether there is a follow-up session or not. All members of the family are encouraged to contact the counselor in the event of a continuing or additional problem.

During its first nine months the project handled 803 referrals involving opportunities for diversion but filed only eighteen court petitions. Court processing was thus necessary in only 2.2 percent of these referrals compared to 30.4 percent brought in on 601 charges in a three-month preproject period and 21.3 percent of the referrals handled in the normal manner in a control group. Youths handled during the first four months were followed for a period of seven months after the initial contact. During this period, 45.5 percent of the control group had been rebooked for a 601 or 602 offense (a 602 offense involves criminal conduct), while the comparable figure for the project group was 35 percent. This is an improvement of over 23 percent in the rate of repeat offenses. For 602 offenses, the rate for the control group was 23.4 percent and 15.3 percent for the project group—a drop in the rate of repeated offenses of 34.6 percent.

Data indicated that project youths required overnight detention in less than 10 percent of the cases while the figure for control cases is over 60 percent.

Foreign Experience—While comparisons are difficult, it appears that many foreign countries without our experience with juvenile courts have gone further on diversion of youths than we have. Juvenile courts have never existed in Sweden. In that country no one less than 15 years old can be prosecuted or put into prison for a criminal act. Child Welfare Councils, of which there are more than a thousand, have absolute jurisdiction over children below the age of 15. Youths 15 to 21 may be diverted from courts to the Child Welfare Councils at the discretion of the public prosecutor. Each council consists of five members, one a pastor of the Lutheran State Church, one a public school teacher, and at least two "chosen for their special interest in and dedication to the care of children and youth." Many cases that in this country would be treated as involving delinquency are seen as welfare problems and are handled as cases of neglect and dependency. Dissatisfaction with the juvenile court system in Great Britain led to the "caution" system used by some British police departments and described earlier in this chapter. We know that other countries deal with juvenile offenders in ways aimed at avoiding institutionalization. For example, a study supported by the Harvard Center for Criminal Justice showed that juvenile court judges in Israel use institutions as a last resort, having as alternative forms of treatment daytime rehabilitation centers, army workshops, assignments to kibbutzim, hostels, and group homes.

DRUG USERS

The tremendous increase in drug abuse in recent years has put enormous burdens on all agencies of the criminal justice system. While there is still a strong punitive element in our society's attitude toward drug users, recognition of the limited effectiveness of severe penalties and the inability of courts and correctional programs to process all potential defendants have led to a search for alternatives. In many jurisdictions marijuana users have been diverted out of the criminal system altogether by more permissive legislation or by police inaction. However, heroin possession and use remain serious crimes and a large percentage of those arrested for theft crimes or prostitution are addicts. For example, one judge in

the District of Columbia found that of 100 randomly selected felony cases coming before him, 72 involved addicts.

The problem of developing alternatives for drug offenders is even
more difficult than for juveniles, because there is so little evidence
that any of the available forms of service or support deal effectively
with addiction. The one possible exception of any quantitative significance is methadone maintenance as an alternative to heroin.
While some methadone projects have reported very high levels of
success in terms of abstention from other drugs and commission of
theft and prostitution crimes, other projects have not found dramatic drops in crime by those on methadone. Nonetheless hundreds
of drug diversion programs built on methadone have developed and
are used by the prosecutors and courts without much concern about
the long-term effect on the addict.

Like most formal diversion programs, the drug programs typically have criteria for what offenses will qualify or disqualify an
arrested person. For example, a program in the Philadelphia Court
of Common Pleas Pre-Indictment Program limits eligibility to a
defendant who has no prior conviction for the crime for which he
is currently charged. Others limit entry to those charged with misdemeanors or those without a record of violence. Because of the
court's desire to avoid having to process drug cases, admission criteria are likely to be liberally construed.

Many of the programs operate on the basis of a conditional suspension of charges with an understanding the charge will be
dropped if the conditions are met. Some require a guilty plea of the
defendant with sentence conditionally suspended. The conditions
typically include not committing future crimes; some will revoke
the suspension if continued drug use is reported or if there are reports that the defendant is not cooperating in treatment. Some programs require urine testing to implement the condition that the
defendant stay off drugs.

Some of the drug programs provide diversion opportunities before an arrested person gets to court. The New York City Police Department program (noted in the second part of this chapter) is one
example. Another is the District of Columbia's program for juveniles
under which Bail Agency personnel see juvenile addicts in the cell
block after their arrest. On the basis of their recommendation the
court may release the addict into the custody of a treatment program. However, the addict does not avoid trial by being in the pro-

gram even if he is being treated successfully, but presumably that success is reflected in the court's disposition.

New York and California have experimented with mandatory civil commitment of addicts, which in a sense is a form of diversion. In effect, civil commitment is a route from the traditional system to a theoretically noncriminal alternative at the sentencing stage. In New York the threat of a three-year civil commitment resulted in the program's being regarded by many as more punitive and severe than full processing by the criminal system. Understandably this view was held most strongly by those who doubted that anything of substantive value was being done that was likely to cure or help the addict.

Present efforts to divert addicts from the criminal system raise a number of perplexing issues. Among these are: (1) Does what addicts are being diverted to offer promise of rehabilitation? (2) Even if it does not, is it better to divert them out of the criminal system? (3) Is one effect of diversion that addicts are subject to some sort of control for longer than they otherwise would be? (4) What, if any, significant effects are the diversion programs in the aggregrate having on the operations of the nation's criminal justice agencies? It is simply too early to make any judgment on any of these issues.

DRUNKS

While programs to divert addicts must take account of punitive attitudes toward heroin users, there is virtually no controversy about the desirability of keeping out of the criminal justice system persons whose only crime is public drunkenness and related disorderly conduct. The President's Crime Commission recommended that public drunkenness not be a crime. Some who oppose this recommendation do so on the basis that probation with a suspended sentence is desirable in pressuring chronic drunks to enter treatment. However, a study by the San Diego Municipal Court showed no significant difference in rate or number of rearrests or time elapsed before rearrest among those referred to an alcoholic clinic, those required to participate in Alcoholics Anonymous, and those receiving no treatment. This study at least casts doubt on the use of criminal processing as a route to treatment. More broadly, it suggests that the central issue with drunks as with addicts is what form of processing of cases is best (least bad) when it appears that we have little hope for improving the defendant's prospects by anything that is done for or to him.

One of the first and best known programs for diverting drunks is the Vera Institute's Manhattan Bowery Project. The program provides a shelter for chronic alcoholics, who are kept on a short-term (usually five days) basis, offered medical care and an opportunity to dry out, and are counseled and assisted into one of 25 aftercare programs offering therapeutic and rehabilitative services. A rescue team, consisting of a rescue aide (usually a recovered alcoholic) and a plainclothes police officer, patrols the Bowery in an unmarked police vehicle. Participants in the project are free at all times to decline services or, if they accept initial treatment, to leave the program at any time. With the cooperation of St. Vincent's Hospital, a broader range of medical services is provided outside the detoxification infirmary.

It was anticipated that many of the project participants would return to the Bowery and a life of drinking, and would be readmitted to the project. Vera reports that in fact,

> during its first three and one-half years of operation, the project admitted about 3500 patients an average of three times each, for a total of about 10,000 admissions . . . Some of the men had been treated as often as 10 or more times. . . . The project has confirmed that rehabilitation for many Bowery men cannot be measured in conventional terms such as permanent sobriety, holding steady jobs, . . . establishing families and other social ties.

On the other hand, the project has discovered that the number of men prepared to accept some form of aftercare plan has risen steadily. Expanded programs for aftercare, including supported work situations, is seen as the next step.

The effect on the criminal justice system is significant. Arrests of derelict alcoholics in the Bowery area have dropped as much as 80 percent. Police officers formerly assigned to derelict control have returned to regular patrol duties.

Projects similar to the Manhattan Bowery Project exist in many other communities. The Boston South End Center for Alcoholics and Unattached Persons offers assistance to skid-row inebriates approached on the streets who agree to accept help. Assistance includes referrals to existing community agencies providing medical, job placement, housing, and welfare services. Eighty percent of the men approached for this project responded willingly, suggesting once more that the threat of passing through the criminal justice system is not needed to motivate chronic drunks into treatment.

Another project with almost the same approach is the St. Louis

Detoxification and Diagnostic Evaluation Center. This program hospitalizes alcoholics for seven days on a voluntary basis, providing medical treatment, social, vocational, and employment counseling; group therapy; lectures, films, and sociodrama; and Alcoholics Anonymous. Aftercare plans include housing, employment, and further treatment if necessary and desired.

An excellent analysis of programs for drunks in various cities appears in Raymond Nimmer, *Two Million Unnecessary Arrests,* published by the American Bar Foundation.

DIVERSION TO PSYCHIATRIC TREATMENT

One of the major but invisible routes of the criminal justice system is by transfer to the mental health treatment system. It is not uncommon that the police make the judgment that a person arrested for a relatively minor offense should be treated as a psychiatric case rather than a criminal one. One of the scandals of the criminal justice operation has been another form of "diversion"— holding defendants in mental institutions as unable to stand trial sometimes for periods far in excess of what their sentences would have been if they had been tried and found guilty.

Diversion to mental health treatment has been one of the informal methods by which prosecutors and judges have been able to avoid placing a criminal stigma on relatively well-to-do persons without substantial criminal records who may be charged with crime. Arrangements may be made to have a defendant see a private psychiatrist or spend time in a psychiatric hospital as a condition of the ultimate dropping of charges. While theoretically the same kind of arrangements might be made for the indigent defendant, he is less likely to have help from his lawyer or family in working out plans that give the courts and prosecutors confidence that some effective treatment will follow.

We know of no data on the effect of psychiatric treatment on those diverted from criminal justice processing, but perhaps this misses the point. Perhaps all that is really sought here, as in the drug area, is some plausible diversion route for those for whom criminal treatment is seen as inappropriate.

A study completed in 1972 by the Georgetown University School of Medicine reports on the impact of a three-year experimental project in which one hundred accused persons in the District of Columbia with possible mental problems were diverted from trial to private or community health programs. These one hundred defendants were compared with one hundred cases going through the regular court processes. The study reported that in general there was not a higher incidence of rearrest among the diversion cases and that costs per person were less. Clearly no single study can tell us much about the possible advantages or disadvantages of diverting criminal defendants to the mental health system. But the Georgetown report is helpful as a reminder that with good research and evaluation we might be able to get some sense of what is at stake with various diversion alternatives.

Issues Relating to Early Diversion

The first part of this chapter outlined briefly some of the reasons for the attempts to divert offenders from the criminal justice system. The second and third parts sought by examples to give an impressionistic picture of what some of these attempts have been and the experience with them. By way of conclusion, this fourth part will suggest, in a necessarily superficial and summary form, what we believe to be the major problems and issues that must be taken account of in deciding what the scope and form of diversion programs should be.

EFFECT OF DETERRENCE

It is probably fair to say that deterrence—the discouragement of potential offenders through the imposition of punishment on one who is caught—is the most important theoretical goal of criminal sanctions. To the extent diversion projects result in a less onerous imposition on offenders than they would have received had they been kept in the traditional criminal justice system, there is the possibility of dilution of deterrence. Of course, many of the diversion programs include obligations or limitations that most people would find undesirable. And many represent a fairer and more rational technique for providing relatively lenient treatment for classes of offenders, some of whose cases might previously have been dropped altogether on an invisible and haphazard basis. (With respect to this latter point, however, some would argue that invisibility and informality may be the best of both worlds—that one can get the deterrent effect of the formal system of penal sanctions while still dropping cases on a bootleg basis.) In any event, it is clearly important before drawing any conclusion as to the likely effect of a particular project to consider its impact on the whole class of potential offenders from whom it draws its population and on potential offenders generally.

Most important, one must be enormously tentative about the effects on deterrence, because so little is known about the extent and method by which the deterrent message is communicated and how effective it is in its impact on any particular group under particular circumstances. The development of the many new diversion projects provides opportunities to begin to seek answers to such questions. But, as noted below, little research of this sort is underway.

FAILURE TO RESTRAIN

Another stated goal of criminal sanctions is taking dangerous persons out of circulation. Proponents of early diversion are met with the argument that they are increasing the general risk to the public by putting offenders back into the community at a relatively early stage. This argument is plausible, but it fails to take account of the possibility that the impact of whatever treatment program follows diversion may make the offender less dangerous than the treatment that follows conventional disposition. To measure the net effect on the offender's dangerousness, we would have to weigh (1) the virtual guarantee that the community will be safe from crime by the offender during incarceration offset by the volume of crime during the offender's lifetime following release from prison against (2) the volume of crime during the offender's lifetime if a diversion alternative is followed. While there is some data (notably from the California Treatment Project) suggesting that recidivism may be lower for persons who have been diverted to treatment in the community, we lack the data that would permit even rudimentary comparisons of the sort suggested. The development of such data may be the most important research need facing criminal justice administration, since it would permit resolution of what is probably the most politically volatile issue in the field. For the present, we have to settle for reminders to those who say diversion programs are endangering public safety that they *may* be wrong—that aggregate exposure to the risk of crime may be decreased rather than increased by diversion away from incarceration. At the same time, those who by reason of hunch or idealism are committed to diversion and deinstitutionalization must be prepared to acknowledge that they may be wrong—that perhaps they are fostering a more dangerous society.

DIVERSION TO WHAT?

Early diversion has become a fashionable concept. Unfortunately, this has led to the widespread and promiscuous use of the diversion label to apply to all sorts of activities. In many instances existing programs have been renamed Youth Services Bureaus or given other diversion-like labels to qualify for funding from Law Enforcement Assistance Administration funds or just to appear to be up-to-date.

One of the most disturbing aspects of this process has been the preoccupation of administrators and funding agencies with the fact and mechanics of diversion, without much consideration of the adequacy of what the offender is diverted to. Many of the reasons for this tendency are obvious. Much of the incentive to develop diversion programs is the reduction of the caseload for jails, courts, and correctional programs and facilities, and the fact of diversion accomplishes this purpose—at least temporarily—even if the offender is being diverted to nothing.

Many of the kinds of services the diverted offenders need are in short supply or are costly and the offender group is likely to be harder to service than others. For example, agencies responsible for job training or placement recognize that their success record will be lower and their headaches greater when they try to help offenders. It is not surprising therefore that with limited resources and enormous demands these agencies respond poorly to offenders unless there is some special pressure or incentive to do so. Indeed, it was in recognition of this problem that the President's Crime Commission proposed the development of youth-serving agencies at the local level with specific responsibility for providing or acquiring services for juveniles diverted from the juvenile court. And it was for similar reasons that the commission and others have proposed service-purchase arrangements under which probation officers or others who represent offenders would have funds with which to buy the services that their clients need.

Of course, to be dropped from the system outright, with no attempt to provide supervision or services, often serves the interests of both the offender and society, but it would be a mistake to allow ourselves to be fooled by the diversion label into believing that we are doing something we are not. This is similar to what commonly happens now when a judge's decision to sentence a person to prison is based in whole or in part on an assumption that it will rehabilitate him, when, in fact, the evidence is to the contrary. Being honest with ourselves will not reform criminal justice administration but it is an absolutely necessary condition to any reform. One danger of the diversion concept is that it will simply become another method of self-deception.

WHO MAKES THE DECISION?

By definition early diversion involves a decision outside the framework of a conventional court or correctional adjudication. Both the decision to divert and the choice of program offered the offender is likely to reflect the discretionary judgment of someone other than a judge or correctional official. In many instances this will be the prosecutor. In some, it will be a police official. In some, it will be a person with presumed expertise in the kind of service being offered.

Two related concerns about such decisions are: (1) they involve broad, unreviewable discretion by the decision-maker that may impose unfair burdens on the offenders; and (2) they are made by persons other than those who now have responsibility for correctional decision-making and therefore may not fairly reflect the interests of society and the rehabilitation needs of the offender.

In evaluating the first of these concerns it is important to bear in mind that in most jurisdictions sentencing decisions by judges and release decisions by parole officials are as a practical matter unreviewable. Nonetheless, the emergence of a new set of "correctional" decision-makers is a realistic basis for concern that offenders may be unfairly imposed upon. While strongly supporting the concept of early diversion, the President's Crime Commission expressed its concern about possible abuse in these terms:

> Experience with civil procedures for the commitment of the mentally ill, for so-called sexual psychopaths, and for similar groups demonstrates that there are dangers of such programs developing in ways potentially more oppressive than those foreclosed by the careful traditional protections of the criminal law. When the alternative non-criminal disposition involves institutionalization or prolonged or intrusive supervision of the offender in the community, the disposition should be reviewed by the court.

More recently Tentative Draft No. 5 of the American Law Institute's Model Code of Pre-Arraignment Procedure has proposed a formal screening conference in the prosecutor's office to make early dispositional decisions. The draft has also provided for both substantive and procedural guidelines for the prosecutor's exercise of discretion.

There would be even greater basis for concern about diversion programs imposing unfairly on their clients if we should discover that such programs include people who would be left alone altogether but for the availability of the diversion alternative. For example, it may be that some types of drug offenders who previously would have been ignored by the system are being arrested and brought to court with the aim of diverting them to methadone maintenance or some other treatment program.

The concern that officials who are not expert in correctional decision-making may be making decisions that fail to reflect society's interest seems to have little substance. In the first place, great dispositional power already resides in prosecutors in connection with plea bargaining and in making sentence recommendations, as well as in their power to dismiss cases. There is no reason to believe that well-designed diversion programs—particularly if they include provision for full information about the offender and the alternatives available—will result in less wise judgments. Nor does it seem likely that the people who would have dispositional authority under diversion programs would be less sensitive to the interests of society than prosecutors are now.

Furthermore, one has to be at least a bit skeptical about how much "expertise" with regard to the rehabilitation needs of the offender would be lost by relieving judges and traditional correctional officials of some of their dispositional power. How much evidence do we have that they operate with the kind of knowledge, consistency, or concern for following up the results of their decisions that would make the introduction of new decision-making processes unwise? In addition many of the new diversion projects involve substantive programs for offenders with which judges and correctional officials have had little or no experience.

LACK OF EVALUATION

It is striking that the emphasis on early diversion of offenders has grown with so little data as to its effect on crime, on the operation of the criminal justice system, and on the quality of treatment afforded. Professor Ward's chapter discusses research and evaluation in the corrections field generally and documents how little we know even about those correctional programs which have been available for evaluation for many years. It should be no surprise that even less is known about the vast number of recently established early diversion projects. As discussed earlier, strong arguments can be made for early diversion in terms of immediate cost savings for the criminal justice system and humane treatment of offenders. It does not seem irrational to seek these benefits, even at a time when the case that diversion reduces crime (or at least does not materially increase it) can be made only in theoretical rather than empirical terms. Perhaps this view is simply a reflection of the sad fact that almost everything we do in the criminal justice field is on the basis of faith, and that there is generally no more empirical support for continuing what is being done than there is for changing.

What is far more disturbing is that so little groundwork is being laid that would permit judgments about the worth of various diversion programs three, five, and ten years from now. The two principal reasons are (1) lack of research funds and (2) chronic reluctance of operating agencies to subject themselves to intensive and possibly critical evaluation. In the late 1960s when the federal government first began providing funds for state and local criminal justice operations, the President's Crime Commission urged that federal support of intensive research be given high priority. Except for the relatively meager funds of the Justice Department's National Institute of Law Enforcement and Criminal Justice and research supported by the Department of Labor on the court employment projects which it finances, the only potential source of funding for research on diversion programs has been the evaluation funds of the state planning agencies which receive and dispense federal funds under the Law Enforcement Assistance Administration program. These agencies have been strikingly unambitious and unsuccessful in developing in-depth research or evaluation of diversion projects—or projects in any other area—and the Law Enforcement Assistance Administration seems to have done little to press for such evaluation.

It thus seems a fair guess that for many years the case for—or against—diversion will continue to be made on the basis of theory, the pressure of backlog in the system, rather superficial cost figures, and views as to the humaneness of more or less coercive treatment.

This paper has not sought to argue the case for early diversion, but rather to provide a basis for consideration and discussion of issues and problems. However, in concluding it may be worthwhile to suggest that arguments for and against diversion in terms of leniency or toughness may miss the most important issue.

In effect, diversion seeks to offer the offender a set of social controls in lieu of the criminal justice system, our most drastic and overpowering form of social control. The assumption is that many who violate criminal laws are people whose lives will always be difficult and who need continuing support and that supervision and supplemental services may be more promising than the combination of a stigma and a cage. Diversion with its gentler, less debilitating controls, may offer the best hope of developing in such people a lasting capacity to deal with a complex and difficult society.

David A. Ward

6

Evaluative Research for Corrections

Most Americans are familiar with the strike and killings at Attica; they know about the shooting of George Jackson at San Quentin and they have heard of the Soledad Brothers. Since 1971 many other states have experienced strikes, demonstrations, riots, and killings that have continued to attract public attention. In addition to inmate leaders and "radicals," citizens have heard the President, the Chief Justice of the Supreme Court, the attorney general, their own governors, and other public figures condemn prisons as "schools for crime" and "correctional institutions that don't correct." The most common theme at the national conferences of American correctional administrators has become "The Crisis in Corrections."

Clearly American prison systems are in trouble and the trouble is not only that there has been violence in the prisons but also that the claim that offenders could be "rehabilitated" in prison has been exposed as a myth. During the 1960s, particularly in the states of California, Minnesota, Wisconsin, New Jersey, and New York, citizens heard much about "treatment" and "rehabilitation" in discussions of prisons but the mass demonstrations, strikes, and riots

DAVID A. WARD *is chairman of the Department of Criminal Justice Studies and professor of sociology at the University of Minnesota. Previously he was assistant director of the California Study of Correctional Effectiveness of the University of California at Los Angeles; he was also consultant to the National Commission on the Causes and Prevention of Violence. With Gene G. Kassebaum and Daniel M. Wilner, Dr. Ward is the author of* Prison Treatment and Parole Survival.

that began at the end of that decade provided dramatic support for inmate assertions that prisons had not become hospitals.

In addition to the protests, it took ten years for researchers to gather enough evidence to convince legislators, judges, and prison administrators that the claim that treatment specialists could make confinement in fortress prisons a positive experience was unfounded.

The purpose of this chapter is to review some of the consequences of introducing the so-called "treatment philosophy" into the largest prison system in America, the California Department of Corrections. Evidence indicating that this philosophy has failed to live up to its advance billing will be reviewed, for in that failure is a lesson that should be remembered as American prison administrators increasingly talk about "community corrections." The new rhetoric of community corrections will be examined in terms of the challenge it poses to those who have learned that pronouncements of the American correctional establishment cannot be accepted uncritically.

Treatment in the "Most Progressive" Prison System

Although in the public mind San Quentin and Folsom are tough, maximum security prisons, they are but two of California's eight major prisons for felons. Several of the other prisons are bounded by security fences rather than walls and Department of Corrections facilities also include reception/diagnostic centers, conservation camps, halfway houses, and a large parole division.

But it has been the number and variety of treatment programs, not new or different physical plants, that have earned California the title of the "most progressive" prison system in the country. (This commendation, it should be noted, was *not* conferred on the department by inmates of California prisons, but emanated instead from the American correctional establishment comprised of prison, probation, and parole administrators and clinical treatment specialists, largely social workers.)

On several counts, persons outside the corrections establishment might agree that the California Department of Corrections has indeed been more "progressive" than any other state system. More new treatment programs have been tried in California than elsewhere and the Department of Corrections has been more open to study by outside researchers. Most of California's major treatment efforts have been systematically evaluated, and department officials have been forced to smile bravely, at least in public, as one study after another found that inmates came back to prison whether they participated in treatment or not.

Other state prison systems have initiated few new programs and they have been uninterested in or even opposed evaluation of existing programs; in fact, a survey of 48 correctional systems in the United States made by Robert Fosen and Jay Campbell, Jr. at the peak of the prison treatment movement determined: (1) that only 19 systems reported any kind of research operation; (2) that only one-third of 1 percent of the total annual budget for adult corrections in the United States was devoted to self-study; and (3) that two systems, California and New York, accounted for over one-half of the total investment in research.

The initiation of few new treatment programs and policies permitting little or no evaluation of new or traditional prison activities has permitted correctional administrators in other states to avoid the embarrassment of disappointing outcome studies. The California Department of Corrections should be given credit for trying harder than any other system to be number one.

PRISONERS BECOME PATIENTS

The claim that prisons could become places where criminality could be "corrected" came into prominence in California in the 1950s when doubts appeared about the effectiveness of imprisonment *per se* as a deterrent for future misconduct. Evidence had accumulated that the return-to-prison rate was high for inmates serving even the longest prison terms. Prisons were also criticized on the grounds that they were inhumane places in which the regimentation and harshness of daily existence promoted continuance of the very behavior for which inmates were locked up in the first place. At the same time, behavioral scientists and clinicians were arguing that criminal behavior was learned, not inherited, and therefore modification was possible.

There is no evidence that in the 1950s the majority of California citizens knew or cared very much about what happened to prisoners, but to certain interest groups—prison administrators, legislators, social workers, and psychologists—the notion that prisons could be settings in which "rehabilitation" occurred represented a promising new development. The old prisons could remain and new prisons could even be built, but within the walls, security fences, and perimeter gun towers inmates would engage in activities that would make them better citizens than when they entered.

Basic to the treatment philosophy were two assumptions: (1) that criminal behavior derives from faulty personality development and (2) that only "professionally" trained persons could treat persons so disturbed.

With regard to the first point, one of the California treatment philosophy's prime spokesmen, Dr. Norman Fenton, stated that "rejection by others, notably parents and others in authority in a person's early life, is a significant factor in arousing and establishing feelings of hostility or resentment." These feelings, Fenton contended, are later expressed in acts of theft, robbery, and assault. From this perspective, inmates were to be seen as people who were suffering from emotional disturbances or arrested psychosocial development and, thus, in need of treatment.

This treatment, however, could not be administered by just anyone. Only trained clinical specialists, social workers, and psychologists could conduct programs that would take into account the special problems of treating "clients" in a prison setting.

The enthusiastic rush to endorse rehabilitation as a new function of imprisonment did result in increased appropriations to expand social casework and individual psychotherapy and to launch the new group counseling program. It soon became clear, however, that even with the increase not enough social workers, not to mention the more expensive clinical psychologists and psychiatrists, could be hired to run the group counseling program.

It was then determined that "nonprofessional" staff members, including guards, would have to be used—under the supervision, of course, of the treatment staff professionals and only after training by the group counseling coordinator—a new position established in each prison.

Along with the treatment professionals and treatment programs came the new rhetoric of treatment. Guards became "correctional officers"; cells became "rooms"; wardens became "superintendents"; prisons were called the California Training Facility (Soledad), California Men's Colony, The California Institution for Men/Women, Deuel Vocational Institution, and The California Medical Facility. Segregation and isolation units (the "hole") were relabeled "adjustment centers" with temporary and long-term residents classified into "acute" and "chronic" cases by "adjustment committees." (It should be noted that San Quentin and Folsom continued to be called *prisons,* and that they were run by *wardens,* and housed *inmates* who lived in *cells*—a clear indication that, at least in the minds of some, there would continue to be inmates "unresponsive" to treatment; San Quentin's "adjustment center" was only for "chronic" cases.)

Other important words introduced to the treatment lexicon were "individualized treatment" and the "indeterminate sentence." The language reveals the influence of the clinical treatment spcialists who entered the prison system and took up places on all departmental and prison committees. But these terms and concepts are more than mere words, they represent interrelated elements of the treatment philosophy and they have had a dramatic impact on the lives of inmates.

Take, for example, the concept of the "indeterminate sentence" whereby the California legislature set the minimum and maximum terms for criminal offenses (e.g., burglary second degree, one to fifteen years; robbery, one year to life; check forgery, six months to two years; sale of marijuana, five years to life). The inmate is remanded to the state prison system for the term prescribed in the law and any release prior to the maximum term is dependent upon the judgment of the parole board. Indeterminate sentencing was enthusiastically endorsed as a means of releasing men from prison *sooner* than was the case when a specific term was imposed by a judge. The introduction of the indeterminate sentence presumed the presence of experts, the treatment specialists, who were expected to decide when the right time was for a man to be released from prison, i.e., when he would be able to "adjust" successfully in the free world.

Over the past dozen years, the key word in the language of both custody and treatment staff members in California prisons has become the word "adjust." The number of amenities which an inmate receives in prison, his chances of being paroled, and his probability of surviving the parole period depend upon his ability to "adjust" as prison and parole personnel define "adjustment."

With the optimism surrounding all these new ideas, new programs, new personnel, and new words, evaluative research was officially encouraged as a means of getting research sociologists and psychologists both inside and outside the Department of Corrections to confirm the success of the new philosophy.

TREATMENT PROGRAM EVALUATION

Given the limits imposed by budget on the number of clinical psychologists and psychiatrists who could be hired to provide individual psychotherapy, the California Department of Corrections moved to make group counseling the major thrust of the treatment effort. Groups of ten or twelve prisoners could be handled at one session, affording considerable economy of time and money, and the social workers who ran the groups were less expensive to hire than psychologists and psychiatrists. Furthermore, group counseling advocates claimed as much for their program as was claimed for individual psychotherapy.

Because of the scope and expense of the group counseling program and because there were still a few skeptics in the state legislature, the Department of Corrections sought the assistance of researchers at the University of California in evaluating the group treatment program.

Procedure—The study, conducted by Gene Kassebaum, Daniel Wilner, and the author,[1] that came out of this request could not begin until some considerable resistance to the idea of a control group was overcome. Several members of the Adult Authority—the parole board—argued that "it was unfair to deny treatment to inmates." That is, even for a study of what group counseling actually achieved which was solicited by the Department of Corrections itself, it was argued that to keep any inmate from participating in the program was to hurt his chances for rehabilitation. The researchers pointed out that having a similar group of men who were not participants was the best way to make a valid test of its effectiveness. (The researchers pointed out that because involvement in group counseling was voluntary some men were already nonparticipants. It was also argued that if the study results were as positive as the Adult Authority members believed, then perhaps all inmates should be required to participate in group counseling.) This reluctance to accept the notion of a control group was testimony to the faith which department officials had in the new group counseling effort.

The evaluation of group counseling was undertaken at California's newest medium security prison, Men's Colony, East, a quadrangular prison comprised of four six-hundred-man units physically separated from each other but all surrounded by a double cyclone fence and eight gun towers. As inmates arrived to fill the prison they were randomly dispersed into a variety of group treatment conditions administered in each of the quadrangles.

[1] Kassebaum, Gene G., David A. Ward, and Daniel M. Wilner, *Prison Treatment and Parole Survival* (New York: Wiley, 1971). (Sections of this paper have been adapted from this report.)

The varied group conditions were: (1) voluntary or required participation, (2) the size of the group, (3) the frequency of group meetings, and (4) the extent of training of the group leaders. Most groups consisted of 10–12 men that met once or twice each week, but there were also three large groups with 50 men each that met daily, each with three leaders. One of the quadrangles (600 men) was designated as the control group. Men in this unit were able to participate in all of the regular programs in the prison—formal education, vocational training, individual psychotherapy, religious and recreational activities. They experienced the same living conditions as the inmates in the different types of group treatment; the only difference was that there was no group counseling program in the unit.

The study incorporated into its outcome criteria both the goals of group counseling as officially stated and the goals which departmental staff specified. The official goals were listed in *The Manual of Instruction for Group Leaders*:

1. To help prisoners adjust to the frustrations that are an unalterable part of life in an institution and in society;
2. To enable the client to recognize the significance of emotional conflicts as underlying criminality;
3. To provide the opportunity for the client to learn from his peers about the social aspects of his personality;
4. To make possible a better understanding of make-believe, of fantasy, and of how costly may be behavioral responses to the antisocial content of daydreams;
5. [To improve] the emotional climate of the institution.

To determine the outcomes expected by the group leaders and other rank and file personnel, the researchers conducted a survey of more than four thousand staff members of the California Department of Corrections. Their predictions became criteria by which the effects of the group treatment program were measured. The most frequently mentioned outcomes in the staff survey were that participation in group counseling would produce: (1) a decrease in inmate hostility toward staff, (2) a decrease in the number of prison rules violations, and (3) a lower return-to-prison rate.

Findings—Six years of study, including a three-year postrelease follow-up of approximately one thousand men, all of whom had participated for at least six months in one of the treatment varieties or who had been in the control group, produced negative findings on *all* predicted outcome criteria. Compared to inmates in the control group—and in terms of statistically significant differences—inmates in *none* of the group treatment varieties (1) were less hostile to staff; (2) committed fewer or less serious prison rules violations; (3) violated parole less frequently; (4) stayed out of prison *longer* before violating parole; (5) committed less serious crimes than their commitment offenses while on parole.

These results were disturbing to correctional administrators and treatment professionals, for much hope as well as money had been invested in the group counseling program. Furthermore evaluative studies of other treatment efforts were reporting uniformly discouraging findings.

For example, a long-cherished notion of the department's parole division was that if the size of a parole agent's caseload could be reduced, closer (i.e., more therapeutic) relationships with the parolee would be possible, thereby reducing the parolees' chances of getting into trouble and eventually being returned to prison. This proposition was tested by comparing caseloads of 70 men with caseloads of 35; additionally small caseloads with intensive supervision during the early months of parole were compared with caseloads calling for "regular" supervision; and finally, caseloads of 15 men were compared with several other types of parole supervision. It was found that neither caseload size nor type of supervision was significantly related to parole survival.

Other programs whose effects were being tested in the mid-1960s in California were the "halfway" house for narcotic addicts and civil commitment of narcotic addicts. (The latter involved confinement in "hospitals" under civil rather than criminal commitment procedures.) Both evaluations produced no evidence that treatment reduced recidivism.

Response—As these studies began to make things uncomfortable for department administrators and for many treatment professionals, researchers heard a growing list of excuses for the failures. In the case of the group counseling study, for example, staff members were confronted with an evaluation that included every element of good research design. The research was done in a prison system that is reputed to be the best in the country. The inmates studied were neither the most violent and habitual offenders confined in maximum security prisons, nor were they the first-term minor property offenders likely to be found in minimum security facilities. The study subjects were representative of the "average" inmate population in a correctional system. Furthermore, they were confined in the most up-to-date prison in the department in terms of physical plant and staffing. In addition, a sufficiently large study population —approximately one thousand men—was used to permit adequate statistical analysis; random assignment of subjects was made to the various treatment and control conditions; contamination of the sample groups was kept at a minimum because of the physical structure of the institution. Also evaluated was a group counseling condition, especially included for this study, in which group leaders were given training beyond that which the present resources of the Department of Corrections could afford. The follow-up was extended for an unusually long period of time (three years) to take into consideration the long-term effects of treatment. To counter the findings of the study, treatment staff members claimed:

—What goes on between a group counseling leader and the group members (the 'therapeutic' relationship) can't be measured by statistics.
—You can't measure what goes on in here (pointing to one's heart) with numbers.
—The impact of the group counseling experience may be so subtle that it may not be felt for perhaps 10 years after the man leaves prison.
—Even though they came back to prison, the inmates are better adjusted (or happier or more emotionally stable) people for having participated in the program.
—The results are not good because we are getting a much worse type of inmate than we got when the program began.
—Actually we were foolish to think that such a limited program would work, what we needed to do was double what we put into the program.

Other reactions cited by Donald Cressey in *Law and Contemporary Problems* included:

—The program is worth it if it saved one man.
—If the treatment had not been introduced, the recidivism rates might have been even higher; the fact that there is no difference really indicates that the technique has been very effective.
—The program certainly *contributed* to the rehabilitation of some of the clients.
—You can't expect any system in which the criminal is seen for only a few hours a week to significantly change personalities which have been in the making for the whole period of the individual's life and which are characterized by deeply-hidden, unconscious problems; we can only keep chipping away.

These defensive reactions constitute what Cressey calls the "vocabulary of adjustment" by which treatment personnel can justify continuing any program as "corrective."

Social workers, in particular, are prone to propose psychologically based treatment programs founded on faith rather than on empirical evidence. New treatment programs are not proposed with the argument that the approach offers promise and that it should be tried as an experiment in one prison, evaluated as to impact by specific criteria and, if demonstrated to be successful, expanded to other institutions. In the 1960s most treatment approaches such as those mentioned were advanced with genuine confidence in their effectiveness, and their implementation at all levels and in all institutions was urged. Goals to be achieved were that offenders would be less likely to return to prison and that in prison they would be less hostile and troublesome for staff. However, when careful evaluations showed that these goals were not being achieved, treatment professionals were forced to move to their second line of defense. Now it is more likely to be contended that the aim of a treatment program is some form of improved inmate or parolee behavior, other than the reduction of recidivism or the maintenance of peace and quiet in the prison. Outcome in many current programs is to be measured in terms of improved parolee performance on civilian jobs or simply maintaining employment; "relating" more effectively to caseworkers, correctional officers, parole agents, or wives; committing fewer or less serious crimes or staying out longer on parole than on previous releases; or simply showing evidence of a "strengthened ego" or the development of greater "emotional stability."

There is nothing wrong or even unusual about evaluating outcome in terms of these criteria, but it should be noted that they have only been advanced after evaluative studies have found no basis for more dramatic claims about treatment impact.

CONSEQUENCES OF EVALUATIONS FOR ADMINISTRATORS

Because administrators of the California Department of Corrections accepted on faith the advice of the treatment experts, they too have experienced embarrassing moments as the results of these evaluations appeared and were publicized. An example of the difficulties the department faced when one of its publicly expressed goals was not achieved involved the project which compared the performances of parolees under the supervision of parole agents with 35-man caseloads with parolees whose agents had 70-man caseloads. When the results were in—negative results—operational instructions were altered by administrative fiat thereby manipulating the outcome statistics to prove the program a success. Paul Takagi reports:

> [A] report was issued on December 22, 1965, and had a devastating effect on the parole agency. In short, there was no difference in parolee recidivism rates between the two types of supervision. The findings were devastating because: the 1964 legislature appropriated funds to initiate ". . . a small caseload program so that: (1) sufficient time be available to the agents to accomplish tasks required of them; (2) the problem of violence be attacked . . . ; (3) the needs of society be protected; and (4) there be differentiated treatment of all parolees" (Agency Document, "Work Unit Evaluation," December 22, 1965, p. 1). The expectations were that the parolees under small caseloads would have favorable outcomes. In response to these discouraging findings, the chief of the parole agency brought together the regional administrators and the district supervisors responsible for the small-caseload program . . . The meeting began with the observation that the small caseloads were not producing favorable results . . . The chief of the agency stated that henceforth the units in the agency will compete against one another to see who can produce the lowest technical violation rate . . . The further requirement was made that copies of such reports will be forwarded to headquarters for review and training purposes and that the material will be utilized to evaluate the performance in the field. The chief of the agency added one final note. All future promotions will be considered in terms of how well the district supervisors and the regional administrators have provided leadership in reducing the technical violation rates. At this juncture in the meeting, my informant indicated one of the participants at the meeting responded to these unwritten policy requirements with an exclamatory: "Bullshit." The chief of the agency turned to the man and said: "Mr. C—, you hold a responsible position in this organization; and, if that is the way you feel, perhaps you should not be in that position."

Headquarters' pressures upon the regional administrators and the small-caseload supervisors served effectively to reduce the technical violation rates in the subsequent months. It is noteworthy that on December 30, 1966, one year later, a report on the small-caseload program was prepared for the members of the Joint Legislative Budget Committee. The coverletter to the report reads as follows:

> The [small-caseload program] originally funded by the 1964 Legislature and placed into effect in early 1965, represents a major breakthrough in its having provided parole service for community protection . . .
>
> As can be seen from the results described in the summary, program outcome has been decidedly positive, with a significant impact having been made on *reduction of felons returned to prison*. During

1965, this program also made possible major savings in institution costs previous to release on parole, accompanied by a higher parole success . . .

Favorable outcome suddenly became an issue in the parole agency, not because of interest in promoting professionalism, nor in effecting administrative efficiency. Rather, the agency's interest in reducing the technical violation rate was in response to pressures from the state legislature to show results in a field where results are difficult to demonstrate. This pressure was the 1¼ million dollars allocated to the parole agency to place one-half of the parolee population in small caseloads, and the legislature wanted to know what services and results were produced for this amount of money. The arguments for small caseload have an intuitive logic similar to the arguments for reducing classroom size, that the professional will have more time to devote to individual client needs and, in this way, be able to achieve the objectives of rehabilitation or educational achievement. When favorable results—in this case, lower technical violation rates—could not be demonstrated, the objectives of the emergency task were re-defined by administrative fiat.

Takagi's report is important not only because it illustrates the impact of evaluative research on agency administrators but also because it serves as a reminder that fluctuations in recidivism rates, in "failure" or "difficulty" rates, or in any other measure of parolee survival may reflect changes in administrative policy, not changes in parolee behavior. (Similarly, changes in the crime rate may reflect changes in police manpower or efficiency or changes in the definition of certain kinds of behavior as criminal.)

LEGISLATIVE REACTIONS TO DEPARTMENT OF CORRECTIONS
REACTIONS TO NEGATIVE FINDINGS

In the late 1960s because of some doubt as to whether the Department of Corrections officials would publicize reports which undercut their own public statements, the California legislature's Office of Research launched a number of very well conceived and carefully conducted evaluations of Department of Corrections programs and policies. One of these reports, *The California Prison, Parole and Probation System*, represented an attempt to find ". . . evidence that correctional programming provides effective rehabilitation." The findings were:

1. There is no evidence to support claims that one correctional program has more rehabilitative effectiveness than another.

2. Statistics on recidivism exaggerate the extent to which convicted offenders return to serious crime.

3. The likelihood of a citizen being subjected to personal injury or property loss can be only infinitesimally lessened by the field of Corrections.

4. The increase in public protection gained by the imprisonment of large numbers of offenders, of whom few are dangerous, is outweighed by the public costs involved.

The above conclusions form the basis of the single recommendation: that no more funds be provided for the construction of state prison facilities.

One of the facts about California penal policies that struck legislators was that from 1960, near the beginning of the push toward "rehabilitation," the average time served by California prisoners had increased, by 1968, from 24 months to 36 months. When questioned about this shift, the California Adult Authority countered with the arguments that the difference in time served was due to the fact that "the inmate today is more hostile, is immature, prone to act out, and less motivated than those sent earlier, and that there has been an increasing number of felons in need of psychiatric care."

The legislature's research group tested this assertion and then reported that "persons committed to prison in 1960 for any offense were essentially the same type of person as those committed for similar offenses in 1968."

What the Adult Authority might have been saying was that during the 1960s perhaps the same types of offenders entered the prisons but while in prison many were politicized or became involved in protest demonstrations against the prison system. The terms "hostile" and "prone to act out" may mean "militant" and the phrase "less motivated" may mean less likely to be obedient to staff directives. It should also be noted that as California moved in the late 1960s into the probation subsidy program large numbers of offenders who had formerly entered the state prison system were kept in county facilities or on probation. In the 1970s most of those offenders who were committed to state institutions had committed crimes of violence or had extensive criminal records.

The California state prison population had dropped from some twenty-eight thousand in the 1960s to less than twenty thousand in 1972. In 1972 with only 6 percent of those convicted for felonies being committed to state prison there was a basis for a claim that the prison population was different.

The problem for the Adult Authority is that they have contended that "a longer exposure to the prison treatment program would improve the response of paroled inmates." This claim has not been supported by any research in California or elsewhere.

In 1970, sociologist Robert Martinson reported to the New York State Office of Crime Control Planning the results of a critical survey of all studies published between 1945 and 1967 which evaluated the effect of any type of treatment applied to convicted offenders. Two hundred and thirty-one studies were found which met requirements for adequate research design, and the review of these studies led Martinson and his associates to the conclusion that ". . . there is very little evidence in these studies that any prevailing mode of correctional treatment has a decisive effect in reducing the recidivism of convicted offenders."

More than a decade of "rehabilitation" programs and rhetoric in California and lesser efforts in other states and the federal prison system produced no clear evidence that treatment made contented inmates or reformed criminals. In fact, the "rehabilitation" phase ended with more trouble in California, New York, and other state prisons than any other period in American prison history. The treatment philosophy was not successful in breathing new life into old prisons.

TREATMENT AS CONTROL

Despite the trial and failure of treatment programs to produce law-abiding—or even obedient—behavior on the part of inmates and parolees, the treatment ideology has proved to be of great value as the latest and most sophisticated justification for controlling the behavior of "militants," "radicals," and "agitators" who threaten the interests of organizational and community power structures. For example, the old system of sentencing felons to prison for a specified period of time meant that no matter what one did in prison, short of committing new crimes involving separate prosecution and conviction, prisoners could plan and orient themselves psychologically to a definite release date. The indeterminate sentencing structure, combined with the new criterion of "good adjustment" (measured in terms of submission to authority), now subjects inmates to a psychological strain that is certain to produce frustration in all, "acting out" by many and, thus, lengthened imprisonment.

The Prison Letters of George Jackson gives a good account of what it feels like to be imprisoned (after driving the getaway car in a $75 robbery) for a term of one year to life, in a system where the criteria of "adjustment" are always changing. Even more frustrating than the "never-knowing system" (as it is called by California prisoners) which characterizes indeterminate sentencing policies is the inability to protest or question this procedure or others that vitally affect inmate lives. Under the treatment ideology "adjustment" is defined, it will be recalled, as *accepting the frustrations that are an unalterable part of prison life.* "Disturbed" persons whose actions show them to be "hostile" are not to be afforded the rights of normal persons and they are certainly not to be permitted a significant role in determining the conditions and the course of their own treatment; that is the job of "professionals." Inmates who protest the psychological warfare between inmates and staff promoted by the treatment philosophy are reported to be not demonstrative of the type of "attitude" that would permit those in authority to release them from "treatment."

While the California State Legislature did dispute the claims of Department of Corrections officials that prisons can produce "rehabilitated" men, this does not mean that the treatment ideology has been discarded by state officials as a rationale for imprisonment. It is still useful to characterize criminal behavior (prison "troublemaking") as stemming from a disturbed emotional state and to argue that the prison system should devote its efforts to "helping" persons so afflicted. Because "correctional treatment" is so ambiguously defined and because it presents such a seemingly up-to-date, scientific and solicitous image, it should be expected that social control agencies will continue to publicly justify imprisonment in its name.

Stated in ideal terms, the treatment approach—whether in the community or in prisons—includes assumptions that even strong critics can endorse. For instance, it recognizes the need to provide individualized or special attention to persons who are genuinely psychologically disabled. It also argues against the belief that criminal behavior is most effectively dealt with by physical punishment or by confinement in traditional fortress prisons.

It has, nonetheless, been overrated as an explanation of and a solution to "the crime problem." It has permitted Americans to pretend that the administration of criminal justice is just and that people who end up in prison deserve to be there because they are really different from the rest of us. Most importantly, it has diverted attention from the social, economic, and political features of American society that promote law violations of one sort or another by almost all citizens and places the responsibility for "crime" upon certain individuals.

Community Corrections: Something for Everyone

The same states that once led the rush to rehabilitate inmates in prison have been arguing, since the late 1960s, that what was needed all along was actually supervision and treatment in the community. Prisons it is now contended should be used only as a last resort for dangerous and habitual offenders. The combined factors of violence and rebellion in the prisons, the negative results of treatment evaluations, and the legislature's own critical studies gave notice to the California Department of Corrections that changes in penal policy were necessary. Further it became clear that if changes did not come from within they would be imposed from without. It should be emphasized that only *after* the claim that offenders could be rehabilitated in prison was tested and found wanting did the move to corrections in the community seem so logical. Before the department began to cast about for new directions it had to be demonstrated that: (1) imprisonment did not deter offenders through severe penalties or long prison terms and (2) there was no evidence to prove that prisons changed men for the better. Several studies which evaluated prison treatment had come to conclusions that paved the way for the next Great Treatment Experiment.

Influential Studies—One of the most significant was the comparison of matched samples of delinquent boys who were sentenced to a regular youth prison and to the Community Treatment Project run by Marguerite Warren and her associates for the California Youth Authority. Initial research findings indicated that the boys in the community treatment program had less trouble with the police and parole authorities than did the control group. A later reanalysis in 1968 by Paul Lerman in *Social Work* led to another conclusion: that the positive results of the experimental group did not reflect differences in the delinquent behavior of the boys but differences in the parole-revoking behavior of the parole agents, namely that the parole agents were less likely to take actions against boys in the experimental group. Nevertheless the study indicated that there was no greater risk to the community to have delinquent boys in the community center than in the prisons and—in the long run it was cheaper. Several studies done for the legislature were also influential.

One report, *Deterrent Effects of Criminal Sanctions,* prepared in 1968 for the legislature's Committee on Criminal Procedure, concluded:

> There is no evidence that more severe penalties deter crime more effectively than less severe penalties.
>
> There is no evidence that prisons rehabilitate most offenders.
>
> There is evidence that larger numbers of offenders can be effectively supervised in the community at insignificant risk and considerable savings in public expense.

Another study begun in 1961 and completed in 1964 was also done at the request of the Committee on Criminal Procedure. This study dealt with a possible expansion of probation and led to a program that has had more dramatic consequences for the California prison system than all the treatment rhetoric and programs —the probation subsidy. The probation subsidy program used cost benefit analysis to compare institutional and community treatment of offenders.

For example, legislators learned from the 1964 probation study that the total minimum career cost of an inmate who served an average term in prison and on parole and who did not violate parole or come back to the system was $5,700. (The figure by 1971 was estimated to be "in excess of $10,000.") The comparative cost for treating one offender on probation under the supervision of a probation officer with a maximum of 50 cases was $142. Furthermore the cost of imprisonment did not include welfare payments to the families of inmates. Combined with the growing evidence of the failure of prison treatment programs to control or correct, the probation subsidy not only represented a new move for the Department of Corrections but it carried with it the winning argument that tax dollars would be saved.

The probation subsidy program, begun in 1966, paid counties a certain sum for each offender who was kept in the county rather than sent to the State Department of Corrections. The argument was that if counties received funds for more probation officers and expanded programs to help offenders, the state could reduce the size of its prison population, which, in turn, would save money. At the same time fewer offenders would suffer the negative consequences of imprisonment. In his review of the probation subsidy program, *A Quiet Revolution*, Robert L. Smith reported that:

> Between 1966 and 1972 California can demonstrate that it has saved $185,978,820 through cancelled construction, closed institutions, and new institutions constructed but not opened. Total expenditure for probation subsidy will be $59,925,705.

Furthermore, Smith indicated that the youth and adult prison populations in California were reduced because 15,487 offenders were not sent to prison during the first five years of the program.

Probation subsidy can be deemed successful if the criteria for success are that it saves taxes and reduces the number of persons confined in state prisons. It is the only program in corrections that has won approval from politicians, Department of Corrections officials, citizens, prison reformers, and offenders. However, if the criterion for success is community *treatment* the evidence is yet to come in.

Smith reported that commitments to the California youth and adult prison systems during the period 1965–70 were reduced 41 and 20 percent respectively:

> During this same 5-year period most indices of crime, such as crimes reported, adult and juvenile arrests, continued upward. None of the increases can be attributed to the probation subsidy since such indices had been increasing for many years before the probation subsidy. Preliminary information for 1970 shows a slight decline in juvenile delinquency arrest rates and in most other indices of juvenile delinquency. Of greater interest perhaps is the fact that superior court probation grants have increased, while violation rates have declined since probation subsidy was enacted. Violators made up 36.3 percent of the total removed from superior court probation for the years 1962–65. This percentage averaged only 33.8 percent for the 1966–69 period. *Other data also suggest that it is reasonable to conclude that the general crime situation in California has not deteriorated since probation subsidy.*

It may be true that the crime picture is no worse since the probation subsidy and community corrections efforts began, but to date we do not know if offenders subjected to community *treatment* commit fewer crimes than if they were simply under routine police surveillance in the community.

EVALUATION PROBLEMS

It appears that the need to demonstrate the "rehabilitative potential," if any, of treatment programs conducted in the community is less urgent to most citizens and even to most offenders than is evaluation of such programs carried on in prison. Community corrections often permit the offender to live in his own home where he can draw upon the assistance of family and friends, and make use of community resources during difficult times. Thus his concern about evaluating community corrections is likely to center on the ways in which supervision intrudes into his life under the guise of treatment. It also seems unlikely that offenders can complain very much about being placed on probation or in community treatment facilities. Unlike the prison situation where little is to be lost by protests over common problems, offenders in the community separated by residence, job, and neighborhood have much to lose. Life in the community would have to be rather bad for offenders to accept the other alternative—prison.

If offenders are not likely to complain, and politicians and citizens are happy about the reduced number of inmates in costly state prisons, then why ask whether community corrections really makes a difference? The answer is that the tendency of organizations is to expand, and in the case of corrections organizations, citizens should be noting that probation officials and those who operate community corrections facilities have begun to ask for increased funds to do the job "right." The argument is now heard that "if community corrections is to be effective it will have to have resources *equaling* the cost of putting offenders in prison." And, despite the failure to make good its claims for the positive value of prison programs the field of corrections has asked for—and received—more, not less, money. Congressional appropriations to the Law Enforcement Assistance Administration increased from $60 million in 1969 to $850 million in 1973. In the late 1960s and early 1970s corrections received about 20 percent of each year's allotment; by 1973 the percentage in some states had increased to 35 percent. State correctional services are financed by both state and federal tax dollars, and a review of applications submitted to state crime commissions (through which LEAA funds are channeled) offers some clues as to what citizens are getting for their money.

For one thing, the flow of federal dollars into the community corrections business has been a bonanza for the field of social work.

The corrections agencies representatives who serve on all local and state crime commissions have argued that funds should not be allotted to community organizations unless "professionals" are in charge. They also contend that the staffing of probation and parole departments, halfway houses, and drug treatment centers will be enhanced by the addition of "para-professionals," volunteers, interns, case aides—and here and there a token ex-offender—provided, of course, that such personnel work under the supervision of the "professionals."

While it may well be true that expansion of community corrections requires more paid workers, it is also the case that community organizations without long histories of involvement in correctional programs might have as much or more to offer offenders than the established agencies. Black, American Indian, and Chicano offenders might be more receptive to the efforts of organizations indigenous to their neighborhoods or run by members of their own racial or ethnic group. Synanon, a California drug treatment organization run exclusively by ex-addicts, is a good example of a program which has dealt with a group of high-risk offenders and has had more success in keeping them off drugs than has any program of the California Department of Corrections. Synanon has never had a "professional" staff of social workers, psychologists and psychiatrists, and it has survived and flourished over the strong objections of the treatment experts in "America's Most Progressive Prison System."

Too often LEAA funds which might have gone to encourage the involvement of all the different communities which make up our cities have been expended for more and better jobs for white middle-class social workers.

Perhaps as a result of lessons learned the hard way, a second feature of the increased federal spending has been a proliferation of programs in which goals are stated in ambiguous terms and where evaluation amounts to little more than "human bookkeeping." Federal guidelines for law enforcement assistance funds require that each request specify an evaluation design; however, this requirement has not been rigorously applied. Consider the goals and proposed evaluation of the following Minnesota grant requests:

> A $60,000 project which "seeks to identify behavior problems of individual students which have prevented them from fully benefiting from the learning process. It will then attempt to alter this behavior by means of the Positive Peer Culture method." According to this proposal "the peer culture of delinquents is of course negative" and a new

culture is to be created which rewards positive behavior (e.g., "class participation," "controlling anger," "is considerate" and "accepting staff directives") and tries to reduce behavior problems (e.g., "authority problem," "bad mouth," "misleads others," "plays the fool," "childish behavior.") Evaluation of the success of the Positive Peer Culture method would be made in terms of "the incidence of negative and positive behavior of students" reported by staff members and "student reactions from standardized tests and attitude inventories."

A $195,000 project for the Minnesota Department of Corrections to establish a community corrections center for adult male parolees: "Evaluation . . . will be limited to information that will demonstrate how well the program has functioned in terms of meeting the goals of the program and goals of developmental plans . . . The program philosophy will stress behavioral and psychological changes over time. Pretests and post-tests of attitudinal and behavioral indices will be administered. Attempts will be made to evaluate the effect of the Community Corrections Center on the client's social adjustment . . . Program impact on the community will be assessed in terms of community involvement."

Regional and state review panels are learning that proposals which provide for evaluations dependent upon: (1) staff assessments of the "positive" and "negative" behavior of program participants, (2) "attitudinal and behavioral indices," and (3) the degree to which "a community becomes involved" assure successful achievement of goals. In addition, they know that such evaluations will preface the request to expand the program during the second year of the project.

Some grant applicants do not even mention the reduction of crime or delinquency as their projects' goals, referring only to gains for the organization itself. For example, a $33,000 project in Minnesota called "Delivery of Service Through Groups" stated its goals: "(1) to utilize group methods as a treatment mechanism; (2) to recruit, screen, train and supervise volunteers to work with former juvenile probationers; (3) to ensure that each child on probation is seen in a group session on a weekly basis; (4) to modify the role of the probation officer to be that of a consultant-supervisor." No information was provided in the proposal about any results *due* to group participation; project goals related only to enhancing the role of correctional workers are likely to be achieved.

If correctional agencies want to argue that they exist not to deal with criminal and delinquent behavior but to help probation officers become "consultant-supervisors" while volunteers carry on the work that probation officers used to do, then legislators and citizens should be in a position to judge whether they wish to support such a goal with tax dollars. Presumably probation and parole departments and all the organizations that are part of community *corrections* were established to reduce the incidence of crime and delinquency, not to promote new careers for social workers. Neither the "experience" of correctional agency administrators nor the rhetoric and formal training of correctional treatment professionals should convince citizens and elected officials that the old goal of reducing crime is no longer the proper measure of organizational performance.

The American correctional establishment claims that community corrections makes a difference, that is, offenders who have gone through their programs are less likely to get involved in crime and delinquency in the future. Community corrections *appears* to offer a cheaper, more humane, and more promising alternative to imprisonment for thousands of offenders. But an earlier period of great hope ended with disappointment and a six months study by a subcommittee of the United States House of Representatives Government Operations Committee concluded that LEAA programs "have had no visible impact on the incidence of crime in the United States."

Social action program evaluation is, however, costly and time-consuming. And community corrections evaluation poses some very difficult research design and data collection problems. For one thing, offenders will not all be conveniently located for an extended period in one place as was the case with prisons. But more significant to adequate assessment is the problem of measuring the impact of any single program given the likelihood that most offenders will be participating in a variety of community programs run by different organizations. That is, it is unreasonable to expect that each community organization can determine the degree to which it has contributed to an offender's "adjustment." The evaluation of numerous services on a community-wide basis should be encouraged, with each agency sharing a part of the cost with the caution that multiple organizational assessment implies agreement as to objectives.

Centralizing evaluation would result in greater consistency of standards, and it would relieve community organizations of the burden of trying to find outside experts to provide evaluation designs for their projects.

While the thrust of this chapter has been to stress the need for evaluation in corrections, it is not contended that all programs require immediate assessment. Neighborhood, racial, and ethnic organizations which are just getting involved in efforts to help offenders might well receive "seed money" on a short-term basis so that they could develop programs which would later be systematically evaluated.

Research funds and the limited number of persons trained to do evaluations should be concentrated on established organizations, particularly state and county prison, probation, and parole systems. Furthermore, every regional crime commission in every state should not be permitted to try out the same programs at the same time. Every probation department in the country does not need to try out a detached worker program, expand casework or group counseling services, or try to provide cultural, counseling, and recreation programs for predelinquents.

Experimental programs should be coordinated by the states and the national headquarters of LEAA to assure that programs are tried in a limited number of settings, that they are accompanied by careful evaluation, and that these evaluations are widely disseminated.

By the same token "criminal justice surveys" undertaken by private firms for local units of government hardly need continued replication. The results of these surveys are usually presented only to the local officials who contracted for them and are not circulated. Private firms have little interest in publicizing their findings since an adjacent municipality or county might want to contract for the same survey.

State universities, with their reservoir of sociologists, political scientists, psychologists, and other research specialists, would seem to have a special obligation to assist in the evaluation of other tax-supported organizations. Under these circumstances, conflicts of interest that exist when a public agency studies its own efforts is reduced and publication of results is encouraged.

Finally it should be emphasized that no successful private industry runs without continual assessment of the efficiency and effectiveness of its methods of operation. Despite the problems cited above, taxpayers have a right to expect routine ongoing assessment of the operations of organizations in the public sector. Evaluation research is one of the few ways of keeping the corrections business honest.

Principal Sources
and Suggested References

Chapter 1

Blumstein, Alfred. "Systems Analysis and the Criminal Justice System." *The Annals of the American Academy of Political and Social Sciences* 374:92–100.

Empey, LaMar T., and Erickson, Maynard L. *The Provo Experiment: Evaluating Community Control of Delinquency.* Lexington: D. C. Heath and Co., 1972.

———, and Lubeck, Steven G. *The Silverlake Experiment: Testing Delinquency Theory and Community Intervention.* Chicago: Aldine-Atherton, 1971.

England, Ralph. "What Is Responsible for Satisfactory Probation and Post-probation Outcome?" *Journal of Criminal Law, Criminology and Police Science* 47 (March–April, 1957):667–677.

Goldman, Nathan. "The Differential Selection of Juvenile Offenders for Court Appearance." In *Crime and the Legal Process.* Edited by William Chambliss. New York: McGraw-Hill, 1969, pp. 264–290.

Grunhut, Max. *Penal Reform.* New York: The Clarendon Press, 1948.

Jessness, Carl F. "The Preston Typology Study." *Youth Authority Quarterly* 23 (Winter 1970):26–38.

Lemert, Edwin M. "The Juvenile Court—Quest and Realities." In *Task Force Report on Juvenile Delinquency and Youth Crime.* Washington, D.C.: U.S. Government Printing Office, 1967.

———. *Instead of Court: Diversion in Juvenile Justice.* Public Health Service Publication No. 2127. Washington, D.C.: U.S. Government Printing Office, 1971.

McCorkle, Lloyd W., Bixby, F. Lovel, and Elias, Albert. *The Highfields Story.* New York: Henry Holt, 1958.

Morris, Norval, and Hawkins, Gordon. *The Honest Politician's Guide to Crime Control.* Chicago: Chicago University Press, 1970.

Palmer, Theodore, and Warren, Marguerite Q. Community Treatment Project, Research Report No. 8, Part I. Sacramento: California Youth Authority, 1967.

Platt, Anthony. *The Child Savers.* Chicago: Aldine Publishing Co., 1969.

Pound, Roscoe. "The Juvenile Court and the Law." *Crime and Delinquency* 10 (1964):490–504.

President's Commission on Law Enforcement and Administration of Justice. *Task Force Report: Corrections.* Washington, D.C.: U.S. Government Printing Office, 1967.

———. *Task Force Report: Juvenile Delinquency and Youth Crime.* Washington, D.C.: U.S. Government Printing Office, 1967.

Robinson, James, and Smith, Gerald. "The Effectiveness of Correctional Programs," *Crime and Delinquency* 17 (January 1971):67–80.

Rubin, Ted, and Smith, Jack F. *The Future of the Juvenile Court.* Washington, D.C.: Joint Commission on Correctional Manpower and Training, 1968.

Smith, Robert L. *A Quiet Revolution: Probation Subsidy.* Department of HEW, Washington, D.C.: U.S. Government Printing Office, 1971.

Street, David, Perrow, Charles, and Vinter, Robert D. *Organization for Treatment.* New York: The Free Press, 1966.

Supreme Court of the United States. *Kent vs. United States.* 383 U.S. 541:555:6, 1966.

———. "In re Gault." *Task Force Report: Juvenile Delinquency and Youth Crime.* President's Commission on Law Enforcement and Administration of Justice. Washington, D.C.: U.S. Government Printing Office, 1967.

Wheeler, Stanton, and Cottrell, Leonard S., Jr. *Juvenile Delinquency: Its Prevention and Control.* New York: Russell Sage Foundation, 1966.

Chapter 2

Advisory Commission on Intergovernmental Relations. *For a More Perfect Union—Correctional Reform.* Washington, D.C.: Advisory Commission on Intergovernmental Relations, 1971.

———. "Jail: History, Significance." *Proceedings of the American Correctional Association.* Washington, D.C.: American Correctional Association, 1970.

Glaser, Daniel, ed. "Some Notes on Urban Jails." In *Crime in the City.* New York: Harper and Row, 1970.

Mattick, Hans W. "Contemporary Jails of the United States." Unpublished manuscript available from the U. of Chicago Law School, 1972.

———, and Aikman, Alexander B. "The Cloacal Region of American Corrections." *Annals of the American Academy of Political and Social Science* 381 (1969): 109–118.

————, and Sweet, Ronald P. *Illinois Jails: Challenge and Opportunity for the 1970's.* Based on the Illinois Jails Survey of 1967–68, 1970.

Moyer, Frederic D., Flynn, Edith E., Plautz, Michael J., and Powers, Fred A. *Guidelines for the Planning and Design of Regional and Community Correctional Centers for Adults.* Urbana, Illinois: University of Illinois, 1971.

Richmond, Mark, ed. *New Roles for Jails; Guidelines for Planning.* Washington, D.C.: Bureau of Prisons, 1969.

Robinson and Smith, 1971. See Chapter 1.

U.S. Department of Justice, Law Enforcement Assistance Administration. *National Jail Census, 1970. A Report on the Nation's Local Jails and Type of Inmates.* Washington, D.C.: U.S. Government Printing Office, 1971.

Chapter 3

Carter, Robert M., and Wilkins, Leslie T. *Probation and Parole: Selected Readings.* New York: Wiley, 1970.

Doleschal, Eugene, and Geis, Gilbert. *Graduated Release.* Washington, D.C.: National Institute of Mental Health, Crime and Delinquency Topics series. Public Health Service Publication No. 2128. U.S. Government Printing Office, 1971.

Empey, LaMar T. *Alternatives to Incarceration.* Washington, D.C.: Office of Juvenile Delinquency and Youth Development. U.S. Government Printing Office, 1967.

Glaser, Daniel. *The Effectiveness of a Prison and Parole System.* Abridged Edition. Indianapolis: Bobbs-Merrill, 1969.

Keller, Oliver J., Jr., and Alper, Benedict S. *Halfway Houses.* Lexington, Mass.: D. C. Heath and Co., 1970.

Chapter 4

Barnes, Harry Elmer, and Teeters, Negley K. *New Horizons in Criminology.* New York: Prentice-Hall, 1945, pp. 457–568.

Carter, Robert M., Glaser, Daniel, and Wilkins, Leslie T., editors. *Correctional Institutions.* Philadelphia: Lippincott, 1972.

Cloward, Richard A., Cressey, Donald R., Grosser, George H., McCleery, Richard, Messinger, Sheldon L., Ohlin, Lloyd E., and Sykes, Gresham M. *Theoretical Studies in Social Organization of the Prison.* New York: Social Science Research Council, 1960.

Cressey, Donald R., ed. *The Prison: Studies in Institutional Organization and Change.* New York: Holt, Rinehart and Winston, 1960.

————, "Prison Organizations." *Handbook of Organizations.* Edited by James G. March. Chicago: Rand McNally, 1965, pp. 1023–1070.

Glaser, Daniel. *The Effectiveness of a Prison and Parole System.* Indianapolis: Bobbs-Merrill, 1964.

Heffernan, Esther. *Making It in Prison: The Square, the Cool, and the Life.* New York: Wiley-Interscience, 1972.

Irwin, John. *The Felon.* Englewood Cliffs, New Jersey: Prentice-Hall, 1970.

Kassebaum, Gene, Ward, David A., and Wilner, Daniel M. *Prison Treatment and Parole Survival: An Empirical Assessment.* New York: Wiley, 1971.

Minton, Robert J., Jr., ed. *Inside: Prison American Style.* New York: Random House, 1971.

Ohlin, Lloyd E. *Sociology and the Field of Corrections.* New York: Russell Sage Foundation, 1956.

Spiegel, John P. "The Dynamics of Violent Confrontation." *International Journal of Psychiatry* 10 (September, 1972):93–108.

Ward, David A. "Inmate Rights and Prison Reform in Sweden and Denmark." *Journal of Criminal Law, Criminology and Police Science* 63 (June, 1972):240–255.

Chapter 5

"Addict Diversion: An Alternative Approach for the Criminal Justice System," *Geo. L. Rev.* 60 (1972):667. (Description of Philadelphia Court of Common Pleas Pre-Indictment Program for addicts and D.C. Juvenile Court Program for addicts.)

Baron, Roger, and Feeney, Floyd. "Preventing Delinquency through Diversion." Davis, California: University of California (The Sacramento County Probation Department 601 Diversion Project, Center on Administration of Criminal Justice), May 1972. (Description of project.)

De Grazia, Edward. "Report on Pre-Trial Diversion of Accused Offenders to Community Mental Health Treatment Programs." Georgetown University School of Medicine, Department of Psychiatry, 1972.

Doleschal, Eugene. "Criminal Justice Programs in Model Cities." National Council on Crime and Delinquency, June 1972. (Description of Des Moines Model Neighborhood Corrections Project.)

Harlow, Eleanor. "Diversion from the Criminal Justice System." National Council on Crime and Delinquency, April 1970. (Description of programs for chronic drunks.)

———. "Intensive Intervention: An Alternative to Institutionalization." National Council on Crime and Delinquency, Feb. 1970. (Description of California Community Treatment Program.)

Hickey, William. "Strategies for Decreasing Jail Population." National Council on Crime and Delinquency, May 1971. (Description of Royal Oak, Michigan, program for misdemeanant probation.)

Hodgson, Tom. "Juvenile Offenders—a Scientific Approach." New Scotland Yard Memorandum, London.

Lambert, Josephine. "Interim Report: Evaluation of Youth Resources Bureaus." Massachusetts Governor's Committee on Law Enforcement and Administration of Criminal Justice, November 1, 1970–May 1, 1971.

Lemert, 1971. See Chapter 1.

"Metropolitan Police—Juvenile Bureaux." Memorandum from Metropolitan Police Office, London, May 1969.

Palmer, Ted B. "California's Community Treatment Program for Delinquent Adolescents." *Journal of Research in Crime and Delinquency* (Jan. 1971). (Description of California Community Treatment Program.)

"Programs in Criminal Justice Reform." *Vera Institute of Justice Ten-Year Report 1961–1971* (May 1972). (Descriptions of Manhattan Bail Project, Manhattan Summons Project, Manhattan Bowery Project, Bronx Sentencing Project, Neighborhood Youth Diversion Program and Manhattan Court Employment Project.)

Seymour, J. "Youth Services Bureaus." Report on a seminar sponsored by the University of Chicago Center for Studies in Criminal Justice, March 11, 1971.

Smith, 1971. See Chapter 1.

Chapter 6

GENERAL SOURCES

Caro, Francis G., ed. *Readings in Evaluation Research*. New York: Russell Sage Foundation, 1971.

Rossi, Peter H., and Williams, Walter, eds. *Evaluating Social Programs: Theory, Practice and Politics*. New York: Seminar Press, 1972.

Weiss, Carol H., ed. *Evaluating Action Programs*. Boston: Allyn and Bacon, Inc., 1972.

ISSUES IN EVALUATION OF CORRECTIONAL PROGRAMS

Cressey, Donald R. "The Nature and Effectiveness of Correctional Techniques." *Law and Contemporary Problems* (Duke University School of Law) 23 (Aug. 1958):754–771.

Hood, Roger, and Sparks, Richard. "Assessing the Effectiveness of Punishments and Treatments." In *Key Issues in Criminology*. New York: McGraw-Hill, 1970.

Lerman, Paul. "Evaluative Studies of Institutions for Delinquents: Implications for Research and Social Policy." *Social Work* 13 (Jul. 1968):55–64.

Logan, Charles H. "Evaluation Research in Crime and Delinquency: A Reappraisal." *Journal of Criminal Law, Criminology, and Police Science* 63 (1972):378–387.

Martinson, Robert. "The Treatment Evaluation Survey." The Office of Crime Control Planning, State of New York, 1970.

Morris, Albert. "A Correctional Administrator's Guide to the Evaluation of Correctional Programs." Bulletin no. 21, Massachusetts Correctional Association, Nov. 1971.

Rabow, Jerome. "Research and Rehabilitation: The Conflict of Scientific and Treatment Roles in Correction." *The Journal of Research in Crime and Delinquency* 1 (Jan. 1964):67–79.

Takagi, Paul. "Evaluation Systems and Adaptations in a Formal Organization." Doctoral dissertation, Stanford University, 1967.

Wilkins, Leslie T. *Evaluation of Penal Measures*. New York: Random House, 1969.

EVALUATIONS OF SPECIFIC CORRECTIONAL TREATMENT PROGRAMS

Empey, 1971. See Chapter 1.

Glaser, 1964. See Chapter 4.

Kassebaum, 1971. See Chapter 4.

Meyer, Henry, Borgatta, Edgar, and Jones, Wyatt. *Girls at Vocational High*. New York: Russell Sage Foundation, 1965.

Index

About The American Assembly

The American Assembly was established by Dwight D. Eisenhower at Columbia University in 1950. It holds nonpartisan meetings and publishes authoritative books to illuminate issues of United States policy.

An affiliate of Columbia, with offices in the Graduate School of Business, the Assembly is a national educational institution incorporated in the State of New York.

The Assembly seeks to provide information, stimulate discussion, and evoke independent conclusions in matters of vital public interest.

AMERICAN ASSEMBLY SESSIONS

At least two national programs are initiated each year. Authorities are retained to write background papers presenting essential data and defining the main issues in each subject.

About sixty men and women representing a broad range of experience, competence, and American leadership meet for several days to discuss the Assembly topic and consider alternatives for national policy.

All Assemblies follow the same procedure. The background papers are sent to participants in advance of the Assembly. The Assembly meets in small groups for four or five lengthy periods. All groups use the same agenda. At the close of these informal sessions, participants adopt in plenary session a final report of findings and recommendations.

Regional, state, and local Assemblies are held following the national session at Arden House. Assemblies have also been held in England, Switzerland, Malaysia, Canada, the Caribbean, South America, Central America, the Philippines, and Japan. Over one hundred institutions have co-sponsored one or more Assemblies.

ARDEN HOUSE

Home of The American Assembly and scene of the national sessions is Arden House, which was given to Columbia University in 1950 by W. Averell Harriman. E. Roland Harriman joined his brother in contributing toward adaptation of the property for conference purposes. The buildings and surrounding land, known as the Harriman Campus of Columbia University, are fifty miles north of New York City.

Arden House is a distinguished conference center. It is self-supporting and operates throughout the year for use by organizations with educational objectives.

AMERICAN ASSEMBLY BOOKS

The background papers for each Assembly program are published in cloth and paperbound editions for use by individuals, libraries, businesses, public agencies, nongovernmental organizations, educational institutions, discussion and service groups. In this way the deliberations of Assembly sessions are continued and extended.

The subjects of Assembly programs to date are:

1951——United States–Western Europe Relationships
1952——Inflation
1953——Economic Security for Americans
1954——The United States' Stake in the United Nations
——The Federal Government Service
1955——United States Agriculture
——The Forty-Eight States
1956——The Representation of the United States Abroad
——The United States and the Far East
1957——International Stability and Progress
——Atoms for Power
1958——The United States and Africa
——United States Monetary Policy
1959——Wages, Prices, Profits, and Productivity
——The United States and Latin America
1960——The Federal Government and Higher Education
——The Secretary of State
——Goals for Americans
1961——Arms Control: Issues for the Public
——Outer Space: Prospects for Man and Society
1962——Automation and Technological Change
——Cultural Affairs and Foreign Relations
1963——The Population Dilemma
——The United States and the Middle East
1964——The United States and Canada
——The Congress and America's Future
1965——The Courts, the Public, and the Law Explosion
——The United States and Japan
1966——State Legislatures in American Politics
——A World of Nuclear Powers?
——The United States and the Philippines
——Challenges to Collective Bargaining